T0393898

Daoism

"Livia Kohn has demonstrated that she presents a view representative of a wide range of texts and approaches. No one has a more comprehensive perspective on Daoist Studies."
— **Alan Fox**, *University of Delaware, USA*

"[N]o one has done more in showing the value of Daoism to scholars both inside and outside of China than Livia Kohn. … This text must be added to the libraries of teachers and students of Chinese religious studies and philosophies."
— **Ronnie Littlejohn**, *Belmont University, USA*

Daoism: A Contemporary Philosophical Investigation explores philosophy of religion from a Daoist perspective. Philosophy of religion is a thriving field today, increasingly expanding from its traditional theistic, Christian roots into more cosmologically oriented Asian religions. This book raises a number of different issues on the three levels of cosmos, individual, and society, and addresses key questions like:

- What are the distinctive characteristics of Daoist thought and cosmology?
- How does it approach problems of creation, body, mind, and society?
- What, ultimately, is Dao?
- How does it manifest and play a role in the world?
- What are the key features of Daoist communities and ethics?
- What role does the body play in Daoism?
- What do Daoists think is the relationship between language and reality?
- What is Daoist immortality?
- How do Daoists envision the perfect life on earth?

The volume delves into philosophical subject matter in a way that is accessible to those approaching the topic for this first time, while also making an original contribution to Daoist philosophy of religion. This volume is suitable for use by undergraduate and graduate students studying Chinese religion and philosophy, as well as more general introductory courses on Daoism.

Livia Kohn is Professor Emerita, Department of Religion, Boston University, USA. Her recent publications include *Guides to Sacred Texts: The Daode jing* (2019) and *Daoist China: Governance, Economics, Culture* (2018).

Investigating Philosophy of Religion
Series editors: Chad Meister, Bethel College and
Charles Taliaferro, St. Olaf College

This is a series of interfaith texts that philosophically engage with the major
world religions in light of central issues they are currently facing. Each work
is an original contribution by a leading scholar from that religious tradition
and incorporates the latest developments in scholarship in the field. The texts
are written for students, scholars, and all those who want a fairly detailed but
concise overview of the central issues in contemporary philosophy of religion
from the perspective of the major world religions.

Judaism
A Contemporary Philosophical Investigation
Lenn E. Goodman

Buddhism
A Contemporary Philosophical Investigation
David Burton

Islam
A Contemporary Philosophical Investigation
Imran Aijaz

Naturalism and Religion
A Contemporary Philosophical Investigation
Graham Oppy

Hinduism
A Contemporary Philosophical Investigation
Shyam Ranganathan

Daoism
A Contemporary Philosophical Investigation
Livia Kohn

For more information about this series, please visit: www.routledge.com/
Investigating-Philosophy-of-Religion/book-series/IPR

Daoism

A Contemporary Philosophical
Investigation

Livia Kohn

LONDON AND NEW YORK

First published 2020
by Routledge
2 Park Square, Milton Park, Abingdon, Oxon OX14 4RN

and by Routledge
52 Vanderbilt Avenue, New York, NY 10017

Routledge is an imprint of the Taylor & Francis Group, an informa business

British Library Cataloguing-in-Publication Data
A catalogue record for this book is available from the British Library

Library of Congress Cataloging-in-Publication Data
A catalog record has been requested for this book

ISBN: 978-1-138-30493-2 (hbk)
ISBN: 978-1-138-30494-9 (pbk)
ISBN: 978-0-203-73143-7 (ebk)

Typeset in Times New Roman
by Newgen Publishing UK

Contents

Dynastic chart

BCE

Xia ca. 2100–1600
Shang 1554–1028
Zhou 1027–221
   Western 1027–771
   Eastern 770–221
      Spring and Autumn 722–48`
      Warring States 480–221
Qin 221–206
Former Han 206–8
     Interregnum 8–

CE

Later Han 25–220
Three Kingdoms 220–265
Western Jin 265–317
Eastern Jin 317–420
Six Dynasties 420–589
   SOUTHERN
      Liu Song 420–479
      Southern Qi 479–502
      Southern Liang 502–557
      Southern Chen 557–589
   NORTHERN
      Northern Wei 386–534
      Eastern Wei 534–550
      Western Wei 535–577
      Northern Zhou 557–681
Sui 581–618
Tang 618–907
     Empress Wu 690–705

Five Dynasties 907–960
     Liao 916–1125
Song 960–1279
     Northern 960–1126
     Southern 1126–1279
Mongol-Yuan 1260–1368
Ming 1368–1644
Manchu-Qing 1644–1911
Republic (Taiwan) 1911–
People's Republic 1949–

Introduction

The nature of Daoism

Compared to other major religions, Daoism tends to be hard to define. Often described as the indigenous higher religion of China, it is multifaceted and often rather amorphous, so that it can be classified neither as an ethnic or a universal religion, but combines elements of both. That is to say, while deeply rooted in Chinese cosmology, society, and language, it is not tribal in the sense that anyone simply by being born Chinese is automatically a Daoist or popular to the degree that it pervades every aspect of traditional living. On the other hand, while exercising a strong appeal to seekers in other cultures and countries and claiming access to universal goals and values, it does not intentionally proselytize or spread actively.

Typically, people who are born into an environment that offers forms of Daoism choose to follow it either as thinkers, devotees, or practitioners of self-cultivation, pursuing the aspect of the tradition that resonates best with them. There is no pressure to join a particular group, obtain a special transmission, or confess to a certain set of beliefs. In fact, a major group of Daoists are intellectuals, thinkers and writers who do not belong to any organized group or engage in obvious rituals or self-cultivation practices yet who "call themselves Daoist and create their identity with the help of Daoist concepts while also forming identity for the religion."[1] If the religion spreads, on the other hand, it is usually as part of something else—literature, medicine, philosophy, governance—so that Daoist ideas, metaphors, images, and practices pervade other East Asian cultures (Korea, Japan, Vietnam) but there are no monasteries, temples, or formal organizations. Only very recently have ordained Daoists begun to initiate foreigners and to support the building of temples and establishment of lineages overseas, supported by the Chinese government as part of their overall expansion and domination policy.[2]

Cultural features

Neither a clearly ethnic or universal religion, another factor that makes Daoism hard to pinpoint is the degree to which it is infused by various other cultural features, so that the boundaries between Daoism and Chinese philosophy, Confucian ethics, traditional cosmology, Chinese medicine, popular religion, and Buddhism are vague at best. That is to say, even in its early stages, the Daoist school was closely related to other forms of Chinese philosophy, the term *dao* being used by all to refer to the underlying patterns of the cosmos and ideal way of governing. It is thus no accident that A. C. Graham entitles his discussion of the Chinese philosophical schools *Disputers of the Dao* and Chad Hansen refuses to acknowledge the very concept of an absolute *dao*, speaking instead of many *dao*s or ways, that is, forms of prescriptive or normative discourse.[3]

Not only sharing its very core term with other schools, Daoism also throughout its history has never lost its close connection to Confucianism, extolling its virtues and integrating its ethical principles, and often working closely with Confucians officials in the government of the empire. Numerous texts outlining organizational precepts emphasize the importance of filial piety toward the parents and loyalty to the ruler, while works on internal cultivation place the five central virtues of Confucianism directly into the human body and link them with the attainment of spiritual perfection. Any Daoist treatise, moreover, that has to do with community and political organization rests heavily in Confucian doctrines, making ample use of Confucian terminology and generally endorsing the mainstream vision.

Another dimension where Daoism is suffused by Chinese culture is classical cosmology, the system of yin-yang and the five phases, a form of correlative thinking that represents reality in terms of two complementary forces (light and dark, high and low, etc.) and five developmental aspects of growth and decay that closely echo the rising and setting of the sun. Pervading Chinese thinking, this cosmology allows the understanding of life through parallels, so that, for example, the patterns of nature also apply in society or family or political structures appear in the human body. In addition, Daoists make ample use, in many different forms and respects, of the *Yijing* (Book of Changes), the traditional calendar, forms of divination (astrology, physiognomy), and various ways of manipulating vital energy (fengshui, music, exercises). Although often called "Daoist" in popular Western writings, there is nothing uniquely Daoist about any of these: they form part of Chinese culture in general and are applied variously in Daoist contexts as and when felt appropriate.

Similarly, blurry boundaries exist between Daoist practice and Chinese medicine. Unlike Indian or Western religions, where the body tends to be seen as the opposite of pure spirit or the soul and therefore constitutes an obstacle to spiritual attainment, Daoists firmly place all and any subtler pursuits into the body. Body and mind (spirit or soul) are part of the same continuum of vital energy (*qi*) and without a healthy, well-functioning physical base there can be no refinement to higher spiritual states. Both in history and today, many Daoists are also healers, practicing classical Chinese medicine in a subtler and more individualized form than the officially sanctioned version of TCM, either as private healers or in temple clinics. Beyond that, Daoist adepts all know the fundamentals of medicine, adjusting their diet, taking herbal supplements, and practicing self-massages along the lines of traditional acupuncture. While there is, therefore, such a thing as "Daoist medicine," the differences to Chinese medicine are subtle and more of degree than substance.[4]

Another area where Daoism is deeply embedded in Chinese culture is popular religion. Today many city god temples, traditionally supported by the community and run by village priests of no particular denomination, are managed by the state with Daoists appointed as caretakers. Vice versa, Daoist deities appear variously in popular temples, notably the Dark Warrior (Xuanwu) and the King of Medications (Yaowang), while popular gods not only receive the common offerings of incense, flowers, candles, tea, wine, fruit, and grain but also writing utensils. The latter are a specifically Daoist feature, symbolizing the high emphasis placed on written communication with the otherworld. Vice versa, although Daoists traditionally reject meat offerings because the pure Dao does not feed on blood, to accommodate folk religious beliefs today they allow meat—even whole pigs—to appear in Daoist-sponsored rites.[5]

The most confusing and most complex facet of Daoism is its relation to Buddhism. After first appearing on the Chinese horizon in the first century CE, it underwent several stages of adaptation and modes of translation to rise to the status of major religion in the 5th. Daoist schools at the time adopted it widely, including aspects of worldview, such as ideas of karma, rebirth, and hell; ethics, notably precepts and monastic vows; and philosophical speculation, such as notions of emptiness and the logic of enlightened states. Buddhist terminology came to pervade Daoist scriptures, Buddhist sutras were copied directly into the Daoist canon (just changing the word "buddha" to "dao"), otherworld levels and rituals were integrated wholesale, and the entire complex of the monastic institution arose as essentially a Buddhist feature.[6]

Still, and despite the close integration of these various outside elements, Daoism is a unique religious tradition with its own particular beliefs and practices that can be summarized as the core focus on the relation of the individual to the cosmos in a positive, productive, and life-affirming way. In other words, unlike Confucianism, classical cosmology, and Chinese medicine, where human society takes center stage, Daoists apply their various ethics, principles, and practices within an encompassing framework, focusing on the personal relationship to the universe at large. Unlike popular religion, where the gods are essentially advanced ancestors in close reciprocity to humankind, Daoist deities are part of a higher, purer level of the cosmos and support life from there, transcendent yet approachable. Unlike Buddhism, which posits life as suffering, Daoists see life as fundamentally good, always suffused by Dao and vital energy. They, therefore, strive for immortality as their ultimate goal, in contrast to the annihilation and personal dissolution in nirvana.

Three features delineate Daoism most specifically: the concept of Dao as the underlying power that creates and supports everything in the best possible way and to which one can relate through personal cultivation; the presence of pure, cosmic deities and transcendent bureaucrats, residing in multiple layers of heaven and aided by human priests who become their equals through ritual transformation; and the firm conviction that the human body-mind as fundamentally consisting of vital energy can be transmuted into an immortal spirit entity through the systematic and persistent application of longevity techniques and advanced meditations.

Three dimensions

Within this overall framework, then, Daoism has several distinct dimensions, commonly described as philosophical versus religious, relating respectively to the early thinkers and the various organized schools of later ages. This division was established by nineteenth-century Protestant missionaries, such as James Legge, on the basis of traditional Confucian views, reflecting the Chinese elite's preference for abstract speculation and their pervasive contempt for popular rituals, deemed superstitious. It has since been discarded as both erroneous and inefficient, replaced by a tripartite division into literati, communal, and self-cultivation.

Literati Daoists are members of the educated elite who apply Daoist philosophical ideas, usually in reference to the early thinkers, to create meaning in their world and hope to exert some influence on the political and social situation of their time. Their identity comes from their dedication to the classical texts of Laozi and Zhuangzi, which they interpret in commentaries and essays, and whose metaphors they employ in stories and poetry. In contrast to the widespread image of Daoists as retired recluses, both historically and today, these literati are highly active in society and can be found in all walks of life: government, academia, business, and more. In terms of outlook, they show the greatest connection with Confucianism and traditional cosmology; in terms of practice, they tend to pursue self-cultivation through philosophical reflection as well as contemplative forms of meditation. Literati Daoists have been part of the tradition since its inception; while the ancient thinkers Laozi and Zhuangzi may well be considered their first example, there are numerous later texts and schools, and the tradition is alive and well today.

Communal Daoists, too, are found in many different positions and come from all levels of society. They are members of organized Daoist groups, complete with priestly hierarchies, formal initiations, regular rituals, and prayers to the gods. Some organizations are tightly controlled fraternities with secret rites or monastic institutions with limited contact to the outside world. Others are part of ordinary society, centered on neighborhood temples and concerned with the affairs of ordinary life—weddings and funerals, protection and exorcism. Believing in a large pantheon of gods and working to keep human life on track with their help, they work with liturgies, prayer hymns, moral rules, and internal energy cultivation. Historically, Daoist religious organizations first appear in the second century CE, soon to adopt a great deal from Buddhism in terms of both doctrines and practices. Today, they are closest to popular religion, Daoist priests managing city god temples and followers worshiping communal, Buddhist, and Daoist deities with equal fervor.

The third group of Daoists focuses on self-cultivation or "nurturing life" (*yangsheng*), utilizing various methods of personal refinement—diet, herbal remedies, sexual hygiene, breathing techniques, exercise, and meditation. They, too, come from all walks of life, but rather than philosophical inspiration or communal rites, their main concern is the attainment of perfect health, extended longevity, and cosmic oneness. They tend to pay little attention to political or community involvement, and their organizations depend strongly on the master-disciple relationship. Their groups can be small and esoteric with only a few active followers, large and extensive with leanings toward organized religion, or vague and diffuse with numerous people practicing a variety of different techniques. Again, historical continuity is strong. The earliest examples of self-cultivation groups are found before the Common Era, tentatively among the followers of Laozi and Zhuangzi, then emerge more prominently among Han-dynasty immortality seekers, eventually even growing into leading Daoist organizations.[7]

Interconnected from the beginning, these three dimensions of Daoism— literati, communal, and self-cultivation—although distinct in their abstract description, are not mutually exclusive in practice. On the contrary, as contemporary practitioners often emphasize, to be a complete Daoist one must follow all three paths: studying worldview and being socially responsible, performing rituals and praying to the gods, and undertaking self-cultivation for health and spiritual advancement.

Periodization

Quite a few features of Daoism can be traced back into prehistory, and the religion in many ways strives to reclaim a time before settled communities and agriculture, when humans lived in small groups in close connection to nature and the universe. Still, its documented history began during the Warring States period (480–221 BCE), with manuscripts and inscriptions describing Dao-based cosmology and energy cultivation. From here it evolved over the course of Chinese history, often in close conjunction with political and economic changes.

This evolution was first divided—along the lines of the distinction into a philosophical and religious branch—into two major phases, called classical and later Daoism, with the dividing line at the beginning of the Former Han dynasty in 206 BCE. From here, as more information on its religious development became available, scholars subdivided later Daoism into an early and a later phase, calling them traditional and new Daoism, respectively, with the beginning of the Song dynasty in 960 as a cut-off point. Since, moreover, the structure of the religion changed drastically with the founding of the Tang dynasty in 618, centralization in government leading to the systematic integration of the many medieval schools, they further divided traditional Daoism into incipient organized and organized.

Expanding this scheme and inspired by research on the development of the deified Laozi, I suggested that two more stages be added: first, a transitional stage between classical and incipient organized Daoism that emphasizes the cataclysmic changes of the Han dynasty, such as the emergence of immortality seekers, the installation of Daoist politics, the increased imperial worship of Laozi as the personified Dao, and the first messianic movements; and second, a stage subdividing new Daoism into a structuring phase during the Song and Yuan and one of increasingly popularization since the Ming.[8]

These days, I see Daoism as evolving in eight distinct stages that each present materials in all three dimensions. Stage One is antiquity, that is, the Warring States. It centers on the early thinkers of Laozi and Zhuangzi and their key works, the most important documents of literati Daoism: the *Daode jing* (Book of Dao and Its Virtue, DZ 664) and the *Zhuangzi* (Book of Master Zhuang, DZ 670).[9] These works, moreover, are supplemented by meditation instructions found in the *Neiye* (Inward Training), reflecting cultivation practices, as well as by a group of newly discovered manuscripts that go back to the mid-fourth century BCE and outline cosmogony and political as well as personal practices. Even then, moreover, there were rudimentary organizations, self-cultivation groups and alternative communities that rejected mainstream culture in favor of a simpler and more primitive life.[10]

Stage Two, matching earlier periodization models, covers both Han dynasties (206 BCE–220 CE), when the empire was unified and religions underwent standardization, various local deities were integrated into the newly dominant cosmology of the five phases, and Confucianism came to form the core of the imperial examination system (136 BCE). This was also the time when Chinese medicine evolved from ritual exorcism of demons thought to cause disease to the energy-centered system of acupuncture and herbal remedies. The first manuals of longevity practices appear, unearthed at Mawangdui (168 BCE) together with two complete versions of the *Daode jing* and other speculative Daoist texts.

In terms of literati Daoism, the dominant school of the time was called Huang-Lao, combining the name of Laozi with that of the Yellow Emperor (Huangdi), a mythical ruler who first instituted Chinese culture (and is still venerated as the father of all Chinese). Described in a group of manuscripts known as the *Huangdi sijing* (Four Classics of the Yellow Emperor), its main feature is the application of cosmological doctrines to active governance, seeing the ruler as sage and formalizing community rules and regulations.[11]

Also, under the Han, Laozi was divinized as Lord Lao, the personification of Dao, leading to a series of revelations in the second century CE that presaged the beginnings of communal Daoism. The earliest organized cults, then, were the Great Peace (Taiping) movement in Shandong and the Celestial Masters (Tianshi) in Sichuan, both led by spiritual masters with divinely sanctioned healing powers, organized into hierarchical social structures subject to strict community rules, and centered on ritual initiations, exorcisms, and cosmic festivals.[12]

After the end of the Han dynasty, the country was divided into Three Kingdoms (220–265), then reunited under the Jin dynasty (265–420). This matches Stage Three, characterized by two major literati developments: the philosophical school of Mystery Learning (*xuanxue*) and the emergence of ecstatic poetry, most importantly among the so-called Seven Sages of the Bamboo Grove. Mystery Learning, sometimes also called Neo-Daoism, arose in reaction to the strong control of intellectual life under the Han, focusing on the search for a more spiritual dimension of life through the recovery and reinterpretation of Daoist classics and the *Yijing*. Its main representative is Wang Bi (226–249), the principal editor of and commentator on the *Daode jing*, closely followed by Guo Xiang (252–312), who created the standard edition of the *Zhuangzi*. They defined and refined a number of key Daoist concepts, establishing a firm intellectual framework for the tradition. Ecstatic poets, too, were members of the aristocracy; however, they found their true satisfaction in seclusion and escaped from the vicissitudes of official life by drinking heavily and taking psychedelic drugs. Their otherworldly experiences then duly recorded in beautiful poems, but they also wrote more theoretical essays on the nature of long life, the importance of music, and more.[13]

All these figures, moreover, actively practiced longevity techniques, and some of them also recorded their preferred methods, such as the *Liezi* (Book of Master Lie) commentator Zhang Zhan of the fourth century, who wrote a major work on longevity techniques. In addition, in continuation of Han immortality seekers, several lineages of alchemists emerged, later codified as the school of Great Clarity (Taiqing). A key figure in this context is the scholar Ge Hong (283–343), a member of the southern aristocracy who studied with a renowned alchemist for five years and wrote down both theoretical and practical guidelines in his *Baopuzi* (Book of the Master Who Embraces Simplicity, DZ 1185).

Alchemy, in conjunction with the teachings of the Celestial Masters, who had become part of the southwestern of the Three Kingdoms in 215 and spread throughout the country, was also at the root of the organized Daoist community known as the school of Highest Clarity (Shangqing). Established in a series of revelations to a spirit medium hired by the Xu family near Nanjing, its members pursued immortality through ecstatic excursions, visualizations, and alchemical concoctions, and over the centuries rose to the leading Daoist school of medieval China.

Stage Four, under the Six Dynasties (420–589), is characterized by the emergence of various new schools and the massive impact of Buddhism. Two communities stand out. One, in the south, was led by Ge Chaofu, a Highest Clarity follower and descendant of Ge Hong. In the 390s, he established his own group, integrating the cosmology of Highest Clarity with the system of the five phases and Celestial Masters ritual. Known as Numinous Treasure (Lingbao), it became dominant in the fifth century and served as the main vehicle of the wholesale adoption of Buddhist ideas and practices into the Daoist tradition. In the north, the Toba rulers sponsored the Daoist theocracy, appointing the new Celestial Master Kou Qianzhi (365–448), who had received various revelations from the deified Laozi, as the leader of a religion-based state administration. Originally Buddhist, they expected Daoists to follow the same model, thus creating the first Daoist monastic institution, complete with celibacy, robes, and rules. It its wake, after state support ceased, Daoist followers established their first independent monastery at Louguan (southwest of Xi'an), allegedly the location of the original transmission of the *Daode jing*.[14]

There they codified the precepts and also created a new and more mystical interpretation of the *Daode jing* in the *Xisheng jing* (Scripture of Western Ascension, DZ 726), integrating religious ideals with classical Daoist thought. In addition, Louguan Daoists were also active in various court debates with Buddhists and helped craft a model for religious integration, sponsored by sixth-century rulers keen on reunification of the empire.

In terms of self-cultivation, adepts of Highest Clarity used various health regimens as preparation for in-depth meditations. In addition, as documented in the *Daoyin jing* (Scripture on Healing Exercises), practitioners adopted Buddhist-transmitted Indian-style exercise sequences, associated them with particular immortals of old, standardized the system of Daoist breathing exercises, and established systematic methods of enhancing vital energy.[15]

Later developments

Stage Five matches the Tang dynasty (618–907), the golden age of Daoism. In terms of community, it saw the integration of the main medieval schools into one organized system, the establishment of major state-sponsored monasteries complete with standardized legal and liturgical rules as well as a formal ordination hierarchy, and the elevation of Daoism to state doctrine under Emperor Xuanzong (r. 713–755).

The main philosophical school at the time was Twofold Mystery (Chongxuan), a reading of the ancient classics under the auspices of Buddhist logic that flourished in the seventh century, followed by other examples of Daoist scholasticism, such as complex considerations of how exactly Dao embodies itself in the world. In addition, the alchemist and master physician Sun Simiao (d. 682), who codified Chinese medicine and is still venerated as King of Medications, and the Highest Clarity patriarch Sima Chengzhen (647–735) created systematic outlines of the self-cultivation and meditation practices of the tradition, elevating the arts of nourishing life to a new and higher level. This great flourishing came crashing down after the An Lushan Rebellion in 755, which initiated widespread unrest and civil war, leading to the systematic dismantling of monastic splendor and spiritual sophistication.

Stage Six signals Daoist renewal under the Song dynasty (960–1279). This period saw major improvements in infrastructure, the wide-spread use of printing as well as increased education, communication, and commerce, leading to the rise of the merchant class. In terms of religion, this meant an overall increase in lay organizations and popular temples and activities as well as a great demand for practical religious aids to daily life. These included talismans for building homes, spells for granting safe passage, exorcisms for healing, as well as rites for business prosperity and services for the dead, provided by Daoist ritual masters in competition with wandering Buddhists, tantric ritualists, and local shamans.

Daoists in this context reorganized both as independent practitioners and in organized schools, many of which were locally centered and focused on an inspired master. The most important new school was Complete Perfection (Quanzhen), which combined worship of these new deities with Chan-Buddhist inspired monasticism and Confucian ethics. In the early thirteenth century, Chinggis Khan appointed its leader the head of all religions of China, making it the most powerful and central organization of the country, under which eventually all other schools came to be subsumed.

As far as self-cultivation goes, this period saw the rise of internal alchemy (*neidan*), a complex system of techniques that integrated meditative longevity techniques, operative alchemy, and the symbolism of the *Yijing*. Its goal was the attainment of immortality as a form of ecstatic otherworld existence through a series of energetic mutations within the body, which would transform it into a spiritual entity known as the immortal embryo. Like popular rituals, longevity techniques spread widely, and officials, intellectuals, and Daoist masters wrote numerous commentaries on the classics and elaborated their worldview in treatises, recorded sayings, and poetry collections.[16]

The trend toward wider popular appeal continued in Stage Seven under the Ming (1368–1644) and Qing (1644–1911) with three important differences. First, all religious organizations and activities were centrally controlled by the state, subject to approval by the Ministry of Rites, which issued ordination certificates and demanded the detailed formulation of priestly regulations. Second, intellectuals matched the unifying efforts of the government by postulating the "unity of the three teachings." They also wrote a number of popular novels featuring Daoist protagonists, most prominently the martial deity Dark Warrior, the Eight Immortals, the Monkey King, the Seven Perfected of Complete Perfection, and Lord Lao. Third, self-cultivation evolved into new styles in close conjunction with martial arts, giving rise most prominently to taiji quan and special practices for women.

Stage Eight, then, began with the founding of the Chinese Republic in 1912. It saw, most importantly the rise of qigong, a Communist-supported adaptation of Daoist longevity and healing practices, which began in 1947 and has since played a major role in Chinese society. In addition, internal alchemy has been simplified and made more accessible to a wider audience. Intellectually, Daoist teachings have spread abroad, leading to a vibrant philosophical dialogue with Western thinkers and practitioners. In terms of religious organizations, the Communist government has continued the tight control of the Ming, so that today all Daoist monks are state employees and have to follow strict guidelines. Still, Daoists are working hard to reinvent themselves to match the times. They increasingly play a role in community organization and are in the vanguard of healthier and more ecological forms of living, supporting businesses and providing self-help advice, psycho-therapy, and medical help.[17]

Notes

1   Kohn and Roth 2002, 9.
2   On Daoism in other East Asian countries, see the articles on Korea and Japan in *Daoism Handbook* (Kohn 2000). For the situation of Daoism today, see Kohn 2018.
3   See Graham 1989; Hansen 2010, 3.
4   On the relationship of Daoism and Chinese medicine, see Kohn 2005.
5   On offerings in Daoist ritual, see Asano 2002.
6   On the Buddhist impact on Daoism, see Zürcher 1980. For more on Daoist identity, see Kohn and Roth 2002.
7   See Kohn 2001, 5–6; Kohn 2008; Kohn and Roth 2002, 9.
8   The first periodization appears in Kirkland 1997, 78; my own outline is found in Kohn 1998, 164.
9   DZ abbreviates *Daozang* (Daoist Canon), the standard collection of Daoist texts put together in 1445. The numbers refer to the catalog in Schipper and Verellen 2004.
10 There are hundreds of translations of the *Daode jing* and many studies. For a comprehensive overview of the text, its history and impact, see Kohn 2019. On the *Zhuangzi*, see Kohn 2014; for the *Neiye*, see Roth 1999. Early manuscripts are aptly presented in Wang 2015.
11 A full translation and detailed study of the medical manuscripts appear in Harper 1998. The four classics associated with the Yellow Emperor are studied in Wang 2015.
12 For more on the early movements, see the article in *Daoism Handbook* (Kohn 2000).
13 A new collection on Mystery Learning that discusses these various thinkers in relation to Daoism is found in Chai 2019.
14 For these medieval schools, see the articles on Highest Clarity, Elixirs and Alchemy, the Lingbao School, and the Northern Celestial Masters in *Daoism Handbook* (Kohn 2000).
15 The *Xisheng jing* is translated and studied in Kohn 2007. A rendition of the *Daoyin jing*, together with other longevity texts, appears in Kohn 2012.
16 For details on Daoism during these periods, see the articles on Daoism in the Tang, Song and Yuan Times, Inner Alchemy, and Complete Perfection in *Daoism Handbook* (Kohn 2000).
17 On late imperial Daoism, read the articles on the Ming and Qing dynasties in *Daoism Handbook* (Kohn 2000). On the situation of Daoism today, see Kohn 2018. The classic study of qigong appears in Palmer 2007.

References

Asano, Haruji. 2002. "Offerings in Daoist Ritual." In *Daoist Identity: History, Lineage, and Ritual*, edited by Livia Kohn and Harold D. Roth, 274–94. Honolulu, HI: University of Hawaii Press.

Chai, David, ed. 2019. *Dao Companion to Neo-Daoism*. New York, NY: Springer.

Graham, A. C. 1989. *Disputers of the Tao: Philosophical Argument in Ancient China*. La Salle, IL: Open Court Publishing.

Hansen, Chad. 2010. "A Dao of 'Dao' in *Zhuangzi*." In *Experimental Essays on Zhuangzi*, edited by Victor H. Mair, 23–55. Dunedin, FL: Three Pines Press.

Harper, Donald. 1998. *Early Chinese Medical Manuscripts: The Mawangdui Medical Manuscripts*. London: Wellcome Asian Medical Monographs.

Kirkland, J. Russell. 1997. "The Historical Contours of Taoism in China: Thoughts on Issues of Classification and Terminology." *Journal of Chinese Religions* 25:57–82.

Kohn, Livia, and Harold D. Roth, eds. 2002. *Daoist Identity: History, Lineage, and Ritual*. Honolulu, HI: University of Hawaii Press.

Kohn, Livia. 1998. God of the Dao: Lord Lao in History and Myth. University of Michigan, Center for Chinese Studies.

Kohn, Livia, ed. 2000. *Daoism Handbook*. Leiden: Brill.

Kohn, Livia. 2001. *Daoism and Chinese Culture*. Cambridge, MA: Three Pines Press.

Kohn, Livia. 2005. Health and Long Life: The Chinese Way. In cooperation with Stephen Jackowicz. Cambridge, MA: Three Pines Press.

Kohn, Livia. 2007. *Daoist Mystical Philosophy: The Scripture of Western Ascension*. Magdalena, NM: Three Pines Press.

Kohn, Livia. 2008. *Chinese Healing Exercises: The Tradition of Daoyin*. Honolulu: University of Hawai'i Press.

Kohn, Livia. 2012. *A Source Book in Chinese Longevity*. St. Petersburg, FL: Three Pines Press.

Kohn, Livia. 2014. *Zhuangzi: Text and Context*. St. Petersburg, FL: Three Pines Press.

Kohn, Livia. 2018. *Daoist China: Governance, Economics, Culture*. St. Petersburg, FL: Three Pines Press.

Kohn, Livia. 2019. *Guides to Sacred Texts: The Daode jing*. New York, NY: Oxford University Press.

Kohn, Livia, and Harold D. Roth, eds. 2002. *Daoist Identity: History, Lineage, and Ritual*. Honolulu: University of Hawaii Press.

Palmer, David. 2007. *Qigong Fever: Body, Science and Utopia in China*. New York, NY: Columbia University Press.

Roth, Harold D. 1999. *Original Tao: Inward Training and the Foundations of Taoist Mysticism*. New York, NY: Columbia University Press.

Schipper, Kristofer M., and Franciscus Verellen, eds. 2004. *The Taoist Canon: A Historical Companion to the Daozang*, 3 vols. Chicago: University of Chicago Press.

Wang, Zhongjiang. 2015. *Daoism Excavated: Cosmos and Humanity in Early Manuscripts*. Translated by Livia Kohn. St. Petersburg, FL: Three Pines Press.

Zürcher, Erik. 1980. "Buddhist Influence on Early Taoism." *T'oung Pao* 66:84–147.

Part I
Reality

1 Ultimate reality

Ultimate reality, the absolute, the core power of all existence, by definition is eternal, self-created, independent, creative, unchanging, as well as omnipresent, omniscient, and omnipotent. Underlying and pervading all, it is a "power or force which centers and gives definiteness to the life of a human community."[1] Being ultimate or absolute, it can never be properly expressed in language, whether abstract in philosophical discourse or concrete in myth, because language is itself part of the created world. Its expression can only approximate, symbolize, or give metaphors for what is forever unknowable and ineffable. Both philosophy and myth, therefore, describe ultimate reality by pointing to primordial chaos, an uncharted void, or formless emptiness, from which oneness arises as the first sign that things have begun to take shape and will eventually become definable, that creation can now proceed.

Existence thus grows from ultimate reality, yet it is never separate from it. When the question is raised whether existence or its underlying formlessness ultimately is the absolute, the answer is always "Both!" The difference between life and its primordial state is never one of fundamental quality but always one of gradation. The ultimate in its concentrated form is in the center, at the beginning of creation; in its differentiated form, it is present in everything that exists—visible, knowable, and capable of being put into words. The transition between the two occurs either through evolution or disruption, either through the interaction of natural elements or the power of a transcendent creator, described in philosophical and cosmological discourse as occurring in phases of cosmic diversification and expressed in myth with the help of various symbols, images, and narratives.[2]

Dao

The ultimate in Daoism is Dao, the concept that gave the religion its name. The word originally means "way" and its character consists of the signs for eye and walking plus a cross indicating direction. Both traditionally and today it is used in this concrete sense, pointing to a road and by extension a method and related explanations. Given this general sense, the term has been used philosophically to indicate the way of the universe, the way human beings are in the world, the best way of social integration, the way of rulership, and more. For the most part, as Chad Hansen points out, it referred to particular ways of doing or managing things, connected to a specific place, time, social setting, and individual.[3]

The more metaphysical dimension of the term appears first in the *Daode jing*, which begins with the famous words, "The Dao that can be dao'ed [told] is not the constant Dao" (ch. 1). That is to say, it postulates that beyond all the various ways of skill mastery, governance, and academic discourse, there is Dao as a cosmic ground, an essence or source of all, an inherent way of being that applies universally. It is constant, invisible, inaudible, and subtle (ch. 14), the origin of heaven and earth (ch. 1), the mother of the universe (ch. 25), always empty yet never exhausted (ch. 4). The core force of the universe, Dao pervades all there is and, however inaccessible to ordinary sensing and knowing, continues to flow in the creative process of all existence free from metaphysical rupture. Without any exterior input or modification, Dao is a *perpetuum mobile* that does not depend on anything. Essentially immanent, it can never become the object of knowing; part of the realm beyond color, sound, and form, before there are things, Dao is free from distinctions, values, and borders. Not a material substance or even energy, it is a process of circular movement, blending and coalescing forces, so that vitality can gush forth in continuous emergence.[4]

Benjamin Schwartz describes it as "organic order." Dao is organic in the sense that it is part of the world and not a transcendent other as in Western religions; it is also order because it can be felt in the rhythms of the world, in the manifestation of organized patterns. Cheng Chung-ying explains its dimensions in terms of language: cosmic Dao is pre-language, whole, and circular; representational Dao is communicable, partial, and linear. Eske Møllgaard speaks of it as both visible and invisible, transcendent and immanent, latent but not beyond, the continuous flow of experience coming into being.[5]

One way to think of Dao is as two concentric circles, a smaller one in the center and a larger on the periphery. The dense, smaller circle in the center is Dao at the root of creative change—tight, concentrated, intense, and ultimately unknowable, ineffable, and beyond conscious or sensory human attainment (*Daode jing,* chs. 6, 14, 25). The larger circle at the periphery is Dao as it appears in the world, the patterned cycle of life and visible nature. Here we can see Dao as it comes and goes, rises and sets, rains and shines, lightens and darkens—the ever-changing yet everlasting, cyclical alteration of natural patterns, life and death (chs. 2, 9, 22, 36). This is Dao as natural transformations: the metamorphoses of insects, ways of bodily dissolution, and the inevitable entropy of life. This natural, tangible Dao is what people can study and learn to create harmony in the world; the cosmic, ineffable Dao, on the other hand, they need to open to by resting in clarity and stillness to find true authenticity in living.

The bipartite division of Dao as manifest and intangible is bridged in communal Daoism by identifying Laozi, the sage at the root of the *Daode jing,* with the central force of his teaching, transforming him into a conscious, active deity who not merely unfolds into the world but actively creates it. Ultimately identical with Dao, he is the entirety of life; with all the powers of a transcendent god, he yet reaches beyond the forces of the universe and manifest on earth in various forms.

The first record of this deification of Dao appears in the *Shengmu bei* (Stele for the Holy Mother) of the year 153 CE, found at a temple in honor of Laozi at his birthplace in Bozhou (modern Henan). It begins,

> Laozi, the Dao:
> Born prior to the formless,
> Grown before great beginning,
> He lives in the prime of great immaculate
> And floats freely through the six voids.
> He passes in and out of darkness and confusion,
> Contemplating chaos as yet undifferentiated,
> Viewing the clear and turbid in primordial union.

Laozi here is a celestial deity who forms part of Dao before creation yet also stands apart from it, being able to float through it and view it as if from a distance. More details appear in the *Laozi bianhua jing* (Scripture of the Transformations of Laozi), a cult-related work dated to around 185. It says,

> Laozi rests in the great beginning and wanders in the great origin,
> Floats through dark, numinous emptiness… .
> He joins serene darkness before its opening,
> Is present in original chaos before the beginnings of time. …
> Alone and without relation, he exists before heaven and earth.
> Living deeply hidden, he always returns to be:
> Latent: primordial; present: a man![6]

Laozi as the body of Dao, therefore, represents the creative, ordering power of the universe that transforms and creates the world. Both primordial and embodied as human, he can be anything and everything, is flexible and yet stable. As the text says,

> Laozi can be bright or dark, latent or present,
> Big or small, rolled up or stretched out,
> Above or below, vertical or horizontal, last or first.
> There is nothing he cannot do, nothing he will not accomplish.
> In fire he does not burn, in water he does not freeze.
> He meets with evil without suffering, confronts disasters without
>   affliction.
> Opposed, he is not pained, harmed, he is not scarred.

> Laozi lives forever and does not die, but merely dissolves his
>   bodily form.
> Single and without counterpart, alone and without dependence,
> He is yet joined with all and never separate.[7]

Here the deity is not merely a personification of Dao, the formless, spontaneous force that creates by unfolding naturally and without external guidance. He is also a conscious creator who stands alone, has knowledge and volition, and takes active steps in guiding the world. He unites the two poles of the absolute, collapses the two circles of Dao into one—representing ultimate reality in all its complexity and contradictions.

Oneness

Another form ultimate reality takes in Daoism is as oneness or "the One" (*yi*), a state of highest unity at the brink of creation, the first level of unified existence after the cosmic void. As the *Daode jing* says, "Dao brings forth the One," which in turn divides into the two, the polar opposites that make up the created world (ch. 42). The *Zhuangzi* has, "In the Great Beginning there was nonbeing. There was no being, no name. Out of it oneness arose. Then there was oneness, but there was no form. Beings realized and came to life. It was called their life force" (ch. 12).

Unifying all things that exist, oneness is not a material or visible entity or a potent creator; it is not a metaphysical reality, a number that initiates all numbers, or a single entity opposite to the many. "The Chinese world," Roger Ames says,

> is not "'one'" in the classical Greek sense of a single ordered "'*uni*'"-verse where some external, independent, and determinative principle provides unity and order to something other than itself. It is not "'one'" in the sense that would make it a closed system, defined in terms of abstract, universal, necessary, and unchanging natural and moral laws."[8]

Rather, oneness signifies unity, uniformity, and nonduality; a fundamental quality of Dao, it makes things and people what they are in the greater scheme of the universe, causing heaven to be clear, earth to be settled, and all beings to live and grow (*Daode jing* 39; *Zhuangzi* 6).

In communal cosmology, the One is close to water as the source of all life and relates to the winter solstice, the point of cosmic renewal in the annual cycle. Above, it is the heavenly pivot or celestial pole, the ultimate geographical core of the universe. The power that controls everything, it is yet not represented by any particular star or constellation and has no "obvious physical presence," but is rather "the marvel of an efficacious 'nothing' at the center of the rotating dome of the sky."[9]

Just as Dao was deified, so the One turned into an astral deity in the official cult of the Han and was installed as the god of the center of the universe. As such, it was further identified with the deified Laozi. As the *Xiang'er*, a third-century Celestial Masters commentary to the *Daode jing*, says, "The One when dispersed is the energy of the world; when concentrated it is the god Laozi. Then he resides on Mount Kunlun and reveals the teaching of Dao." The *Laozi zhongjing* (Central Scripture of Laozi; DZ 1168) similarly describes the One as "the father of Dao, older than heaven and earth. He resides in the heaven of Great Clarity above the nine heavens." Later Daoist mythology, moreover, has him also appear in female form. Thus, the Goddess of the Great One (Taiyi yuanjun), part of cosmic primordiality, one with Dao, and well-versed in its arcana, instructs the newly born divine Laozi in the basic principles of Dao and world.

Activated also in self-cultivation, the One is further—together with other celestial phenomena—placed inside the human body, generally seen as a microcosm of the universe. Thus, the *Taiping jing* (Scripture of Great Peace, DZ 1101), a sixth-century reconstruction of materials from the organized Great Peace movement of the second century, says:

> In the head, the One is the top;
> Among the seven orifices, it is found in the eyes;
> In the center of the body, it is the navel;
> Among the five organs, it is the heart;
> Among the members of the body, it is the hands;
> Among the bones, it is the spinal column;
> In the flesh of the body, it is found in the five organs and the stomach.

According to the *Baopuzi*, the One is

> 0.9 inches in length in the male, and 0.6 inches in the female. Sometimes it is in the lower elixir field, 2.4 inches beneath the navel. At other times it rests in the central elixir field in the heart, the Golden Tower or Purple Palace."
>
> (ch. 18)

In medieval Daoism, the One becomes a particular deity who looks like a new-born baby, is clad in purple robes, and sits on a golden throne. His residence is the Scarlet Palace of the heart or the Purple Chamber of the head, that is, the upper elixir field. The three elixir fields (*dantian*) are key energy centers of the body, located in the center of head, chest, and abdomen, respectively, and representing the three levels of heaven, humanity, and earth. In addition, and reflecting his celestial status, the deity holds the handle of the Northern Dipper, the pivot of Daoist astral mythology, controlling agent of all activities, and master of human destiny.[10]

Stages of unfolding

The way ultimate reality relates to the world is typically described in terms of several stages that begin with oneness and unfold into two and from there into three and thus multiplicity. Thus, the *Daode jing* famously has,

> Dao gives birth to one,
> One gives birth to two,
> Two give birth to three,
> And three give birth to the myriad beings.
>
> (ch. 42)

The *Huainanzi* (Book of the Master of Huainan) of about 150 BCE provides an interpretation. "Dao begins with oneness. Oneness alone, however, does not give birth. Therefore, it divided into yin and yang. From the harmonious union of yin and yang, the myriad beings were given birth."

Other versions of Daoist cosmogony appear in manuscripts recently excavated from southern China. Thus, the *Fanwu liuxing* (All Things Flow in Form) describes universal unfolding in terms of beginning with oneness, which brings forth to the two and the three, and from there proceeds to the mother to eventually lead to the integrated combination of all. The mother, as is well known, is a common Daoist metaphor of cosmic origin, applying the human relationship of mother and children to the universe and the myriad beings. However, rather than being a metaphor for Dao as it is in the *Daode jing* and thus resting at the very source of existence (chs. 1, 25, 52), here it appears at a later stage, at the brink of ultimate integration, that is, the emergence of the myriad beings.

The *Taiyi shengshui* (Great Oneness Gives Birth to Water) was discovered at Guodian in the same cluster of bamboo slips as fragments of the *Daode jing*, dated to around 350 BCE. The text clearly shows its influence in both its key concepts, "one" and "water," which it expands to great oneness as the core creative factor of the universe. Its emphasis on the notion that "the Dao of heaven values weakness," too, connects to the *Daode jing*, which favors weakness and softness over aggression and competition. While the *Taiyi shengshui* begins with the One, it does not go on to two but has the universe evolve by moving on to water, from which heaven and earth arise. They in turn connect back to Great Oneness and water. Once these are established, spirit and light emerge, and only then do the two of the *Daode jing* come into play: yin and yang arise together with summer and winter, cold and heat, dampness and dryness, to eventually result in the ongoing cycle of the years.[11]

A yet different version of early cosmogony appears in the *Hengxian* (Constancy Before). The term *heng* means "constant" and appears in the very first line of the *Daode jing*. Constancy is another key characteristic of Dao, indicating the unchanging and invariable nature of the ultimate. In this version, then, the universe begins with constancy. From here, the text says, "space arises. Once there is space, there is vital energy. Once there is vital energy, there is material existence. Once there is material existence, there is a beginning. Once there is a beginning, there is the passage of time." The ultimate is defined as unmoving as well as having no material existence, being instead "simplicity, stillness, and emptiness." No material existence means that there is nothing, that life is in a state of latency, nothingness, or non-being, formless and undifferentiated, not yet manifesting in concrete things, often also called "vessels." This gives rise to vital energy, which in turn leads to presence, existence, or being, and eventually initiates entropy and thus the flow of time.[12]

Medieval communal Daoists, too, present various outlines of the world's unfolding, integrating the understanding of yin, yang, and water energies with divine entities and heavenly spheres. For example, the fifth-century *Santian neijie jing* (Inner Explanation of the Three Heavens), a mythical outline of Celestial Masters' history, begins with Dao as the underlying creative power of the world, "dark and obscure, vast and open, and without prior cause." Revolving in emptiness and natural so-being, it brings forth a figure called the Elder of Dao and Virtue, immediately followed by the three highest heavens.

Next, "in the midst of emptiness and pervasion, Great Nonbeing was born. Great Nonbeing transformed and changed into the three energies: primordial, mysterious, and beginning." They in turn "intermingle in chaos, following each other, then transform to bring forth the Jade Maiden of Mystery and Wonder." She, then, gives birth to the celestial Laozi through her left armpit—imitating the hagiography of the Buddha. The god in this version is not Dao himself but its direct product, mediated through a series of transformations that bring forth heavens, spiritual powers, pure energies, and a mother figure. Born supernaturally, his emergence from the left armpit borrows on the story of the birth of the Buddha, who leaves his mother through her right hip.

Next, Lord Lao creates the world. Under his guidance, mysterious energy rises up to form heaven, beginning energy sinks down and becomes earth, while primordial energy flows everywhere and turns into water—thus forming the three basic realms of the Celestial Masters' universe. In addition, the god creates three major continents with three countries each, where he places people and religions: Daoism in the center (China), Buddhism in the west, and the "Way of Clear Harmony" in the south, bringing the world with its main continents and religions into existence.[13]

Another example appears in the *Kaitian jing* (Scripture of Opening the Cosmos) of the sixth century. Here Laozi is Dao, described in terms closely echoing the *Daode jing*:

> Lord Lao, Dao, was at rest in open mystery, beyond silent desolation, in mysterious emptiness. Look and do not see, listen and do not hear. You may say it is there and do not see a shape; you may say it is not there, yet all beings follow it for life. Beyond the eight bounds—slowly,

slowly—first it divides, sinks to form the subtle and the wondrous, to make the world.[14]

The seed of order in the midst of chaos, Dao as deity then guides the universe through various stages of evolution, "descending from barren emptiness to be their teacher," in each case his mouth emitting the appropriate scripture, written in celestial script and consisting of millions of words. He begins in Vast Prime, a phase of undifferentiated oneness, "mysterious barrenness and silent desolation," then moves on to Grand Antecedence, separating heaven and earth and establishing the celestial bodies of sun, moon, and stars. After this came Grand Initiation, the "beginning of the myriad beings," followed by Grand Simplicity, when people lived on sweet dew and pure essence, attaining long life in harmony with nature, and eventually moving on to develop culture and create the world as we know it.[15]

Underlying structures

All these variations of Daoist cosmogony have in common that they describe the contrast between the absolute and the world in terms of binary opposites, such as the One and the many, stillness and movement, formlessness and form, beginning and completion. Later thinkers, moreover, have expressed this fundamental division in a variety of ways, adding intricacy to the understanding and enhancing its philosophical subtlety.

A major player in this regard is Wang Bi, the prime commentator and editor of the *Daode jing*. He developed the concept of original nonbeing, giving identity and outline to Dao as well as a distinct role in the world, describing it as the root versus the branches, as inherent substance versus external function. For Wang Bi, oneness is no longer merely an attribute of Dao, but identical with it. He reduces the depth of the ground, gives a name to the ineffable and describes its activity in clear-cut patterns. Original nonbeing points to Dao as the root and origin of the world, relating it to the world of being as silence does to language: while silence is the absence of language, it is yet more than that; silence underlies language, which punctuates it only fleetingly. Similarly, nonbeing lies beneath all being. It is its absence and yet more; it is its cause and its reason. As Wang Bi says,

> All being originates from nonbeing. Therefore, the time before there were forms and names is the beginning of the myriad beings. When forms and names are there, Dao raises them, educates them, adjusts them, and causes their end. It serves as their mother. Dao creates and completes beings on the basis of the formless and the nameless. They are produced and completed but do not know how or why. Indeed, it is mysterious and again mysterious.
>
> (ch. 1)[16]

A different take on the issue appears further in an eighth-century text known as *Daoti lun* (Embodiment of Dao). A highly metaphysical discussion, it presents a lengthy, abstract dialogue on the original nature and active presence of Dao in the world. Complex and intricate, the text looks at problems from many different angles and, integrating Buddhist Madhyamika thought, gives paradoxical definitions using patterns like "both" or "neither." It divides into three parts, focusing in turn on the *Daode jing*, the nature of Dao, and its embodiment.

It begins by making a distinction between Dao and virtue, separating the transcendent principle at the root of creation from its embodied aspect and active principle in the world.

> Dao is all-pervasive; it transforms all from the beginning. Virtue arises in its following; it completes all beings to their end. They thus appear in birth and the completion of life. In the world, they have two different names; fulfilling their activities, they return to the same ancestral ground. They are two and yet always one. … Dao is always there, yet eternally other. Beings need Dao to embody themselves. At the same time, Dao needs beings to embody itself. Beyond the inherent oneness of all, there are good and evil, right and wrong, life and death, opposition and conformity.

Dao and beings, therefore, depend on each other, just as Dao and virtue form two aspects of the creative power of life. They are different yet the same, separate yet one, nameless yet named, at rest yet in constant movement. Dao cannot be without embodiment; embodiment is an inherent aspect of Dao. Invisibility and ineffability stop here. Although in essence beyond human reach, Dao is yet always also embodied in all things. This means that Dao, however eternal, also lives and dies along with all things. "Since beings live and die, Dao also lives and dies. … Still, Dao contains all equally and is free from life and death." Looking at the problem from the perspective of the living and dying of beings, Dao is inherent yet beyond, changes as beings change yet stays always and ultimately the same.

Next, the text makes the same point in terms of identity and difference, emphasizing that "in their perfection, they culminate in the absence of identity and difference." Dao and beings are both identical and different, and neither identical nor different. As Dao is and is not all living beings, Daoist cultivation is noncultivation, necessary despite the fact that there is no essential gap to bridge—echoing the Mahayana Buddhist position that everyone is already enlightened. One must cultivate because "cultivation makes up for the discrepancy, however slight, between the root and its embodiment, and leads back to original nonbeing," here integrating Wang Bi's core concept.

Dao, through its embodiment, can therefore be known; the Daoist teaching becomes a teaching with words that can be followed to overcome the gap between world and pure Dao. Names and intellectual distinctions, sacred chants and scriptures like everything else participate in Dao and embodiment. Moving from embodiment back to Dao, adepts strip off names and mental classifications to attain true Dao-nature (reflecting the concept of Buddha-nature) by reaching the state of Chaos Perfected, a state without distinctions, total, and centered in itself, the closest any living being can come to true realization.[17]

Notes

1 Sproul 1979, 29.
2 Sproul 1979, 10; Biallas 1986, 44.
3 Hansen 2010, 35.
4 This discussion is based on Moeller 2004, 98; Møllgaard 2007, 23. See also Kohn 2014, 79.
5 These statements appear in Schwartz 1985, 195; Cheng 2004, 145; Møllgaard 2005, 2–5.
6 This translation follows Seidel 1969, 62.
7 Both early documents are translated and studied in Seidel 1969. For a discussion in English, see Kohn 1998a.
8 Ames 1998, 228. For a more detailed discussion, see also Kohn 2014, 83.
9 Pankenier 2014, 92. On the communal take on oneness, see also Robinet 1993, 121.
10 This discussion follows Kohn 1989, 135–36. The *Baopuzi* passage is translated in Ware 1966, 302.
11 Wang 2015, 8.
12 The manuscripts are discussed and translated in Wang 2015. The passage from the *Huainanzi* appears in Major et al. 2010, 133. A detailed study and complete translation of the texts from Guodian is found in Cook 2012.
13 This discussion follows Kohn 1998a, 15–16. For a study and translation of the text, see Bokenkamp 1997.
14 Kohn 1993, 36
15 Kohn 1993, 36–9. The names of the stages go back to the *Yijing*.
16 This discussion follows Kohn 1992, 61. A complete translation of Wang Bi's commentary appears in Rump and Chan 1979.
17 For more on this text and on Daoist scholastic endeavors in general, see Kohn 1998b.

References

Ames, Roger T. 1998. "Knowing in the *Zhuangzi*: From Here, on the Bridge, over the River Hao." In *Wandering at Ease in the Zhuangzi*, edited by Roger Ames, 219–30. Albany, NY: State University of New York Press.

Biallas, Leonard J. 1986. *Myths: Gods, Heroes, and Saviors*. Mystic, CT: Twenty-Third Publications.

Cheng, Chung-ying. 2004. "Dimensions of the Dao and Onto-Ethics in Light of the *Daode jing*." *Journal of Chinese Philosophy* 31.2:143–82.

Cook, Scott. 2012. *The Bamboo Texts of Guodian: A Study and Complete Translation*. 2 vols. Ithaca, NY: Cornell University Press.

Hansen, Chad. 2010 [1983]. "A Dao of 'Dao' in *Zhuangzi*." In *Experimental Essays on Zhuangzi*, edited by Victor H. Mair, 23-55. Dunedin, Fla.: Three Pines Press.

Kohn, Livia. 1989. "Guarding the One: Concentrative Meditation in Taoism." In *Taoist Meditation and Longevity Techniques*, edited by Livia Kohn, 123–56. Ann Arbor, MI: University of Michigan, Center for Chinese Studies.

Kohn, Livia. 1992. *Early Chinese Mysticism: Philosophy and Soteriology in the Taoist Tradition*. Princeton, NJ: Princeton University Press.

Kohn, Livia. 1993. *The Taoist Experience: An Anthology*. Albany, NY: State University of New York Press.

Kohn, Livia. 1998a. *God of the Dao: Lord Lao in History and Myth*. Ann Arbor, MI: University of Michigan, Center for Chinese Studies.

Kohn, Livia. 1998b. "Taoist Scholasticism: A Preliminary Inquiry." In *Scholasticism: Cross-Cultural and Comparative Perspectives*, edited by José Ignacio Cabezon, 115–50. Albany, NY: State University of New York Press.

Kohn, Livia. 2014. *Zhuangzi: Text and Context*. St. Petersburg, FL: Three Pines Press.

Major, John S., Sarah A. Queen, Andrew S. Meyer, and Harold D. Roth. 2010. *The Huainanzi: A Guide to the Theory and Practice of Government in Early Han China*. New York, NY: Columbia University Press.

Moeller, Hans-Georg. 2004. *Daoism Explained: From the Dream of the Butterfly to the Fishnet Allegory*. La Salle, IL: Open Court Publishing.

Møllgaard, Eske. 2005. "Zhuangzi's Notion of Transcendental Life." *Asian Philosophy* 15.1:1–18.

Møllgaard, Eske. 2007. *An Introduction to Daoist Thought: Action, Language, and Ethics in the Zhuangzi*. London: Routledge.

Pankenier, David W. 2014. *Astrology and Cosmology in Early China: Conforming Earth to Heaven*. Cambridge: Cambridge University Press.

Robinet, Isabelle. 1993. *Taoist Meditation: The Mao-shan Tradition of Great Purity*. Translated by Norman Girardot and Julian Pas. Albany, NY: State University of New York Press.

Rump, Ariane, and Wing-tsit Chan. 1979. *Commentary on the Lao-tzu by Wang Pi*. Honolulu, HI: University of Hawaii Press.

Schwartz, Benjamin. 1985. *The World of Thought in Ancient China*. Cambridge, MA: Harvard University Press.

Seidel, Anna. 1969. *La divinisation de Lao-tseu dans le taoïsme des Han*. Paris: Ecole Française d'Extrême-Orient.

Sproul, Barbara C. 1979. *Primal Myths: Creating the World*. San Francisco, CA: Harper & Row.

Wang, Zhongjiang. 2015. *Daoism Excavated: Cosmos and Humanity in Early Manuscripts*. Translated by Livia Kohn. St. Petersburg, FL: Three Pines Press.

Ware, James R. 1966. *Alchemy, Medicine and Religion in the China of AD 320*. Cambridge, MA: MIT Press.

2   The world

Once human beings find themselves living in the world, they begin to build structure and create meaning. Human life itself is an ongoing exercise in sense-making, so that, as Peter Berger puts it, "every human society is engaged in the never completed enterprise of building a humanly meaningful world." Both society and the individual must, in their efforts to justify and interpret existence, by necessity resort to means that lie beyond the basic facts of existence as such. They therefore transcend reality while searching for explanations. As Peter Berger has further shown, the explanations themselves turn around in due course and become realities of their own. The interpretative framework begins to demand certain actions, adaptations of concrete reality and human psychology, in order to remain valid, while itself subject to change and transformation, variations, and revisions.[1]

Most fundamentally, human world-building relies on the propensity for order. To establish a meaningful world, people must organize random data into a systematic whole. Underlying this process is a fundamental human faith in order as such, a need of the human being to feel integrated and properly positioned. This is evident already in the behavior of children who demand the reassurance that everything is in order, that their caregivers are there and do exactly what they should be doing. It also emerges in the conviction that people and things can be proper and improper both in a simple everyday fashion and also in a religious and sacred way. Yet, the basic assumption that there needs to be order is already a step beyond concrete reality, since it implies the existence of transcendent principles. It signals that people are in the world yet also creating the world they are in.[2]

Typically, this philosophical world-building involves identifying key building blocks of existence, such as the atoms and elements in ancient Greece, as well as the systematization of reality according to central numbers, for example, the Babylonian focus on seven. It also usually involves a connection to the stars, the identification of key planets and constellations, as well as the structuring of land and sea, and the determination of essential landscape features.

Vital energy

Existence in Daoism—as much as in Chinese cosmology in general and also in Chinese medicine—is built on vital energy (*qi*). The basic material of all that exists, it animates life and furnishes functional power of events. There is only one *qi*, just as there is only one Dao. Yet it, too, appears on different levels of subtlety and in different modes. At the center, there is primordial, prenatal, true, or perfect *qi*—intangible, invisible, inaudible, dark, and mysterious. At the periphery, there is postnatal or earthly *qi*—like the measurable Dao, it is in constant motion and perceptible in form, sound, and light.

Life happens when *qi* comes together, while death is its dispersal—not a loss or elimination of energy but a change in density and constellation. Whether present or latent, all aspects of the universe are forms of *qi*, which can flow faster or slower, be looser or denser, lighter or heavier. For example, at the time of creation, primordial light *qi* rose up to create heaven while heavy *qi* sank down to form earth. *Qi* can be evaluated in terms of quantity, since having more *qi* means stronger function, but quality of flow is what really counts. Each and every person, animal, plant, rock, river, starry constellation, and social unit has the amount and flow ratio of *qi* that is just right, creating perfect balance, health, and harmony.[3]

Flowing *qi* makes up everything, envisioned as a complex system of interconnected pools and channels on all levels of existence. Within the human body, for example, as reflected in the names of acupuncture points, it centers in the Ocean of *Qi* in the abdomen and from there flows into rivers through the upper torso, arms, and legs. In addition, there are springs of *qi* in the wrists and ankles and wells of *qi* in the fingers and toes. The system is holographic—everything interconnects with everything else, and a disturbance at even a small spot impacts the whole. Like quanta, moreover, that can appear both as waves and particles, *qi* is nonlocal: it can be anywhere and exchange information with anything else instantaneously. To express it with a metaphor from physicist Itchak Bentov, all reality can be imagined as a huge bowl of fairly rigid jelly with raisins in it. Vibrate one part of it, and the rest also vibrates. One section cannot move without the other, and even the slightest touch to one single raisin will immediately transmit movements to all the others and the body of the jelly.[4]

The same also holds true for human beings. Every individual has electrical charges in and around him, which are measurable and can be felt. These charges are the body's energy field: it interacts not only with its own organs and parts but also with the field of things around it and the greater universe— all the way through the galaxies.[5] In other words, *qi* is everything, connects everywhere, and pervades all. Rather than striving for accumulation or preponderance of any particular portion of this *qi*, then, the overarching goal is to achieve overall balance and smoothness, a great harmony of the entire system.

Harmony occurs when *qi* is just right and flows smoothly: this is called proper or upright *qi*. It manifests in people as a sense of vibrant health and in nature as regular weather patterns and the absence of disasters. In society it appears as the peaceful coexistence and strong community among families, clans, villages, and states, and is evident on the cosmic, galactic level in the regular course of the planets. This presence of a steady *qi* flow everywhere—from the farthest reaches of the universe to the minutest cells in the individual—is what the Chinese call the state of Great Peace, an ideal venerated by Confucians and Daoists alike.

The opposite is wayward or deviant *qi*, which occurs when *qi* has lost its harmonious pattern and no longer supports the dynamic forces of change. Whereas proper *qi* moves in a steady, harmonious rhythm and effects daily renewal, wayward *qi* is disorderly and dysfunctional, producing change that violates the normal order. When wayward *qi* becomes dominant, the *qi*-flow can even turn upon itself and deplete resources. Then the individual, community, or state no longer operates as part of a universal system and is not in tune with Dao (see Figure 2.1).

Wayward *qi* appears when *qi* moves too fast or too slow, is excessive or depleted, or creates rushes or obstructions. *Qi* can become excessive through too much heat or cold or too much open space or stimulation. Excessive *qi* can be moving too fast or be very sluggish, as in the case of excessive dampness. Whatever the case, from a universal perspective there is no extra or new *qi* created, but localized disharmonies have arisen because the ongoing *qi* process has become excessive and thus harmful, distorting the subtle patterns of energetic vibrations.

Similarly, *qi* can be in depletion. There may be a tense flow due to restriction or overbuilding, or volume and density have decreased, which would be the case in serious prolonged violation of nature or personal illness. However, more commonly depletion occurs when the *qi* activity level is lower, its flow is not quite up to standard, or there is a thinner than normal concentration of *qi* in one or the other part. Thus, perfection of *qi* means the optimal functioning of vital energy in its various dimensions, while control of *qi* means the power to guide the energetic process to one or the other part, enhancing overall health and harmony.[6]

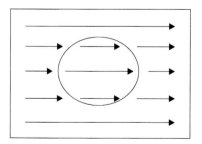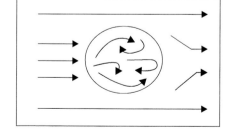

Figure 2.1 Proper and wayward *qi*.

The world being a conglomeration of various vibratory fields, there can never be just one single cause for any given situation, but the interconnection of the whole needs to be examined. Corrections, while diagnosed typically in terms of excess and insufficiency of flow, come accordingly in many different forms and should have an effect on the entirety of the system, applying a strong harmonizing rhythm to any given part of the vibrational pattern. Chinese medicine applies this to restore health to individual bodies; governance in China works to affect it in the society as a whole. Daoists integrate both but in addition they also see the cosmic dimension, relating people and social structures to nature and the workings of the stars, whether in abstract thought, through ritual activities, or in personal self-cultivation.

Yin-Yang and the five phases

Again, common to all of Chinese culture is the understanding that the rhythm of *qi*-flow functions in terms of the numbers two and five. While the number one represents cosmic unity and the energy underlying all, two characterizes its movement in terms of yin and yang: up or down, forward or back, rising or falling. Originally indicating the sunny and shady sides of a hill, yin and yang soon acquired a series of associations: bright and dark, light and heavy, strong and weak, above and below, heaven and earth, ruler and minister, male and female, and so on. Commonly presented in the well-known circle with two black and white curved halves, they represent the interlocking of energy patterns in an ongoing process of balancing and ordering, of continuous enfolding and unfolding (Figure 2.2).

While Westerners commonly assume that yang is "better" than yin, the Chinese view demands that neither is better, stronger, brighter, or more preferable, and the two forces do not represent good and evil. On the contrary, the yin aspect of things is just as important as the yang, because one cannot be without the other. They are neither substance nor opposites but complementary phases of *qi*-flow, one bringing forth the other in close mutual interdependence, one inevitably necessitating the other.[7]

The underlying structure of this particular world-building is a form of correlative thinking. More ancient than Western linear analysis that focuses on logic and the law of cause and effect, it is not unique to China but can also be found in other traditional cultures, such as ancient Greece, and in the West is still used in occultism and magic. It represents a basic pattern of the human mind clearly present in the way we acquire language. For example, to build the plural of *shoe*, we add the letter "s" to get *shoes*. The same applies to cat/cats, stone/stones, road/ roads. But then we learn that this correlative pattern when applied to the word *foot* is wrong and instead of *foots* we use another pattern and go from *foot* to *feet*, then apply the same to get goose/geese, and so on. In all cases, the organization of language is based on a simple pattern that is correlated and repeated in different instances.

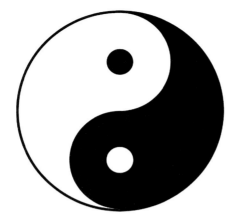

Figure 2.2 The Taiji Symbol. Wikimedia Commons.

Correlation also comes into play in a more general understanding of reality. For example, the working of the human body may be applied to politics, so that the mind in relation to the body is understood as similar to the ruler's relation to his subjects, or vice versa. A more mechanical vision of the body may see it as a complex engine, while a more cosmological understanding (as in Daoism) may envision it as the residence of starry deities. In all cases, similarities and differences between patterns are recognized and reality is understood in terms of the interaction of different aspects that impact on each other. At the same time, the pattern itself also creates a specific vision of reality—as correlated and interactive—leading to the formation of new structures in the world.[8]

The binary division into yin and yang pervades the Chinese world on all levels and is activated in every aspect of Daoism, be it the theoretical understanding of heaven and earth, themselves a binary pair; the activation of ritual, where officiants are two if female and one if male (odd numbers being yang); as well as in self-cultivation, whose methods differ according to times of day and year (midnight to noon as well as spring and summer being yang) and work strongly with the ongoing rise and fall of vital energy.

From here, moreover, the Chinese also work with a system of fives, known as the five phases (*wuxing*). Essentially there are subtler aspects of energy dynamics, designating an initial rise, a heightened state, a turning point, a beginning decline, and a deep trough. These five are then called minor yang, major yang, yin/yang, minor yin, and major yin, respectively, and associated with five natural materials—wood, fire, earth, metal, and water.

In their natural rhythm, the five materials produce each other continuously in a harmonious cycle. Thus, water comes about through rainfall. It makes things grow, so that there is lush vegetation and wood arises. Wood dries and becomes fuel for fire, which burns and creates ashes. Ashes become earth, and earth over long periods of consolidation grows metals in its depths. Metals in the depths of mountains, moreover, attract clouds and stimulate rainfall, thus closing the cycle. At the same time, however, the five materials also have a relationship of mutual control. Thus, water can extinguish fire, fire can melt metal, metal can cut wood, wood can contain earth, earth can dam water, and water can again extinguish fire. Hence, there is an inherent dynamic among them that can be either productive or controlling.

In the early Han dynasty, cosmologists began to associate the five energetic phases as defined through those materials with all different aspects of life:

phase	dir	season	color	planet	organ	flavor	sense	emotion
wood	east	spring	green	Jupiter	liver	sour	eyes	anger
fire	south	summer	red	Mars	heart	bitter	mouth	euphoria
earth	center	Sept	yellow	Saturn	spleen	sweet	touch	worry
metal	west	fall	white	Venus	lungs	spicy	nose	sadness
water	north	winter	black	Mercury	kidneys	salty	ears	fear

This system not only forms the basis of abstract speculation but is activated in many ways, so that, for example, the ruler would perform rituals to deities of the various directions during the appropriate season, clad in the right color, eating matching foods, and so on. It is also at the core of Chinese medicine, which balances the energy in the organs through acupuncture, massage, herbal remedies, dietary modifications, and seasonal adaptations, using the productive and controlling cycles. Daoists, in their turn, adopted it not only in their overall world-making, classifying everything in groups of five and activating it in ritual, but also used medical diagnosis and healing as the foundation of their self-cultivation practices.[9] Their more cosmic orientation plays out particularly in their vision of the five phases as representing the horizontal dimension of cosmology (the five organs in the body), while the three levels of heaven, humanity, and earth stand for its vertical aspect (the three elixir fields). They all, moreover, are understood as celestial palaces and starry constellations, nurtured by cosmic energy and inhabited by powerful deities that represent pure, cosmic Dao.

The world in nines

A yet different way of making sense of the world in traditional China centers on the number nine, three squared and thus representing a high potency of yang. It first appears in the understanding of the world as consisting of a square earth covered by the round dome of heaven, which gives it the overall shape of a turtle. The earth, moreover, was seen to consist of nine concentric squares, with China in the center (the Middle Kingdom), friends and allies in the cardinal directions, and the so-called barbarians on the periphery. The country itself was further divided into nine provinces, the capital city was laid out to have nine major wards, and the palace contained a ritual space to show the world in miniature.[10] When Yu the Great, the mythical founder of the Xia dynasty—today tentatively associated with a chalcolithic site at Erlitou in Henan (1900–1600 BCE)—tamed the flood, he moved back and forth through the nine provinces, establishing order and claiming power over the country.

Early cosmologists integrated the nine squares with the number five in two major ways, placing the numbers one through nine into them to represent a vertical and horizontal aspect as well as the distribution of forces before and after creation. The vertical, pre-creation chart looks like a cross and shows three concentric spheres, with the number five in the center, the numbers one through four in the narrow circle, and the higher numbers on the periphery. Facing south as all traditional Chinese maps do, it has the yin numbers at the bottom (toward the north) representing the cosmic beginning and yang numbers at the top, showing completion. The horizontal, post-creation chart retains the nine squares. It, too, has the number five in the center, but places the odd (yang) numbers into the cardinal directions and the even (yin) numbers in the intermediary positions. The two charts, moreover, supposedly were delivered directly from heaven via markings on the back of a sacred dragon (yang) and turtle (yin) who emerged from the central rivers of China. They are known as the *Hetu* ([Yellow] River Chart) and *Luoshu* (Writ of the Luo [River]; Figures 2.3 and 2.4).[11]

Daoists activate these charts variously. Besides using them in abstract cosmological speculation and number analysis, they form the basis of a ritual dance known as the Pace of Yu (*yubu*), which imitates the ruler's wanderings while taming the floods and allows the priest to take possession of the world. In addition, the magic square is also transposed into the stars, associated with the nine stars of the Dipper (seven regular plus two invisible ones), activated in ritual and personal cultivation in an ecstatic excursion known as "pacing

```
                    7
                    2
        8    3      5    4    9
                    1
                    6
```

Figure 2.3 The *Hetu* numbers

```
    4          9          2
    3          5          7
    8          1          6
```

Figure 2.4 The *Luoshu* numbers

the heavenly net." Beyond that, the nine appear in the head in the form of the Nine Palaces (*jiugong*). The center here is the upper elixir field, also known as the Niwan and traditionally the residence of the chief deities of the universe. Surrounding it are four palaces that serve as the residences of the Great One, the Highest Lord, the Lord of the Great Ultimate, and the Goddess of Highest Clarity. The remaining four palaces house lesser but still essential cosmic gods, such as the Jade Emperor (Yuhuang) and the gods of light. Matching the central area of the brain with its major control centers and ventricles, the Nine Palaces are activated in meditation to create a cosmic connection and strong internal control.[12]

Another scheme that works with the number nine goes back to the *Yijing*, the main divination manual of the Zhou dynasty. It works with a system of universal unfolding that is different from that of the *Daode jing*. While also acknowledging Dao as the "pivot of emergence and master of growth" and emphasizing its unfolding into the two forces yin and yang, it moves on to claim a fourfold pattern as the next stage. Depicting the two as lines, single (yang) and in two parts (yin), it combines them in four ways (two yang, two yin, yang over yin, and yin over yang), creating the so-called four images or emblems (*sixiang*), which in turn produce the eight trigrams (*bagua*) by combining the lines into sets of three.[13] The eight trigrams in turn symbolize various features of the world, such as heaven and earth (6, 2 in the chart below), water and fire (1, 9), mountain and lake (8, 7), thunder and wind (3, 4). Daoists integrate them with the *Luoshu*, centered around a core pivot that represents the planet as a whole and also connects to the Great One as empty vastness. They use them variously to designate directions, alchemical substances, and internal energies as well as symbolize major aspects of life, and apply them in philosophical speculation, divination, fengshui, and internal alchemy (Figure 2.5).

Beyond this, the number nine is ubiquitous in Daoist ritual and cosmology. For example, the

4	9	2
3	5	7
8	1	6

Figure 2.5 The Eight Trigrams in the *Luoshu*. Daoist Canon.

Daoist's staff, a sign of sacrality and authority, is made from bamboo and has nine knots, named after planets, lunar stations, and starry constellations. In the otherworld, Daoists occupy nine celestial ranks, and many dignitaries wear robes of nine colors. Scriptures, rules, heavens, and more all come in multiples of nine, the numbers thirty-six and eighty-one appearing most often.

With respect to the world, the most important feature in this context is the belief in thirty-six grotto heavens (*dongtian*) and seventy-two auspicious spots or blissful lands (*fudi*) that create an intricate network of cosmic energy throughout the landscape and allow adepts to relate intimately to its subtle flow of *qi*. The Chinese generally see mountains as connectors between heaven and earth, and particularly worship the five sacred mountains—peaks that rise prominently from the plains located in the five directions and matching the five phases.

Daoists in addition honor mountains that have deep grottoes or caverns, which they understand as alternative worlds, immortal realms, deep wombs of pure energy. They have their own heaven and earth, sun and moon, landscape and community, albeit of a different order, so that night is bright and daytime couched in darkness. Ruled by perfected beings sent from heaven and inhabited by earth immortals, they are only accessible to selected adepts after extensive periods of purification and preparation. The grottoes, moreover, are not isolated but connect to each other in a system known as earth meridians, matching the *qi* conduits in the human body, to create a potent energy web within the depth of the earth. Doubling the traditional number five, Daoists acknowledge ten major grotto heavens, including the well-known ritual centers of Wangwu shan (Henan), Qingcheng shan (Sichuan), and Luofu shan (Guangdong), plus thirty-six lesser ones that also include the five sacred mountains. Lesser peaks, then, form the seventy-two auspicious spots, which are not as potent as the grotto heavens but provide and excellent environment for practice and connection to the divine.[14]

Notes

1   Berger 1969a, 27, 17.
2   Berger 1969b, 68.
3   See Kohn 2016, ch. 2.
4   Bentov 1977, 29.
5   See Oschman 2000.
6   See Kohn 2005.
7   See Wang 2012.
8   See Graham 1986.
9   Kohn 2016, ch. 4.
10   On ancient cosmology, see Allan 1991; Wheatley 1971.
11   Robinet 2008. For more, see also Saso 1978; Major 1984.
12   On ecstatic excursions to the stars, see Robinet 1989; for "pacing the net," see Andersen 1990; on the Nine Palaces, see Réquéna 2012, 149.

13 This cosmogonic scheme appears in the Great Appendix to the *Yijing*. See Wilhelm 1950, 319; Sung 1971, 299.
14 See Miura 2008.

References

Allan, Sarah. 1991. *The Shape of the Turtle: Myth, Art, and Cosmos in Early China.* Albany, NY: State University of New York Press.

Andersen, Poul. 1990. "The Practice of *Bugang*." *Cahiers d'Extrême-Asie* 5:15–53.

Bentov, Itchak. 1977. *Stalking the Wild Pendulum: On the Mechanics of Consciousness.* New York, NY: E. P. Dutton.

Berger, Peter. 1969a. *The Sacred Canopy.* Garden City, NY: Doubleday.

Berger, Peter. 1969b. *A Rumor of Angels.* Garden City, NY: Doubleday.

Graham, A. C. 1986. *Yin-Yang and the Nature of Correlative Thinking.* Singapore: Institute for East Asian Philosophies.

Kohn, Livia. 2005. *Health and Long Life: The Chinese Way.* In cooperation with Stephen Jackowicz. Cambridge, MA: Three Pines Press.

Kohn, Livia. 2016. *Science and the Dao: From the Big Bang to Lived Perfection.* St. Petersburg, FL: Three Pines Press.

Major, John S. 1984. "The Five Phases, Magic Squares, and Schematic Cosmography." In *Explorations in Early Chinese Cosmology*, edited by Henry Rosemont, 133–66. Chico, CA: Scholars Press.

Miura, Kunio. 2008. "Grotto Heavens and Blissful Lands." In *The Encyclopedia of Taoism*, edited by Fabrizio Pregadio, 368–73. London: Routledge.

Oschman, James. 2000. *Energy Medicine: The Scientific Basis.* New York, NY: Churchill Livingstone.

Réquéna, Yves. 2012. "The Biochemistry of Internal Alchemy: Decapitating the Red Dragon." *Journal of Daoist Studies* 5:141–52.

Robinet, Isabelle. 1989. "Visualization and Ecstatic Flight in Shangqing Taoism." In *Taoist Meditation and Longevity Techniques*, edited by Livia Kohn, 159–91. Ann Arbor, MI: University of Michigan, Center for Chinese Studies.

Robinet, Isabelle. 2008. "*Hetu* and *Luoshu*." In *The Encyclopedia of Taoism*, edited by Fabrizio Pregadio, 483–85. London: Routledge.

Saso, Michael. 1978. "What Is the Ho-t'u?" *History of Religions* 17:399–416.

Sung, Z. D. 1971. *The Text of Yi King.* Taipei: Chengwen.

Wang, Robin R. 2012. *Yinyang: The Way of Heaven and Earth in Chinese Thought and Culture.* Cambridge: Cambridge University Press.

Wheatley, Paul. 1971. *The Pivot of the Four Quarters: A Preliminary Enquiry into the Origins and Character of the Ancient Chinese City.* Chicago, IL: University of Chicago Press.

Wilhelm, Richard. 1950. *The I Ching or Book of Changes.* Translated by Cary F. Baynes. Princeton, NJ: Princeton University Press.

3   Heavens and hells

The human penchant for order also extends to realms beyond the visible and tangible world we live in. With regard to heaven and hell, there are three fundamental philosophical positions. The materialist position, dominant in modern Western thinking, radically denies any form of otherness beyond this world and only allows for things it can see, touch, and manipulate. The spiritist conviction, central to traditional Indian thought, assumes that only the pure realm of the divine is real while this world is ultimately an illusion (*maya*) and has to be overcome or set aside to perceive ultimate reality. The third, common to most cultures, typically works with three levels—our own plus one above and one below. That is, they postulate an upper, celestial realm where stars and gods reside, and an underworld, where the shades of the dead and various demonic forces hang out.

The most ancient and pervasive form of religion that holds the latter view is shamanism, by Mircea Eliade characterized as "archaic techniques of ecstasy." Very much like Daoists, shamanic cultures generally assert that nature is a living force, where all entities are imbued with life energy and jointly participate in the greater cosmos. Reality is fluid, manifest in constant change, consisting of a complex set of multiple layers that are interdependent and permeable and allow open-ended yet always mysterious transformations, so that whatever happens in our world is caused or influenced by supernatural powers. Shamans as mediators of the divine go into trance, then travel in their souls to the otherworld to connect to spirit beings and collect information. They guide the dead to their proper level and ensure that all agents are in harmony and at peace. In some traditions, they also open themselves to the presence of divine entities, housing the spirits in states of possession. "Shamanic processes construct social and personal consciousness through conceptualizations of 'others' as embodied in the spirit world, the socialization of self through internalizing 'sacred others,' and the construction and diversification of self as exemplified by the guardian-spirit complex."[1]

Astrophysicists, too, allow for other worlds, described in terms of alternative universes or the multiverse. Given the sheer size of the universe with billions of galaxies, it is quite likely that there are other solar systems with conditions equally conducive to life and thus other worlds. As Marcelo Gleiser says,

> Imagine a vista with valleys and peaks stretching in the distance. Different valleys in the landscape correspond to different universes, each with its own properties, possibly even with distinct values for the constants of Nature. In some, the speed of light may be greater than ours; in others, lesser. In one, light does not exist; and in another, electrons have different electric charges and masses. There is no time in the landscape; it represents only a mapping of potential universes.[2]

Similarly, representatives of string theory propose the concept of parallel universes that are right next to ours but work in a different dimension, infinitely big and enveloping space in a bubble, so that the cosmos is not a universe but a multiverse, where we occupy only a tiny pocket. Universes here come in various forms and shapes, opening the possibility of life forms vibrating in different energetic frequencies and with constituents and intelligences, potentially even self-aware beings quite different from us, living literally next door.[3]

Gods, ancestors, and immortals

The Chinese certainly agree with this notion. To them, the otherworld and its inhabitants are completely real and very close, constituting the yin complement to the yang world of tangible living. All equally participate in *qi*, together forming an integrated and fundamentally harmonious cosmos. At the same time, the energy of the otherworld is subtler and thinner, a shadowy latency as opposed to manifest solidity.

There are two basic types of otherworldly beings in Chinese religion, forces of nature and the dead. Each of these, again in traditional yin-yang pattern, come in a light and dark form, leading to a fourfold division into gods and demons, ancestors and ghosts. Both are called by the same terms (*shen/gui*), showing that, although different in position and power, there is not ultimately a significant distinction between them.

Forces of nature in this context include gods of wind and rain and earth, five mythic emperors who represent the five phases, the sun god, the lady of the moon, the various powers of the planets (and especially the Dipper), and other marvelous deities. All these have highly specified and benevolent functions in the workings of the cosmos, representing pure powers of life and creation that help to steer the universe in its right course. On the darker side, natural forces also manifest as demons that bring disasters and epidemics, cause earthquakes and locust plagues, and in general make life difficult for people. There are demons of fire that burn down houses, demons of thunder and clouds that create bad fortune, and demons of cold and wind that cause sickness and infertility.[4]

People, too, have their yin and yang parts, especially in their spirit and material souls (*hun/po*) that join from heaven and earth to constitute the person and after death return to their native realms. As a result, the yang part is worshiped spiritually in an ancestral tablet while the yin part is buried with proper ceremony—ensuring in each case the continuation of both a heavenly and an earthly form of existence for the individual.

The dead become ancestors only if both parts of their being are taken care of properly. They are then worshiped for several decades, a typical Chinese lineage including male forebears and their spouses for five generations. Ancestors are basically beneficent in that they direct good fortune toward their descendants in return for prayers and feeding, but they can also be a source of trouble if they are not happy in their otherworldly existence or have accumulated a great burden of bad energy during life, which is duly visited upon their kin in the form of bad fortune, described in terms of "inherited evil."

Ghosts are the lost dead, people who have died violently or far from their kin, otherworldly manifestations of unfortunate animals, or otherwise harmed creatures who cannot find rest. They are exceedingly numerous and typically hungry, with a limited degree of consciousness that guides them to possible sources of food—food in general being one of the leading motives in Chinese religion and ritual. They gobble up sacrifices originally meant for *bona fide* ancestors, seek sexual congress with beautiful girls or boys, possess harmless people to get them to do their wishes, and in general wreak havoc wherever they appear. A typical countermeasure is to throw a shoe (presumably a slipper that can be taken off quickly) as soon as one spots them, calling out their names if one can identify them, or shooting arrows at them made of special wood (often peach). Talismans and exorcisms complete the armory of unsuspecting citizens constantly surrounded by otherworldly malevolence.

The basic division into gods, ghosts, and ancestors is still relevant today, with nature gods joined by successful ancestors and transformed ghosts. In the case of ancestors, it is typically felt that the benevolent energy of an important personage should not be limited to their own families but be made accessible to the population at large. A good example is Guan Yu, originally a martial hero of the Three Kingdoms who today serves as the highly popular god of war and wealth. In the case of ghosts, the care for a deserted, unknown corpse found near a village goes by default to the community as a whole and, if its worship leads to miracles, in some cases gives rise to a new deity cult. These corpses often being discolored is the reason why some popular deities appear black.[5] The major characteristic of this mainstream understanding of otherworldly beings is their close, mutual interaction with the living. The dead and the living help or harm each other and exist within a codependent relationship, matching the cosmic pattern of yin and yang.

This is not the case in the Daoist vision. Although the Daoist otherworld is also populated by gods and demons, ancestors and ghosts, they are secondary to the immortals. Immortals, too, are of two kinds: either uncreated or created, born form pure celestial energy or transformed from a human base. Uncreated immortals include the pure gods of Dao, who are not forces of nature but stand beyond nature at the root of existence and represent the core heavens and scriptures of the religion. Created or transformed immortals, on the other hand, are human beings who, either through an elixir or through a variety of self-cultivation practices have found a new identity as spirit beings of Dao.

In either case, immortals are part of the pure level of the cosmos at the root of creation and thus beyond the yin-yang division. They stand alone and interact with other beings entirely on their own terms. No feeding or forcing is possible. Like bodhisattvas (with whom they are linked in due course), one can pray to them but their response, if it ever comes, is entirely an act of grace and not based on a mutual relationship of any kind.

Immortals are physical beings, as everything in the Chinese universe is physical in a more or less subtle form. But while the gods of the mainstream pantheon consist of high yang energy and the dead of high yin, immortals are beyond either, having bodies of the ultimate pure yang that makes up the root of all other forms of *qi* and is part of original oneness. According to early sources, they reside in Penglai, a group of five islands in the eastern sea that are carried on the backs of supernatural turtles, or on Mount Kunlun, the Daoist mythical world mountain located in the western region, where the Queen Mother of the West (Xiwangmu) rules and the peaches of immortality grow. To transcend there, human beings—who consist of a lucky mix of yin and yang—have to undergo long periods of self-cultivation to create a new, transcendent type of body. Eventually they pass through death, experienced as shedding the body "like the skin of a cicada" and fly off into the empyrean.[6]

Underworld administration

In medieval Daoism, the successfully transformed immortal is duly rewarded with a position in the celestial administration, the supernatural hierarchy that keeps track of people's good and bad deeds and issues rewards and punishments. First documented in a manuscript at Fangmatan, which describes the resurrection of a man named Dan in 297 BCE and his report on otherworld conditions, it was formalized under the Han dynasty and located to the depth of Mount Tai. Numerous bamboo slips found in tombs of the period accordingly contain petitions addressed to the Yellow Lord, the Lord of the Earth, or the Lord of the Underworld, including lists of grave goods and presents to be given to the responsible bureaucrats. In addition, there are funerary texts that function as a kind of "passport or letter of introduction," by which a celestial envoy "recommends the deceased to the netherworld authorities, thus assuring the newly arrived shade of a satisfactory integration into the subterranean territory."[7]

In Highest Clarity Daoism, the realm of the dead is located in the so-called Six Palaces of Fengdu. As the ritual manual *Tianguan santu jing* (Three Charts of the Heavenly Pass, DZ 1366) describes it,

> Mount Fengdu is located in the north, in the position of the celestial stem *gui*. Therefore the northeast is known as the Gate of Demons [*gui*], the root of the energy of death. The mountain is 2,600 miles high and 30,000 miles in circumference. Its grotto heaven begins right beneath the mountain; it measures 15,000 miles in circumference… .
>
> Its Six Palaces are governed by the Northern Emperor. They are the Six Heavens of the demons and the ghosts of the dead. Here the institution that governs people's death is located. In all cases, a death summons is issued at these Six Palaces on Mount Fengdu.[8]

The Six Palaces are hell-type places, where the dead are not only administered but also punished. They have picturesque names, such as Palace of Infamy, Destruction, and Ancestral Misdeeds, and are run by officials of rather low rank, who work their way up to the higher realms in centuries of dedicated service. They are often—as are also the denizens of the upper reaches—identified as meritorious ancestors of devout Daoists and the popular gods of the mainstream pantheon. Populated thus by familiar figures, the Daoist otherworld actively continues earlier beliefs while yet transforming them in a new way.

A more elaborate hell system emerges with the school of Numinous Treasure in the early fifth century. Under Buddhist influence and its doctrine of karma and rebirth, the administrative heavens of the dead here morphed into the "three bad destinies and five deepest hells." As the *Santu wuku jing* (Scripture of the Three Bad Rebirths and Five Sufferings, DZ 455) notes,

> The three bad destinies are: the hells, where one is held accountable for former misdeeds; life as an animal, where one has to repay previous karma; and life as a hungry ghost, where suffering is most intense. Thirsty, one wishes to drink, but the liquid turns into fire; hungry, one wishes to eat, but the food is burning charcoal. The five deepest hells, then, are the mountain of knives, the tree of swords, the hot iron pillar, the boiling cauldron, and the pool of blood.

With this increase in mythological complexity, the moral demands also rose. People were supposed follow the five precepts, abstaining from killing, stealing, lying, sexual misconduct, and intoxication, lest they find their way into hell. To keep sinners and good people apart, moreover, and to ensure that the right kind of punishment was meted out for the right kind of sin, the administration mushroomed. As described in the *Siji mingke* (Illustrious Regulations of the Four Ultimates, DZ 184), a text of Highest Clarity provenance, there are three basic officers who administer people's sins: an officer on the left who presides over yang transgressions, such as killing, theft of religious valuables, unwarranted leakage of sacred texts, as well as cursing and swearing; an officer on the right who rules over yin transgressions, which include harboring schemes, disobedience, planning to harm others, and never remembering Dao; and a central officer who governs all transgressions caused by doubts and duplicity, such as lack of reverence and faith in heavenly perfection, desecration of heavenly treasures, thoughts of removing the scriptures, or of defiling perfected writings. Far from handling all this on their own, these officers control a big staff, including numerous divine guards and bailiffs.

In addition, they also extend their supervision to earth, where a vast supernatural staff resides in the nine prefectures, centered in the grotto heavens of the sacred mountains. It typically includes 120 officials, 1,200 bailiffs, and 50,000 troops who manage the souls of the dead, keeping them in the rebirth cycle for eons, ever renewing their punishments of pain and torture.[9]

The heavens

The upper reaches of the otherworld, too, are structured in multiples of three. As outlined in the *Jiutian shengshen zhangjing* (Stanzas of the Vital Spirit of the Nine Heavens, DZ 398) of the fifth century, the three energies at the root of creation—beginning, primordial, and mysterious, in their distinctive colors green, yellow, and white—form the three highest heavens of Highest Clarity, Jade Clarity, and Great Clarity. These are the residence of the central gods known as the Three Pure Ones, and the location of the holiest of scriptures, classified in the Three Caverns.

They are wondrous realms, as the *Fafu kejie wen* (Rules and Precepts Regarding Ritual Garb, DZ 788) describes it,

> made from flying clouds and floating mists, pure spontaneity and wondrous energy, brought forth from the precious radiance of all nine colors … As for all the various cities and townships, palaces and halls, towns and terraces, plants and animals, carriages and utensils, pennants and awnings, and all kind of ritual implements—they are all made from pure spontaneity and appear in accordance with prevailing causes. None of them have any material solidity whatsoever. They appear and disappear without constancy.[10]

Integrating Buddhist cosmology, Daoist heavens grew to a total of thirty-six, besides the Three Clarities including the four so-called Brahma Heavens, named after the central deity of the Hindu pantheon who represents the purity of the universe and the four ideal mental states (*brahmaviharas*) of equanimity, love, compassion, and sympathetic joy. They are reserved for true believers, human beings who have attained a very high level of purity in their lives and after death are transposed into these divine realms of pure bliss. From here, they can advance to become immortals in the Clarities or, like bodhisattvas, decide to return to the lower realms if they decide to assist humanity in its quest for peace and perfection.

Below these seven heavens are twenty-eight existential dimensions known as the Three Worlds. The lowest six form the World of Desire; the following eighteen are the World of Form; and the four heavens above them constitute the World of Formlessness. This is more or less the world people inhabit, their level determined by their dominant way of life. Are they mainly guided by desire and is their life governed by passion? Or do they follow fundamental principles, ethical rules, and inherent virtues that go beyond desire yet can still be expressed in form? Or are they spiritually advanced and have developed a strong intuition, a sense of rightness in themselves and in the universe, subject neither to desire nor to limiting rules? Only the highest of beings participate in the World of Formlessness and at death are poised for ascension into the Brahma Heavens or even the Three Clarities.

Above all this, moreover, is the Heaven of Grand Network (Daluotian) with its capital of Mystery Metropolis, also known as the (Mountain of) Jade Capital. "Golden towers of purple subtlety, soaring trees of the seven treasures, cosmic unicorns and wondrous lions live in this realm." Here the great celestial scriptures are stored, managed and guarded by the highest of deities, powerful representatives of Dao and the most distinguished among elevated immortals.[11]

The denizens of these divine realms are ranked in nine levels in close imitation of the imperial bureaucracy on earth. Thus, leading celestials can be Dao-kings in the Clarities, rulers of the Brahma Heavens, or governors of the Three Worlds. Others can occupy the positions of dukes, ministers, or officials, in all cases classified according to the ranks of sages, perfected, and immortals, matching Jade, Great, and Highest Clarity respectively.

Members of each rank within this hierarchy—again like on earth—have to conform to a particular style of dressing, may use only particular colors, fabrics, and materials, and are obliged to appear with certain ritual objects and specific insignia of rank and office. They also have to go to work. Typically, beginners work in the underworld levels managing the dead in Fengdu, eventually rising to serve in the Department of Destiny, which administers the life expectancy and destiny of human and other beings. They may also become officials in the Department of Pestilence, which takes care of the proper distribution of plagues and illnesses among the living, punishing the sinful and relieving the good. They may administer the Department of Rain and Wind, largely under the control of dragons and responsible for the timely appearance of the natural forces that the make crops grow and give the soil its rest. Or they may become active in the Celestial Treasury, where people are given the loan of life and their repayments or further debts are closely monitored.

Immortals serve in these departments in various bureaucratic functions, gradually attaining higher rank and developing in status. The main difference to the officials in the world is that immortals hold more power and have more ease, that they are free from the burdens of physical existence and need not to worry about the well-being of either family or ancestors. Other than that, the rules are the same. Exemplary performance in office is lauded and rewarded with promotion, mistakes are punished, and serious errors may lead to demotion or even exile among mortals.

On the more positive side, once immortals have served with merit in various offices, they may take a period of leave. They may whirl around the heavens in free enjoyment of pure movement; they may also, for the pure fun of it, go back to the world of mortals, be born as emperors and kings, as court ladies or as wandering mendicants. Already immortal to begin with, they are strange among mortals and can fly off again any time. Immortals returning to the world are just as before they left it, but with a celestial certainty behind them that makes ascension less urgent. Given the toil they face in the administration above, it is small wonder that some decide to prolong their stay on mortal shores.

However, even those eccentrics have the guarantee of eternal life and the knowledge of the ultimate joy of immortality. They know they need only to ascend to be full members of the parties, banquets, and audiences among the heavenly host. With dragons and phoenixes dancing and singing, with the celestial halls decked out in miraculous splendor, with the peaches of immortality in full ripeness and the elixir pure ambrosia, with delightful jade maidens and celestial lads hovering to serve one's every whim—the paradisaical joys of the immortal life eventually entice even the most earth-bound back to the heavens. The administration once forgotten, celestials dress up in their fancy garb and dance and sing to their heart's delight. This, then, is the ultimate reward of the seeker's quest, the end of the Daoist journey, the paradise won and never to be lost.[12]

Transition

The otherworld being thoroughly bureaucratic, transition to it also involves an administrative act: the removal of the adept's name from the registers of the dead in Fengdu and its entry in the ledgers of life. Ritual incantations repeatedly emphasize this point. For example, the *Tianguan santu jing* has,

> Oh, Yang Brightness of Mystery Pivot,
> Spirit Soul and Spirit of the Heavenly Pivot!
> Oh, Nine Lords of Highest Mystery—
> Merge and transform into one single spirit!
> Cut off my route to death at the Gate of Demons,
> Open my registers of life in the Southern Office!
> Let my spirit soul be free from the three bad rebirths,
> Let me come to life again as an immortal![13]

The self-cultivation practice that goes with an incantation like this is two-fold: a visualization of the divine representatives of Dao and an ecstatic excursion to the heavenly abodes. Visualization typically begins with a period of purification (fasting, bathing, no contact with blood or dirt) and takes place in an oratory, where adepts burn incense, bow to the ten directions, click their teeth to indicate their readiness, and loosen their clothing to settle in meditation. Then they visualize various celestials descending and offering protection. Together with these gods, they ecstatically travel to the far reaches of the earth, then move on to match the movements of the sun and the moon. From here, adepts reach out to visit the higher heavens and petition to have their registration transferred and be given an official position in the otherworld. As the *Tianguan sandu jing* has,

> I am a minister of the Lord Emperor of Heaven,
> My name is registered in Jade Clarity.
> From there on down to the Six Palaces,
> To all the demon abodes of the Northern Emperor,
> All realms are under my control.
> They are all part of my jurisdiction—
> How would any demon dare to go on living there?[14]

In terms of communal ritual, transfer registration is undertaken on behalf of someone else, notably at the time of burial. According to the *Mingzhen ke* (Rules for the Illustrious Perfected, DZ 1411), one should set up sacred talismans with divine writing on tables in the courtyard to face the five directions, placing five gold dragons next to them. The rite ensures that the deceased is protected by the right spells during his transition, while the dragons carry the message of his impending transfer to the relevant spirit officers. Another way serves more distant ancestors and involves the casting of statues of Daoist gods, notably Lord Lao, with inscriptions that implore the deity to grant entry into the heavenly halls. An example is the statue commissioned by Yao Boduo, dated to 496, which has,

> We pray that
> All the members of Daoist Yao Boduo's family—
> His three forebears and five ancestors,
> His fathers and mothers of seven generations,
> All his relatives, long deceased or dead lately—
> If currently in the three bad rebirths,
> May speedily be rescued and liberated!
> May they forever be separated from
> The suffering of the dark hell prisons,
> And ascend to the Southern Palace,
> The true home of the immortals!
> Should they, again, be reborn as humans,
> May they have lords and kings for their fathers![15]

The goal in Daoist practice is to have all one's ancestors transferred to heaven and thus removed them from the mutuality-based relationship between the dead and the living, so that they need no more feeding and can no longer cause havoc among their descendants. The transfer of one's ancestors to the heavenly halls of pure light thus simultaneously means the complete exoneration of the descendants from all kinds of inherited evil, assuring those presently living of a highly prosperous and fortunate life and increasing their own chances of a successful ascent. Both self-cultivation and ritual practice, therefore, serve the same purpose, to create a higher level of cosmic harmony within the various realms of this and the other world.

Notes

1 Winkelman 2002, 74. See also Eliade 1964.
2 Gleiser 2010, 70.
3 Greene 2011, 132, 136.
4 See Harper 1985; Loewe 1988.
5 On the division, see Jordan 1972. For inherited evil, see Hendrischke 1991. A discussion of souls appears in Yü 1987.
6 See Kohn 1990.
7 Seidel 1987, 228. See also Harper 1994; Teiser 1988.
8 Kohn 1993, 265. See also Mollier 1997.
9 Kohn 2004, 16. See also Kohn 2019.
10 Kohn 1993, 340.
11 Kohn 1993, 69–70,
12 Kohn 1993, 333–4.
13 Kohn 1993, 259.
14 Kohn 1993, 266.
15 Kamitsuka 1998, 75–6.

References

Eliade, Mircea. 1964. *Shamanism: Archaic Techniques of Ecstasy*. Princeton, NJ: Princeton University Press.

Gleiser, Marcelo. 2010. *A Tear at the Edge of Creation*. New York, NY: Free Press.

Greene, Brian. 2011. *The Hidden Reality: Parallel Universes and the Deep Laws of the Cosmos*. New York, NY: Alfred A. Knopf.

Harper, Donald. 1985. "A Chinese Demonography of the Third Century BC." *Harvard Journal of Asiatic Studies* 45:459–98.

Harper, Donald. 1994. "Resurrection in Warring States Popular Religion." *Taoist Resources* 5.2:13–28.

Hendrischke, Barbara. 1991. "The Concept of Inherited Evil in the *Taiping Jing*." *East Asian History* 2:1–30.

Jordan, David K. 1972. *Gods, Ghosts and Ancestors*. Berkeley, CA: University of California Press.

Kamitsuka , Yoshiko. 1998. "Lao-tzu in Six Dynasties Sculpture." In *Lao-tzu and the Tao-te-ching*, edited by Livia Kohn and Michael LaFargue, 63–85. Albany: State University of New York Press.

Kohn, Livia. 1990. "Transcending Personality: From Ordinary to Immortal Life." *Taoist Resources* 2.2:1–22.

Kohn, Livia. 1993. *The Taoist Experience: An Anthology*. Albany: State University of New York Press.

Kohn, Livia. 2004. *Cosmos and Community: The Ethical Dimension of Daoism*. Cambridge, MA: Three Pines Press.

Kohn, Livia. 2019. "Armored Gods: Generals, Guardians, Killers, and Protectors." *Journal of Daoist Studies* 12:35–64.

Loewe, Michael. 1988. "The Almanacs (*jih-shu*) from Shui-hu-ti: A Preliminary Survey." *Asia Major*, Third Series 1.2:1–29.

Mollier, Christine. 1997. "La méthode de l'empereur du nord du Mont Fengdu: une tradition exorciste du taoïsme médiévale." *T'oung Pao* 83:329–85.

Seidel, Anna. 1987. "Post-Mortem Immortality: The Taoist Resurrection of the Body." In *Gilgul: Essays on Transformation, Revolution, and Permanence in the History of Religions*, edited by Shaul Shaked, David Shulman, and Guy G. Stroumsa, 223–37. Leiden: Brill.

Teiser, Stephen F. 1988b. "Having Once Died and Returned to Life: Representations of Hell in Medieval China." *Harvard Journal of Asiatic Studies* 48.2:433–64.

Winkelman, Michael. 2002. "Shamanism and Cognitive Evolution." *Cambridge Archaeological Journal* 12.1:71–101.

Yü, Ying-shih. 1987. "O Soul, Come Back: A Study of the Changing Conceptions of the Soul and Afterlife in Pre-Buddhist China." *Harvard Journal of Asiatic Studies* 47:363–95.

Part II
Humanity

4　The body

The body is the central vehicle for human beings to experience, understand, and modify the world. While physically the same for everyone, it is not a natural, fixed, and historically universal entity. Rather, it is defined differently in various cultures, both in terms of abstract concepts and metaphors and through applied usage. Marcel Mauss has called this usage "body techniques," i.e., "ordered, authorized, tested actions," sanctioned by a given society or community, which serve to shape the reality and identity of its members. Ranging from body movements (walking, squatting) through ways of caring for the body (washing, grooming) to consumption techniques, they include attitudes to food, authority, sexual relations, nakedness, pleasure and pain, medicine and healing, and the use of "body" metaphors. The particular vision and use of the body thus creates a sense of culturally and communally determined identity that is realized in ordinary, daily life and lays the foundation of all religious experience.[1]

Pierre Bourdieu develops Mauss's notion further and notes that the body has "an infinite capacity for generating products-thoughts, perceptions, expressions, and actions—whose limits are set by the historically and socially situated conditions of its production." The various ways in which the body is understood and used, therefore, create a specific set of feelings, conceptions, and expressions that both reflect the culture and society that instilled them and give them enduring structure. The body, in other words, is the seat of a pervasive metaphysical and cultural commitment, highly charged with social meanings and values. It consistently instills bodily knowledge, i.e., knowledge realized through active embodiment in physical reality and transmitted through bodily experience. Religious experience, then, is both the foundation and the result of constructed bodies, specifically oriented senses, and arranged bodily perception, so that in the end the ability to live fully in the world and enter into communion with higher spheres is a function of how the body is perceived and used.[2]

Modern Western cultures tend to see the body as essentially mechanical, a machine consisting of parts that function more or less well and can be repaired or changed as necessary. Here the body is like a processing plant or a car, which should not be driven appropriately, be the right kind of fuel, and be regularly serviced. Having a physical is thus like an annual car inspection, and going on vacation becomes "recharging your batteries." Illness, moreover, is a separate thing, an alien force that attacks and invades the body from the outside and has to be driven out by waging war. Health is the successful defense against invaders, germs that are constantly on the warpath. Tonics and vitamins bolster the body's defenses, getting better happens because people fight the disease. The immune system is an armed guard standing ready to ward off and do battle at any moment. Medications are used to fight pain and suppress symptoms: many of them are actually called "killers." Doctors in this system are strategists, generals, and officers in a constant war effort, with large numbers of troops—human, mechanical, and chemical—and at their beck and call. The patients and their bodies are the battlefield whose defenses have let them down.[3]

Dimensions

The Daoist take on the body could not be more different. There is nothing firm, stable, or separate about it but, like everything else, it consists of *qi* and is thus essentially the same as the cosmos. The body is the visible expression of the universal flow of energy, a dynamic field of multiple forces and tendencies, a continuous process of materialization, animation, disintegration, and reconstitution. Still, just as Dao and *qi* work on various levels, *so* the body has different dimensions, and human beings can use it more or less in its original cosmic nature.

The most cosmic body in Daoism is called *ti*, signaling "a boundless organism with infinite boundaries." Like the body of a plant, each part of which is interconnected with each other part and can propagate and replicate it in its entirety, so the concept of organism indicates the limbs and parts of the human body that together form one whole. By extension, it also means the human body as part of a much larger social and cosmic corpus, "consubstantial with the bodies of ancestors and descendants" and "all the people with whom it engages in exchanges of labor and food." The boundless organism is like an extended network: each individual contains many different organic structures within himself and is outwardly bound in with numerous others. "The largest unit of the *ti* is the cosmos itself, … a wholeness that can encompass life and death, heaven and earth, and all beings."[4]

From here, the body appears as individualized physical form (*xing*), a discrete, visible shape or mass whose edges and outlines stand in contrast to the formless. As pure form, this body matches the creation of being, the unfolding of multiplicity, the manifestation of matter evolving from pure Dao. Dao is above form, while form is beneath Dao, a notion reflected in the modern word for "metaphysics," literally "above form." Similarly, Dao as much as the cosmic organism is boundless, while form has distinct and discreet boundaries. Although bound, the body as form is not circumscribed by cultural norms or defined through social values. Rather, it is part of the natural world, and animals have it as much as human beings. It functions smoothly and harmoniously, following the natural laws, fully defined through the energies that constitute it. If left to its own devices, without cultural interference, it will grow, mature, decline, and die—all in its own good time, never leaving its ultimate cosmic embeddedness.[5]

However, while people are continuously connected to the boundless organism of life and endowed with pure physical form at birth, they subject them to cultural patterning. As they grow up and interact with the world, learning the body techniques of their particular society, they superimpose structure and create a yet different dimension of the body: the personal body (*shen*). The lived, relational body, this is the way people shape themselves as embodied persons; although rooted in nature, it is artificial and contrived. The *Daode jing* says that this body is "the reason why I have great afflictions" (ch. 13). Li Rong, seventh-century philosopher of Twofold Mystery, explains this in terms of sensory involvement and the development of particular desires.

> Having a personal body means having vexations and adversities. Frustrated by sight and hearing, tortured by taste and smell, one is subject to pain, irritation, heat, and cold … As soon as there is a personal body, the hundred worries compete to arise and the five desires hurry to make their claims.[6]

In other words, the personal body is the self-image people create on the basis of their physical experience as shaped through social realities and learned reactions to sensory experiences, creating emotional patterns, personality boundaries, and a stereotyped vision of life that gets more rigid over time.

Eventually this leads to the tightly controlled, sanctimonious body that is favored in Confucian literature (*gong*). "The *gong* body is that aspect of the human body or person most closely associated with the ritualized performance and public, visual display of character, conduct, and values." Written with the combination of the words for "body" and "bend," *gong* graphically illustrates the ritual action of bending at the waist and bowing in formal ceremony. Reflecting a fixed mindset within and linked with ritual life, it provides an outward presentation of the person on ceremonial display, controlled and constrained, unyielding and inflexible.

Daoists, not surprisingly, have only contempt and criticism for this kind of body. As the *Zhuangzi* puts it, "With likes and dislikes, sounds and colors you cripple what is on the inside; with leather caps and snipe-feathered bonnets, batons stuck in belts and sashes trailing, you cramp what is on the outside" (ch. 12). What is seen in Confucian sources as the "purveyor of ideal conduct is conceived here as exhibiting little more than artifice."[7]

Internal structure

Whichever dimension of the body people activate, it always has a set internal structure. For one, it represents heaven and earth. As the *Huainanzi* says,

> The roundness of the head is an image of heaven, the square of earth is the pattern of earth. Heaven has four seasons, five agents, nine directions, and 360 days. Human beings have similarly four limbs, five inner organs, nine orifices, and 360 joints. Heaven has wind, rain, cold, and heat. Human beings have the actions of giving, taking, joy, and anger. The gall bladder corresponds to the clouds, the lungs to the breath, the liver to the wind, the kidneys to the rain, and the spleen to the thunder.
>
> (ch. 7)[8]

For another, as also outlined in Chinese medicine, it grows from core energy lines, functional containers of primordial *qi* that arise at early stages of embryonic development. Most important and most primordial among them is the Penetrating Vessel, which runs right through the center of the body. It begins at the perineum, a small cluster of muscles located between the anus and the genital organs, passes through the central torso, and ends at the crown of the head, a point known as Hundred Meeting in Chinese medicine and as the Heavenly Pass in Daoism.

The second major energy line is the Belt Vessel, which runs around the abdomen a few inches below the navel, connecting the Ocean of *Qi* in front with the Gate of Destiny in the back. Next come the Conception and Governing Vessels, which run along the front and back of the torso respectively, reaching from the pelvic floor to the head. They are cosmic channels of yin and yang energy that serve to mix *qi* and blood and are essential for guiding *qi* through the major Daoist centers of the body.

These centers or elixir fields represent the body's vertical structure. Located in the head, solar plexus, and lower abdomen, they match the three cosmic levels of heaven, humanity, and earth. The upper elixir field in the head, also called Niwan, is at the center of the Nine Palaces. From here celestial energies are accessed and the spirit embryo ascends to the otherworld. A major center of energetic processing, it houses the spirit and manages the close connection of humanity to heaven.

The middle elixir field, next, is in the solar plexus, between the nipples. Called the Cavity of *Qi*, it is the center of humanity and seat of pure *qi* within the body, collecting and holding it for dispersal either through ordinary activity or for spiritual cultivation. The heart is its primary organ, seconded closely by the lungs, thus relating to both emotions and breathing. Governing also fire and the blood circulation in the body as well as controlling the major yin organs, it plays also a key role especially in women's practice.

The lower elixir field is commonly placed about 1.3 inches beneath the navel, in the center of the abdomen. Also called Ocean of *Qi* and identical with the *hara* in Zen, it is the point where Daoists find their center of gravity, their reproductive power, and their stability in the world. The home of primordial *qi*, the original life force of the world, it is closely connected to earth and linked with the reproductive energy known as "essence" (*jing*), the indeterminate aspect of *qi* that forms bones, hair and brain, and also manifests as semen.[9]

Next, the body is structured horizontally along the lines of five phases cosmology, again applying notions common throughout Chinese culture and essential in medicine. There are five central storage organs, understood to be yin in nature, and five processing viscera, defined as yang, all matching the various colors, directions, seasons, and other dimensions of the known world. They are:

phase	yin organ	yang organ
wood	liver	gall bladder
fire	heart	small intestine
earth	spleen	stomach
metal	lungs	large intestine
water	kidneys	bladder

These organs, moreover, are energetically connected with other physical aspects, such as body parts, fluids, and forms of *qi*:

organ	parts	fluids	energies
liver	joints	tears	blood
heart	vessels	sweat	defensive *qi*
spleen	muscles	mucus	pulse
lungs	skin	nasal	protective *qi*
kidneys	bones	saliva	essence

Each inner organ, that is to say, matches a particular body part, fluid, and form of *qi*, reflecting the vision of world and body as an intricate network of energy patterns. All these dimensions, moreover, continuously transform and mutate into one another, following the basic cycle of the five phases and thus matching the rhythm of the day and the succession of the seasons.

The organs, moreover, have their own energy lines, called meridians, channels that run to the right and left, connecting organs and extremities as well as providing communication between the upper and lower, interior and exterior aspects of the body. As *qi* flows through them, it moistens the bones and tendons, provides nutrition to the joints, and balances yin and yang.

There are twelve pairs of organ-based meridians, documented in medical textbooks since the Han dynasty. They match the five yin and yang organs and also include a sixth set, the pericardium (yin) and the Triple Heater (yang). A uniquely Chinese entity, the latter connects lungs, stomach, and intestines, integrating the nourishment extracted from air and food as well as managing its transport, utilization, and excretion. The six yin meridians, then, run along the inside of the extremities: either full or empty, they store and process essential *qi* and are a function of overall health. The six yang meridians flow along the outside of arms and legs: either replete or exhausted, they process active *qi*, run closer to the surface than their yin counterparts, and help with the digestion of food and the transmission of fluids.[10]

People activate the internal structure differently, depending on which dimension of the body they dominantly live in. Those whose lives center on the sanctimonious and personal bodies create much stress and tend to have wayward *qi* flow. Their organ systems are full of negative emotions and toxic energies, their meridians tend to get clogged, and their elixir fields remain essentially dormant, leading to ill health, chronic disease, and early death, in addition to an overall disconnect from community and divinity. People who are mainly in their physical form are more relaxed and at ease in life and know who they are. Reaching out to realizing their full potential in this world, their *qi* flow is proper, their organ systems are healthy, their meridians open, and their elixir fields active, so that they live in harmony with the world around them. Those, finally, who have activated their body as cosmic organism are strong in organs, energy conduits, and elixir fields. Of superior spirituality, they no longer see themselves as separate individuals but work in synchronicity with Dao and *qi*. Sagely in their attitude and behavior in the world, they are on their way to becoming immortals.

Body gods

Daoists have a variety of techniques that enhance identity on the levels of form and organism besides various physical exercises, dietary recommendations, and herbal supplements they share with Chinese medicine. A prime method is known as the Five Sprouts and first documented in medieval Highest Clarity documents. It involves activating the cosmic energy of a given organ by facing the matching direction, visualizing its energy in the appropriate color on the horizon, then gradually shrinking it to the size of a concentrated pill. After chanting an invocation to the relevant deity, adepts guide the energy pill toward themselves, swallow it and direct it to the organ in question, envisioning it functioning perfectly, consistently connected to, and supported by, the gods and energies of the greater cosmos.[11]

The modern version of this is called the Inner Smile. Adepts begin by placing a smile on their face, then they take the smiling feeling lower along the face into the throat area to the thyroid and parathyroid glands. From here, they let the smiling energy flow down to the thymus gland in the solar plexus, the seat of love and enlightenment, and allow it to moisten and grow bigger. Next, they visualize *qi* flowing to the five organs in turn, envisioning them with their respective colors, appreciating them for their work, and allowing negative emotions to leave and positive virtues to enter.[12]

Another way involves the visualization and activation of numerous divine entities in the body, commonly known as body gods. For example, as first outlined in the *Huangting jing* (Scripture of the Yellow Court, DZ 403) of the early Highest Clarity school, the five inner organs are first of all inhabited by the heraldic animals, massive constellations in the cardinal directions of the night sky that comprise a number of stars not unlike Western zodiac images. They include the green dragon (liver), vermilion bird (heart), white tiger (lungs), and the turtle-and-snake known as the Dark Warrior (north).

In addition, the organs are also the residence of celestial deities, notably Lord Lao in the center, the spleen-stomach area, more formally known as the Yellow Court. He is accompanied by the god known as Prime of White in the lungs, the Flowery Canopy, also the name of the constellation Cassiopeia. "The lungs," as the *Huangting jing* says, "form the residence of this lord and his attendants who regulate the breath, communicating to the outside through the Central Peak of the nose." The liver, moreover, contains

> a deity called Dragon Mist, alternatively known as Embodying Light or Nonviolent. He sometimes transforms into two jade lads, one dressed in green cloth, the other in yellow. Each is nine inches tall and holds jade liquids from the liver."

Next,

> the god of the kidneys is called Mysterious Darkness, also known as Raising Offspring. He wears a cloud skirt of dark purple brocade with patterns of curling dragons, reaching up into the sky and swirling like mist around the sun and the moon. The kidneys are like a hanging garden of dark, yin energy, housing the god who rules over the six viscera and the nine sources of fluids. They communicate with the outside through the ears and the hundred waterways."

The heart, finally,

> is like a verdant lotus blossom. Its deity is called Prime of Cinnabar or Guardian of the Numinous. He wears a flying robe of cinnabar brocade and a skirt of jade-like gauze, a golden bell pendant hanging from his vermilion sash. He controls all heat and cold as well as protective and nutritive energies, regulates the blood and manages people's destiny, keeping their bodies from decaying."

These deities, moreover, function analog to the imperial administration, as already pointed out in the medical classic *Huangdi neijing suwen* (Inner Classic of the Yellow Emperor, Simple Questions, DZ 1021).

The heart is the residence of the ruler, spirit and clarity originate here. The lungs are the residence of the high ministers of state, order and division originate here. The liver is the residence of the strategists: planning and organization originate here. The gall is residence of the judges: judgments and decisions originate here. In addition, the center of the breast is the residence of a special task-force: joy and pleasure originate here. The stomach is the residence of the granary administration: the various kinds of taste originate here. The large intestine is the residence of the teachers of Dao: development and transformations originate here … The kidneys are the residence of managers: activity and care originate here.[13]

In medieval Daoism, this system was further expanded to include a vast force. For example, the *Laozi zhongjing* another early meditation manual, places eight administrative deities into each organ, in charge of 3,600 minor officials, riding around in carriages of the appropriate color, drawn by the heraldic animals.

To enhance the function of the body as form and cosmic organism, adepts are to envision these deities in their full splendor and functioning perfectly, thereby to maintain both internal integrity and a cosmic connection. They do the same with the three elixir fields, the residence of the Three Ones, direct manifestations of the three energies of creation. They in turn govern twenty-four fundamental powers in the human body, which correspond to the twenty-four solar periods of the year and the twenty-four major constellations in the sky.

The exact procedure of the meditation varies according to season but, if at all possible should be performed at the solstices and the equinoxes. For example, to activate the Upper One, adepts visualize a ball of red *qi* in the Niwan center, allowing a red sun to appear that is about nine inches in radius. Its brilliance envelops practitioners to such a degree that they enter a state of utter oblivion. As soon as they have reached this state, the god Red Child becomes visible. The ruler of the Niwan, he holds a talisman of the white tiger, the sacred animal of the west. He is accompanied by an attendant, the god of the subtle essences of teeth, tongue, and skull, who holds a sacred scripture. Working similarly with the other Ones, practitioners reorient their body to be the container of heavenly palaces and deities, to be in fact a cosmos itself, and thus attain oneness in body and spirit with the cosmic dimensions of the universe. Their very physicality turns into a cosmic network and becomes the celestial realm in which the gods reside.[14]

Dynamic landscape

Not only stationary palaces and resident gods, the body also contains dynamic features and is understood as a universe in miniature. In charts first found in Song-dynasty sources, it is depicted as a sacred mountain, containing a landscape complete with hills, rivers, fields, and more (see Figure 4.1).

Figure 4.1 The body as landscape. *Duren jing neiyi* (Internal Meaning of the Scripture on Salvation, DZ 91, dat. 1227).

The more recent *Neijing tu* (Chart of Internal Passageways, dat. 1898) expands on this, showing the three elixir fields as a multiple mountain peaks in the head, a yin-yang spiral in the chest, and four connected spheres in the abdomen. The head here matches the immortals' paradise of Mount Kunlun and shows key deities above and below the mouth. Between the eyes which represent the sun and the moon, there is the Hall of Light, the first among the Nine Palaces. Best reached by passing through the deep, dark valley of the nose, it is guarded by the two high towers of the ears. To attain entry one has to perform the ritual exercise of "beating the heavenly

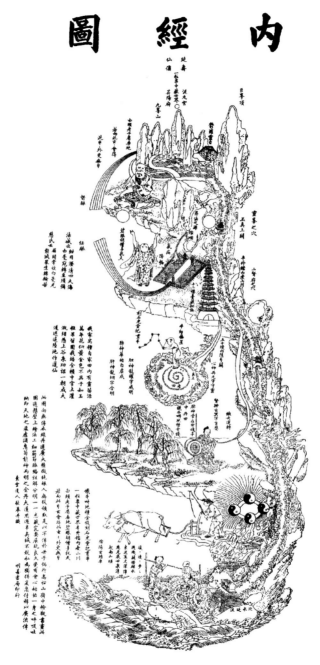

Figure 4.2 Neijing tu (Chart of Internal Passageways, dat. 1898). Stone Stele at Baiyunguan, Beijing.

drum": with both palms covering the ears, snap the index and middle fingers to drum against the back of the skull (see Figure 4.2).

Again, beginning with conscious breathing at the nose, adepts may also travel downward through the nose valley to find the mouth in the form of a small lake. Filled by divine fluid that is experienced as saliva, this regulates the water level of the upper lake in the head and raises or lowers it as necessary. Crossing the mouth-lake over a long bridge (tongue) and moving further down, adepts reach the twelve-storied tower of the throat, then come to the Flowery Canopy (lungs), the Scarlet Palace (heart), the Yellow Court (spleen), the Imperial Granary (stomach), the Purple Chamber (gall bladder), and various other starry palaces transposed into the body's depth. Going ever deeper, another cosmic region is reached, with another sun and moon (kidneys). Beneath them, the Ocean of *Qi* extends with another Mount Kunlun in its midst. Various divine beings reside throughout, creating vitality and providing spiritual resources.

To activate the *qi* flow along the spine, depicted here as a mighty river, adepts begin by focusing on the Tail Gate, an architectural structure at the bottom of the image. Here two children, representing yin and yang, work a water wheel to send *qi* up along the spine. It soon reaches the important passage of Narrow Strait, depicted as a gate-like building halfway up the spine, about level with the stars of the Dipper, wielded by a lad standing on a spiral. From here the path leads into the verdant plains at the foot of Mount Kunlun.[15]

In an integrated practice known as the microcosmic orbit, essential to the practice of internal alchemy, adepts not only run the energy up along the spine and into the head, but across the face and back down along the front of the body. Doing so, they combine the fundamental energy lines of the Governing and Conception Vessels, placing the tongue at the upper palate in the mouth to connect them.

Another practice of internal alchemy, documented in the *Jinguan yusuo jue* (Instructions on the Golden Gate and Jade Lock, DZ 1156), a text of Complete Perfection and closely associated with its founder Wang Chongyang, consists of a spiritual journey through the body. Here, too, the body appears as an inner landscape, with rivers and mountains, gardens and palaces, guards and gods, witches and demons. More specifically, adepts floating in a boat on the internal river first come to three deep torrents that represent the three teachings, then arrive at six deep ditches that stand for the six bodhisattva virtues, internal attitudes that help purify the senses. Moving on, they see three freshly built rafts, different dimensions of spiritual purity, then pass the Fruitbearing Garden, guarded by an old man, where they can lay down their accumulated karma of the past. A few miles further on, they notice an enormous tree with a golden ox tethered to it. At this point several splendid terraces appear on the bank of the river, which they must never lose sight of, lest they are attracted by three women who turn into evil witches.

Next, there is a huge mountain, with different animals: a black water buffalo on the eastern slope, a white ram in the west, and a yellow goat to the south. Representatives of the teachings of Laozi, Confucius, and the Buddha, they lead the adepts into the mountain, the symbolic representation of the ultimate teaching. Inside, adepts find a walled city with four gates that represent the eyes, ears, nose, and mouth and lead to four grottoes and four temples that stand for the four stages of enlightenment. Eventually, adepts reach the Nine Palaces and connect with the celestial deities—all present in the body and accessible at any time.[16]

Notes

1 Mauss 1979, 98–100, 117–18.
2 See Bourdieu 1990.
3 See the various articles in Coakley 1997.
4 Sommer 2010, 223–24. See also Jullien 2007.
5 Pregadio 2004.
6 Kohn 1991, 249.
7 Sommer 2010, 215. See also Kohn 2014, ch. 6.
8 Kohn 1991, 227. For more on the cosmology of the *Huainanzi*, see Le Blanc 1985.
9 See Kohn 2016, ch. 5.
10 See Kaptchuk 2000.
11 Kohn 2006, 2012, ch. 10.
12 Chia and Chia 1986, 145.
13 Kohn 1991, 231.
14 Kohn 1991, 237.
15 See Komjathy 2008, 2009.
16 Kohn 1993, 174–80. See also Komjathy 2007.

References

Bourdieu, Pierre. 1990. *The Logic of Practice*. Stanford, CA: Stanford University Press.

Chia, Mantak, and Maneewan Chia. 1986. *Iron Shirt Chi Kung*. New York, NY: Healing Dao Center.

Coakley, Sarah, ed. 1997. *Religion and the Body*. Cambridge: Cambridge University Press.

Jullien, François. 2007. *Vital Nourishment: Departing from Happiness*. Translated by Arthur Goldhammer. New York, NY: Zone Books.

Kaptchuk, Ted J. 2000. *The Web That Has No Weaver: Understanding Chinese Medicine*. New York, NY: Congdon & Weed.

Kohn, Livia. 1991. "Taoist Visions of the Body." *Journal of Chinese Philosophy* 18:227–52.

Kohn, Livia, ed. 2006. *Daoist Body Cultivation: Traditional Models and Contemporary Practices*. Magdalena, NM: Three Pines Press.

Kohn, Livia. 2012. *A Source Book in Chinese Longevity*. St. Petersburg, FL: Three Pines Press.

Kohn, Livia. 2014. *Zhuangzi: Text and Context*. St. Petersburg, FL: Three Pines Press.

Kohn, Livia. 1993. *The Taoist Experience: An Anthology*. Albany, NY: State University of New York Press.

Kohn, Livia. 2016. *Science and the Dao: From the Big Bang to Lived Perfection*. St. Petersburg, FL: Three Pines Press.

Komjathy, Louis. 2007. *Cultivating Perfection: Mysticism and Self-Transformation in Quanzhen Daoism*. Leiden: Brill.

Komjathy, Louis. 2008. "Mapping the Daoist Body (1): The *Neijing tu* in History." *Journal of Daoist Studies* 1:67–92.

Komjathy, Louis. 2009. "Mapping the Daoist Body (2): The Text of the *Neijing tu*." *Journal of Daoist Studies* 2:64–108.

Le Blanc, Charles. 1985. *Huai-nan-tzu: Philosophical Synthesis in Early Han Thought*. Hong Kong: Hong Kong University Press.

Mauss, Marcel. 1979. *Sociology and Psychology, Essays*. London: Routledge & Kegan Paul.

Pregadio, Fabrizio. 2004. "The Notion of 'Form' and the Ways of Liberation in Daoism." *Cahiers d'Extrême-Asie* 14:95–130.

Sommer, Deborah. 2010. "Concepts of the Body in the *Zhuangzi*." In *Experimental Essays on Zhuangzi*, edited by Victor H. Mair, 212–27. Dunedin, FL: Three Pines Press.

5 Mind, thoughts, and emotions

There is no fundamental difference in substance or function between body and mind in Chinese thought: they form part of the same continuum. Fundamentally monistic, this vision is yet neither physicalist nor idealist, but proposes an underlying energy (*qi*) that can manifest as either body or mind, the two thus forming an interlocking web of fields that each pulsate at their own rate. This vision matches the understanding of modern physics, which sees all reality as made from highly ordered, crystalline material, tiny atoms vibrating in groups along coiled molecules. The patterns are constant, rapid, and orderly undergoing modifications or changes upon being subjected to various influences. The mind in this vision is essentially the same as the body: there is no separation of consciousness from physical existence. Both are energy fields, they just vibrate at different speeds: 1,022 Hz for the atomic nucleus, 1,015 for the atom itself, 109 for molecules, and 103 for cells. Sensations in the body accordingly do not come from specific sense organs but arise through the fluctuation of different vibratory fields—all of which are immediately linked with consciousness in a nonlocal way, and in fact, *are* consciousness.[1]

This oscillating energy-mind, then, involves several specific faculties. These are awareness and perception as well as reflective or discriminating consciousness. Awareness and perception are a biological given and find prime expression in the emotions, inherent response tendencies to sensory data that incorporate muscle tension, hormone release, cardiovascular changes, facial expressions, attention, cognition, and more. A primordial form of consciousness, emotions arose in living organisms as a way "for the brain to represent biological survival values to the evolutionarily emergent cognitive deliberation." They come in two major forms: withdrawal and approach, i.e., defensive and inviting or negative and positive. Matching the universal tendency to seek comfort and avoid discomfort, they are essentially reaction patterns that increase chances of success in three major areas of life: material supplies (object acquisition), physical integrity (reproduction), and social connection (interaction with others). The three dominant emotions associated with these are anger, fear, and sadness, respectively, socially activated and influenced by cultural structures into particular forms of expression.[2]

Discriminating consciousness, on the other hand, is a specifically human ability that came about as the result of an ongoing process of evolution and differentiation, language and culture. A unique mode of dealing with reality, consciousness required an enhanced long-term memory and opened more refined ways of representing reality in complex theories, increasing differentiation and facilitating social change. Consciousness made it possible for human beings to recognize, monitor, evaluate, encourage, and remind themselves. It also created the recursive mind and theory of mind, that is, the ability not only to reflect upon our own thinking but also to simulate the minds of others. Like language, precise imitation, and abstraction, it made it possible for humans to gain control over the environment and grow into new and ever more potent dimensions. However, it also alienated them from the body, nature, and the greater universe, limiting perspective and blocking cosmic wholeness.[3]

Major levels

Infinitely faster and subtler in its energy oscillations and vastly more powerful than the body, the mind in Daoism matches its dimensions and equally evolves on four distinct levels. To begin, connecting to the body as cosmic organism, the mind is a vast abyss (*yuan*), pure flow and limitless vacillation of universal energy, manifesting in various states. As the *Zhuangzi* has it,

> From a state of being that has not yet emerged through the vastness of primeval chaos and the beginning stages of heaven and earth that are without name or substance but already working all the way to the pattern of earth—still and silent, nothing moving, nothing standing up.
>
> (ch. 7)

Unlike other levels, where mental activities are written with the "heart" radical, this mind is all water: its activities are running, gurgling, springing, whirling, eddying, and more. The river of life itself, it flows in us and through us, and we merge with it in vastness.

Next, more individualized and matching the body as form, there is what the *Zhuangzi* calls heaven's storehouse—"one fills it, yet it is never full; one drains it, yet it is never empty" (ch. 2). Also described as "one-with-heaven" (ch. 15) and the "numinous terrace" (ch. 11), this is mind as pure, cosmic spirit (*shen*). Spirit is the core level of all consciousness and mentation, a powerful indwelling agent as well as a holy force to be held in awe. As the *Zhuangzi* says,

> "Pure spirit reaches in the four directions, flows now this way, now that: there is no place it does not extend to. Above, it brushes the sky; below, it coils on the earth. It transforms and nurses the myriad things, but no one can make out its form. It is one with heaven.
>
> (ch. 15)

The active, organizing configurative force and transformative influence in the person, spirit is without limit or judgment and comes before thinking and feeling. An integrated whole that is not subject to increase or decrease, it works mainly with precognition and intuition, opening us to heaven and cosmic oneness. Manifest in individual consciousness and impossible to be perceived directly—as when concentrated in gods, ancestors, and other divine forces—its vitalizing force exerts a transformative influence on all aspects of the human being.[4]

Spirit, however, in most people does not remain pure for long but through cultural programming evolves into the heart-mind (*xin*), matching the personal body. The seat of both cognitive and affective functions, motivational and emotional patterns, the mind on this level is a structuring force within the person that can be open and fluid or regulating and tight, most commonly working with preference and aversion, approval and disapproval. The chief of the inner organs and functions of the body, the heart-mind supervises and manages the senses, like an emperor ruling his officials. As in real-life bureaucracy, the more the mind leaves the senses to do their thing, the better they work. When it gets into micromanagement or superimposes its particular tendencies or preferences, i.e., socially determined, induced desires or specific concepts, the senses will stop functioning fully and only report pertinent information. Imposing restrictions on the body's functions, the heart-mind comes to predispose sensory data, limiting perception of reality in favor of preconditioned responses.

The senses, moreover, provide input in the form of emotions (*qing*), feelings of like and dislike that settle in the five organs, so that anger rests in the liver, euphoria in the heart, worry in the spleen, sadness in the lungs, and fear in the kidneys. They represent a directed flow of vital energy in response to sensory experiences, combined with various mental and affective functions. The heart-mind as manager moves along with the emotions throughout the different parts of the body, makes sense of the body sensations, creates a narrative around them, keeps a record in memory, and establishes set behavior patterns and conscious judgments. In doing so, it makes clear choices, either opening itself to all sorts of inputs and moving along freely with the world or concentrating in one specific body part or sense organ and restricting information flow. Ideally, people should be able feel the steady flow of *qi* as sensory data in a state of empty, open, non-judging awareness, keep their heart-mind steady, and refrain from superimposing its patterns on experience.[5]

Typically, however, they get caught up in judgments of right and wrong and before too long develop a fixed mind (*chengxin*), full of assumptions, preconceived notions, and prejudices. Corresponding to the sanctimonious body, this mind is rigid and tight, manifesting rote responses, inflexibility, and stereotypes. In terms of judgment, it means predictability and prejudices; in terms of personality, it means stiffness and set ways. The mind at this level is no longer free and easy, but covered in weeds and brambles, as the *Zhuangzi* describes it (ch. 1). It may also turn into a "mechanical mind" that sees the world in terms of personal gain and loss and strives to impose its own preferences on life (ch. 12). The source of all errors, the fixed or mechanical mind holds on tight to its set structures and established norms. Rather than expressions of spontaneous goodwill and joyful relationships that change over time, these norms become restrictive, stifling corsets of mind and life.

Psychological forces

Again matching the body, the mind in both in Daoism and Chinese medicine is understood in terms of the five phases and linked to the five organs, where it manifests in personalized aspects of the individual and functions through distinct psychological forces, emotions, and virtues—all manifestations of one cosmic *qi*, flowing more or less smoothly and directed alternatively toward the greater good or personal enhancement.

The first among them is spirit itself, pure cosmic energy as it flows through the heart, creating a form of awareness that aids the overall functioning of life and allowing the arising of consciousness. The heart is the key factor in the management of spirit; the emotion associated with it, that is, the overly intense or rushed flow of energy as directed toward personal benefit, is euphoria or excessive joy, the tendency to get carried away and lose sight of what is appropriate. To counter this, its dominant virtue and more altruistic attitude is propriety (*li*), a word whose graph combines the symbol for "spirit" with the image of a basket full of beans. That is, it presents a visual expression of ritual offerings and by extension indicates the sense of reverence and awe in the face of the numinous and the divine. In ancient Chinese thought, propriety describes the clear inner awareness of social distinctions and personal potentials, the ability to maintain moderation and exhibit an appropriate and respectful response in all kinds of situations. Propriety or moderation keeps the heart on an even keel, supporting its ongoing work, and allowing spirit to function optimally.[6]

Next human beings have something called the spirit soul, a directional and individualized aspect of cosmic energy. Coming from heaven and yang in nature, it resides in the liver, linked also with the gall bladder and described as the residence of strategists and judges. The spirit soul is the origin of all planning, organization, judgments, and decisions; it pulls people toward heaven, purity, and goodness, enhancing their artistic, intellectual, and spiritual growth. That is to say, it is the personalized dimension of cosmic spirit in terms of professional and spiritual development, the unique expression of Dao within the individual that determines his or her natural aptitudes and inherent urges toward the finer dimensions of life.

The spirit soul has the ability to leave the body while the person is asleep and travel through the spirit realm, observing and learning and gaining insights that manifest as dreams. All our dreams—whether at night or as visions of the future—are expressions of this potency: it guides people toward the ideal expression of spirit in their particular uniqueness. In addition, it governs human interaction with other people and their role in society and the world, finding expression in courage and enthusiasm. However, there is also the potential for excess, leading to the negative emotions of anger and aggression that manifest in impatience, annoyance, irritation, frustration, resentment, fury, and even rage. The main counterbalancing attitude or virtue—which the spirit soul thrives on—is humaneness (*ren*), also translated as kindness, benevolence, goodwill, generosity, and compassion. The character shows the word for "person" combined with the numeral "two," indicating its focus on interpersonal connection.

Next, there is the material soul, coming from earth and representing the power of yin. Its home is in the lungs and large intestine, the place of breathing as well as of digestive elimination, in body cosmology understood as the seat of administration, order, and structure. Where the spirit soul focuses on cultural attainments, the material soul represents the physical base of life, activated in instincts of survival that make sure people get enough food, drink, sleep, and sex. In other words, the material soul makes sure that human beings have a sufficient and sustaining material foundation of life, uniquely tailored to the particular situation and culture of the individual.

It, too, has a tendency to go to extremes, leading to the loss of vital energy in sexual passion or its dissipation through hankering after luxury and ease. On the negative side, it may cause fears of deprivation or starvation, bringing forth greed, stinginess, jealousy, and envy, and making people lose sight of purity and simplicity. If material goals and social support, moreover, are not forthcoming, people may suffer from sadness, also expressed as melancholy, depression, grief, sorrow, or despair—an emotional reaction that often finds physical expression in constricted breathing or tightness in the chest.

The virtue associated with the lungs that optimizes the functioning of the material soul is righteousness (*yi*), the sense of familial duty and social obligation that reaches beyond the interpersonal and takes the greater good into account. The character consists of the two words for "I" and "sheep," suggesting the connection of the self to the flock of humanity. In addition, Daoists emphasize the fundamental attitude of enoughness or sufficiency, the innate feeling of how material objects and money move through life in a current, constantly coming and going yet always providing just the right amount.[7]

The two remaining organs are the kidneys and spleen, which house the psychological forces of will and intention. The will here means the specific direction of effort toward one's specific vision of ideal life and perfect accomplishments, closely matching people's particular circumstances as well as their unique natural aptitudes. The intention indicates a more generic way of thinking, the way one connects to the world and relates to one's self-identity. A key factor in creating the particular form life takes for the individual, it is the central power that directs *qi*. As first noted by the Confucian thinker Mencius and since repeated many times by Daoists and qigong masters alike, "where the intention goes, *qi* follows."

Will and intention are linked organically with the kidneys and bladder as well as the spleen and stomach. The kidneys regulate the water household of the body and are closely connected to primordial *qi*, the original potency humans receive from heaven and earth. Here people come truly into their own, forming their unique personal determination, life purpose, and sense of wholeness. The potential pitfall in this area is fear in all its forms: unease, nervousness, anxiety, fright, scare, even terror, the pervasive doubt that one is not ready or good enough to attain one's dream. It is thus no accident that the key stress hormone is adrenaline, literally "ad-renal," which means "next to the kidneys."

The positive attitude or virtue to counterbalance this is wisdom (*zhi*), whose graph shows the combination of "speech" and "arrow," indicating the mental direction underlying vocal expression. It signals the appreciation of the individual's unique values and abilities as well as the awareness of the inherent, self-generating, and self-organizing order of the universe. Realizing that one forms an integral part of universal evolution and is at all times connected to the vastness of spirit, one can step forward with confidence to live one's best life.

The intention, finally, resides in the very center of the body, where the spleen and stomach form the core repository and food is turned into vital energy. Their main task is planning and organization, which easily leads into the negative tendency of overthinking and worry. Most important here is to enhance the virtue of personal integrity as it manifests in fundamental honesty, integrity, trustworthiness, and faith (*xin*), a word that combines the graphs for "human being" and "speech." This indicates the sense of personal truth and inner authenticity, being true to one's particular disposition while maintaining a pervasive connection to the original, underlying perfection and wholeness of Dao.[8]

Cognitive functions

Within this system, Daoists acknowledge a hierarchy among cognitive functions, outlined particularly in the fifth-century *Xisheng jing* (Scripture of Western Ascension), a text of the Northern Celestial Masters at Louguan. It recounts the oral instructions Laozi gave when he transmitted the *Daode jing* to Yin Xi, the Guardian of the Pass, integrating religious ideals with classical Daoist thought.[9]

The text uses two words for cognitive processing, "thought" (*si*) and "thinking" (*nian*). *Si* is a compound of the pictograms for skull or brain plus heart or feeling; it indicates the interchange between these two aspects of the mind. *Nian*, also written with the "heart" radical, contains the word for "now" and thus points to the active, ongoing act of thinking. Both have in common that they are non-evaluative and merely denote a specific mental activity. The *Xisheng jing* employs *nian* in most instances in the sense of "to recollect" or "be mindful." That is to say, it takes up the religious meaning of the term as it is found in the Buddhist use of *nianfo*, i.e., "to be mindful of the Buddha," in practice the recitation of the Buddha's name, either verbally or mentally. Using this implication of *nian*, the *Xisheng jing* admonishes its readers to continue reciting the *Daode jing* and never stop recollecting and thinking of Dao. *Si* is used very similarly. It frequently refers to a concentration on Dao that indicates a form of meditation.

At the same time, the text employs the two terms positively only when directed toward Dao. When directed toward ordinary life and the artificial superstructure of reality, thinking turns into a destructive force and thought ceases to be neutral. From straightforward, plain thought it turns into something else: planning, yearning, worry, care, or concern. "When you try to force Dao, it will not come. Why is this so? Because trying involves having yearning and concerns. This goes against Dao" (18.2–3). Especially *si* is then often used in conjunction with "planning thought" (*lü*), also the term used for the negative emotion of worry. In this specific combination, the term refers to thoughts that are not directed toward the present and life at hand but toward the past or the future. Once out of touch with immediate reality, thoughts become regrets and worries, longing and yearning, directly related to emotions, passions, and desires. The practitioner's task consequently lies in reducing and eventually abandoning this misdirected power of thought, in keeping all thinking in the present and on Dao through meditation and recitation.

Moving into the deeper structures of the human mind, the will becomes apparent. It is the force that exists immediately behind the function of thought and forms the root of all thinking. As such it has to be strictly controlled to prevent it from leaping out of bounds. Like thought, the will can be a formidable asset in attaining oneness with Dao, yet it also tends to run wild and concern itself overly much with the affairs of this world. While one is still trying to impose one's will on the affairs of this world, one cannot possibly reach a state of natural nonaction. As the *Xisheng jing* has it, "As long as your will is fixed on existence, your nonaction will be ailing" (14.4). Properly directed, thought is thus essential to progress toward Dao, but can only be attained when the will is solidly under control. Holding "the will dispassionate and remaining in nonaction" (12.4), one can keep it on a right leash and turn it into a servant of Dao.

Coupled with the will is the intention, crucial to the workings of the mind. The *Xisheng jing* defines it in ordinary people as a misdirected form of conscious thinking that "arises through yearning for some state of the body" (7.9) and is concretely felt as an emotion or desire. Thus "mind and intention are afflictions" (17.3) and constitute "a bondage to life" (29.4). The intention is on equal footing with the personal body or self as a conglomerate of sensory desires. As the Tang meditation manual *Neiguan jing* (Scripture of Inner Observation) says,

"The eyes covet color, the ears are obstructed by sound, the mouth is addicted to tastes, and the nose depends on smell. One's intention thus is turned to either craving or aversion, and one's personal body continues to desire to be slimmer or fatter.

In the same vein, the *Xisheng jing* insists that one has to "reject all that the self or intention desire" (12.13). One must take care to "never let the intention run loose" (14.7) and control it stolidly just as one keeps an iron fist on the will. In due course, the intention as determined by the conscious mind and the senses becomes weaker and weaker, and there is no more conscious knowledge. Ultimately it dies.

> "When the intention dies, stillness arises and life is recovered. As life immerses me more and more, excitement and agitation cease altogether. I am full of the undifferentiated source of Dao, enveloped by primordial energy … utterly empty and free from desires.
>
> (38.1-4)

Although without thought, will, or intention, Daoist masters still function actively and consciously in the world. The *Xisheng jing* explains this paradox by saying that only the intention defined through the senses and serving the artificially created self must die. The intention as pure spiritual or mental force, on the other hand, is part of Dao: it represents the inner need for harmony and the intuitive sense of true integrity. In itself good and necessary, it is spoiled by desires, the dependence on the senses, and the demands of social structure and convention. Twisted and warped, it becomes a cognitive function that must die to allow the deeply buried intention for inner truth and oneness with Dao to surface. This pure intention, like will and thought, is recovered by reducing directional thinking to neutral psychological activity, to plain conscious thinking. "Keep your will dispassionate and remain in nonaction; meditate with concentrated imagination and active conscious thinking," the *Xisheng jing* advises (12.4).

Forms of meditation

Daoists use various forms of meditation to retrain the mind toward a more primordial level of purity, toward the recovery of the active functioning of cosmic spirit within. The *Neiye*, a fourth century practice manual, about one third the length of the *Daode jing* and close to it in terminology and outlook, works largely with concentration. Its main practice is breath control combined with focus on a single object described as "embracing oneness," as well as holding on the spirit and material souls. It also recommends moderating food intake, letting go of desires and emotions, and reducing sensory stimulation. Doing so, adepts attain the fourfold alignment of body, limbs, breath, and mind, an overall state of stillness and stability, internal virtue, and the energetic balance of upright *qi*, and find a single-minded focus that leads to a cultivated, stable and well-ordered mind. This, in turn, allows *qi* to flow harmoniously through the body and Dao to pervade one's life, leading to a state of serenity and repose that resembles the clarity and stillness proposed in the *Daode jing* (ch. 45). Adepts move through life in harmony with all, untouched by danger and harm, their bodies unimpaired. At peace in themselves and in alignment with the world, they reach a level of physical health that keeps them fit and active well into old age.

The *Zhuangzi*, too, has a method of concentration and sensory withdrawal it calls mind-fasting (*xinzhai*). It says,

> Unify your will and don't listen with your ears but listen with your mind. No, don't listen with your mind, but listen with your *qi*. Listening stops with the ears, the mind stops with matching [perception], but *qi* is empty and waits on all things. Dao gathers in emptiness alone. Emptiness is mind-fasting.
>
> (ch. 4)

This involves the systematical release of sensory processing until, instead of hearing with the ears and the mind, one is only aware of the steady flow of vital energy manifesting as sounds in a state of empty and open, nonjudging awareness. Another way the *Zhuangzi* describes this is as "making the body like a withered tree and the mind like dead ashes" (chs. 2, 24). Eliminating the fixed mind as well as the heart-mind, this recreates the natural spontaneity of childhood: "The infant acts without knowing what he is doing, moves without knowing where he is going. His body is like the branch of a withered tree; his mind is like dead ashes" (ch. 23). The person who achieves this state is "perfected in reality and perception. He never looks for reasons. Dim and dark, dark and dim, no-mind complete: one can't plan anything with him" (ch. 22). Part of the overarching harmony of heaven, a person in this state is "truly authentic," resting in "self-forgetful sleep-informed non-self-awareness."[10]

The *Zhuangzi* also outlines a different form of meditation it calls "sitting in oblivion" (*zuowang*), which is a complete letting-go of all personal identity and conscious functioning. "I let my limbs and physical structure fall away, do away with perception and intellect, separate myself from body-form and let go of all knowledge, thus merging in great pervasion" (ch. 6). Unlike in concentration, where adepts focus on one object mentally, here the mind is relaxed, and the main effort is physical. One should sit with legs crossed or folded, back straight but light, stomach empty, head drawn upward, eyes holding a relaxed gaze, tongue touching the roof of the mouth, hands resting comfortable in lap, breath flowing gently, and in complete silence then release all effort and "just sit." Historically linked with, and similar to, Zen practice, this leads to a state where one can just be: all visceral awareness of emotions and desires is lost, and all sense perception is cut off. Completely free from bodily self-consciousness and dualistic awareness, it represents a state of deep immediacy and no-mind, open to all things and vibrantly connected to Dao.

In the Tang dynasty, Sima Chengzhen, in his treatise called *Zuowang lun* (Sitting in Oblivion), expanded this practice to integrate it with Buddhist mindfulness, especially as described in the then-popular Tiantai school. Mindfulness or "inner observation" (*neiguan*) involves establishing a detached, objective observer or witness consciousness, allowing the mind to roam and observe all experiences as if from a distance. It also comes with a particular perspective, seeing the world in terms of flow and change, and with an emphasis on positive mental attitudes, such as compassion and calmness. Thus Sima Chengzhen encourages adepts to understand the interconnectedness of all phenomena and realize the full power of karma and retribution, to see worldly necessities as food and clothing as a mere vehicle for temporary use, and to let go of the personal self in favor of the body as form, seeing it merely as "the shape one has taken in this particular life." All this helps to release the mind, to take it back from its dualistic tendencies as heart-mind to working as the conveyor of pure spirit in body and life.[11]

Notes

1 See Targ and Katra 1999.
2 On emotions, see Panksepp 1998.
3 Corballis 2011, 133–8.
4 On spirit, see Roth 1990; Puett 2003.
5 On emotions, see Hansen 1995; Puett 2004. For more, see Kohn 2014, ch. 6.
6 For more on the "heart," see Enzinger 2002.
7 On the souls, see Harrell 1979. For more on sufficiency, see Twist 2003.
8 For more on the mind, see Ishida 1989.
9 For the text, see Kohn 2007, ch. 6, which discusses the mind.
10 For the *Neiye*, see Roth 1999. On withdrawal practice in the *Zhuangzi*, see Santee 2011.
11 See Kohn 2010.

References

Corballis, Michael C. 2011. *The Recursive Mind: The Origins of Human Language, Thought, and Civilization*. Princeton, NJ: Princeton University Press.
Enzinger, Irmgard. 2002. "Bedeutungen des Begriffes "Herz": Das Körper-Denken in *Mengzi* und *Zhuangzi*." *Monumenta Serica* 50:95–170.
Hansen, Chad. 1995. "*Qing* (Emotions) in Pre-Buddhist Chinese Thought." In *Emotions in Asian Thought: A Dialogue in Comparative Philosophy*, edited by Joel Marks and Roger T. Ames, 181–212. Albany: State University of New York Press.
Harrell, Stephen. 1979. "The Concept of 'Soul' in Chinese Folk Religion." *Journal of Asian Studies* 38:519–28.
Ishida, Hidemi. 1989. "Body and Mind: The Chinese Perspective." In *Taoist Meditation and Longevity Techniques*, edited by Livia Kohn, 41–70. Ann Arbor: University of Michigan, Center for Chinese Studies.
Kohn, Livia. 2007. *Daoist Mystical Philosophy: The Scripture of Western Ascension*. Magdalena, NM: Three Pines Press.

Kohn, Livia. 2010. *Sitting in Oblivion: The Heart of Daoist Meditation*. Dunedin, FL: Three Pines Press.

Kohn, Livia. 2014. *Zhuangzi: Text and Context*. St. Petersburg, FL: Three Pines Press.

Panksepp, Jaak. 1998. *Affective Neuroscience: The Foundation of Human and Animal Emotions*. New York, NY: Oxford University Press.

Puett, Michael J. 2003. "Can Nothing Overcome Heaven? The Notion of Spirit in the *Zhuangzi*." In *Hiding the World in the World: Uneven Discourses on the Zhuangzi*, edited by Scott Cook, 248–62. Albany: State University of New York Press.

Puett, Michael J. 2004. "The Ethics of Responding Properly: The Notion of *Qing* in Early Chinese Thought." In *Love and Emotions in Traditional Chinese Literature*, edited by Halvor Eifring, 37–68. Leiden: Brill.

Roth, Harold D. 1990. "The Early Taoist Concept of *Shen*: A Ghost in the Machinery?" In *Sagehood and Systematizing Thought in the Late Warring States and Early Han*, edited by Kidder Smith, 11–32. Brunswick, ME: Bowdoin College.

Roth, Harold D. 1999. *Original Tao: Inward Training and the Foundations of Taoist Mysticism*. New York, NY: Columbia University Press.

Santee, Robert. 2011. "The *Zhuangzi*: A Holistic Approach to Healthcare and Well-being." In *Living Authentically: Daoist Contributions to Modern Psychology*, edited by Livia Kohn, 39–58. Dunedin, FL: Three Pines Press.

Targ, Russell, and Jane Katra. 1999. *Miracles of Mind: Exploring Nonlocal Consciousness and Spiritual Healing*. Novato, CA: New World Library.

Twist, Lynne. 2003. *The Soul of Money: Transforming Your Relationship with Money and Life*. New York, NY: W. W. Norton.

6   The human condition

Going beyond the intricacies of body and mind, the human condition describes the overall position of humanity in the world, in relation to other human beings, to animals and nature, and to the divine. The latter provides its most fundamental definition, creating deeply conditioned beliefs and constricted views of humanity. For example, the prevailing view of humanity in Western religions is determined by the Biblical injunction in Genesis:

> And God said: Let us make man in our image, after our likeness; and let him have dominion over the fish of the sea, and over the fowl of the air, and over the cattle, and over all the earth, and over every creeping thing that creepeth upon the earth.
>
> (1:26)

This gives human beings the right and even the duty to dominate and use animals and the natural world for their own purposes, leading to an overall relationship of conquest and control. In India, in contrast, human beings are isolated soul-entities moving through a world that is ultimately illusory, locked into a close relationship with nature and animals in endless cycles of transmigration and rebirth.

An overarching distinction of the human relation to the divine is oneness versus independence, what Maria Colavito has called the "mythic model of the One" as opposed to that of the Zero. In a world rooted in underlying oneness, "everything manifest would of necessity be a copy of that which exists within the One .... with the One the only original." Any object or being consequently partakes of the One yet can never be the One itself, which remains formless at the root of creation. Everything thus has always only partial access to the unity of the original, is never fully whole. One-centered cultures typically rest their entire thinking on the One and strive for the return to wholeness and completion.

Zero cultures, in contrast, hold on to two basic principles, "that each thing is independent unto itself; and that that which is, is that which manifests." In a world based on these principles, the role and importance of all things is only determined by themselves: they work only for their own interest, there is no need to justify any action, and "if things *could* be done or created, they *would* be." Death being not a return to one's true home in the One but the end of all existence, there is an endless struggle for stability and solidity, found only in the things of this world, leading to the dominance of materialism over spiritual attainment. Closely related is the fundamental sense of being in a world that is essentially harmonious versus one that is unstable, unpredictable, and disorderly, leading to a dominant feeling of integration rather than alienation and to gentler and harsher ways of promoting individual discipline and social order.[1] In other words, how cultures perceive of the human condition is elementary in the way they construct reality on all levels.

Life and world

Within this framework, Daoists definitely belong to the model of the One, seeing life and world in an affirmative mode rather than as threatening or a source of suffering. It is good, natural, and real to be human. People are part of the universe, not separate or created special. If they functioned as they were originally intended, intelligent yet non-evaluative, responsive to nature's changes without getting upset, the world would flow along in perfect harmony and function to the benefit of all.

Harmony, then, is an important category defining the human condition in China. It is the acknowledgment of a true and pure state of natural flow that can be disrupted—typically either through excess or deficiency, torrents or obstructions. This can happen naturally by an occasional excess or deficiency in *qi*, but it can also be the result of intentional or willful human action. Consciousness, the power to think and act in a harmonious or disharmonious way, is what sets human beings apart from the rest of creation. Humanity is not only in a position of central importance but also in one of highest responsibility. Earthquakes, floods, and tornadoes are people's fault, indications that all is not well in society and government. The category of harmony thus includes the notions of interactivity and of responsibility for the state of the world. This again contrasts sharply with Western notions of separate and unique individuals and Hindu ideas of soul-entities. Personal realization in China is never individual but always interactive, be it in obligation to society or in reaching oneness with the cosmos.

Another key category in this context is the understanding of the cosmos as dynamic versus static, flowing rather than substantial, a process of becoming rather than a state of being. There are no elements in the Greek sense in the Chinese universe, no firm indissoluble entities that exist from the beginning and remain forever. All life consists of a continuous flow of dynamic energy interaction that never stops and always moves in one direction or the other. What counts are "the implications of tendencies rather than linear causes and effects"—replacing the idea of "effect" with that of "efficacy," the force created by the dynamics of a specific set of circumstances. Seeing events under the auspices of synchronicity as developed by Carl Jung, Daoists understand reality as an ongoing process of change in a diagrammatic configuration. Key factors here are time, place, and circumstances, the latter expressing "the particular configuration (disposition, arrangement)," the ongoing tendency or propensity of reality in an inherently dynamic universe.[2]

On the level of human affiliations, the Chinese vision of the human condition is clearly hierarchical as opposed to egalitarian, focuses on groups and social obligations rather than on the rights and autonomy of individuals, and sees human activity as bound by cosmic commandments instead of personal decisions. While this vision is strongly Confucian, it also plays a major role in Daoist thinking and the structure of communities. All social standing and activities in the world are determined by a hierarchical structure, without any clear notion of equality. The same hierarchical thinking also applies to humans vis-a-vis outsiders or savages (barbarians) and animals, so that humans, and particularly the Chinese, are considered the most spiritual of all without, however, being thought of as their masters. The continuity of all life and its manifestation in different patterns of *qi* ensures a clear structure of ranks while at the same time reaffirming the basic commonality among all living beings.

In addition, hierarchies ensure that all obligation is circumscribed firmly by the individual's status, while the interactivity of the system causes virtues to be predominantly social (loyalty, filial piety) rather than personal (integrity, perseverance). Honesty in this context is still a virtue but interactive rather than of character. Instead of referring to a person's allegiance to a generally acknowledged objective and irreversible reality, it indicates the best possible behavior in the light of social harmony. For example, "if a host is caught by his guest with his pants down, there is no apologizing or confusion; instead there is a social agreement that the event simply never happened."[3]

Justice, too, is a group affair, often entire families being executed for the treason of one. Even the individual's intention in committing a breach is ignored in favor of the effect of his deed on the harmony of the whole. Thus, in formal legal codes the killing of a father is not measured according to its being accidental, manslaughter, or murder, but taken as a major disruption of social coherence and punished accordingly.[4] Tragedy in the Western sense is thus unknown—conflicts between two contradictory inner inclinations commonly being resolved by the social rightness of one over the other.

On the level of human affiliations, therefore, the Chinese understanding of the human condition shows a certain similarity with other socially focused religions, such as Judaism, Islam, or Hinduism. Religious realization is attained through a wholesome and lawful life within society, the religious community is the same as the social, supernatural structures match earthly bureaucracies, and many aspects of daily life are defined by rules. In contrast to other religions, however, norms in China are not derived from a divine source but depend on the cycle of nature and the patterns of human interaction; their main commandments are not unchangeable laws but vague rules that are adjusted according to changing circumstances. The main purpose, moreover, is the attainment of harmony both in nature and society, making the Chinese idea of obligation similar yet different.

Inner nature

Harmony manifests when everybody does exactly what he or she is supposed to be doing in the greater scheme of life—described sometimes in musical terms as consisting of various instruments playing together, each contributing its voice and piping its own pitches, yet together creating a harmonious tune. The key factor in this is inner nature (*xing*), a word that consists of the characters for "heart" and "life." In early China, the concept occurred mainly in the context of longevity practices and the cultivation of health; later it came to indicate the inherent tendencies and functional dispositions of the human being, the unique way spirit and the various psychological forces manifest as inborn talents, predilections, and tendencies.

Physically inner nature appears as genetically determined characteristics, such as size, stature, fingerprints, hand lines, and more. Psychologically it indicates the predisposition toward certain preferences, behaviors, and skills. Both are obvious from birth, just as no two infants are ever completely identical: they each react to the world differently, so that the same picture or gesture may make some smile, some cry, and others go to sleep.

There are two fundamental models of looking at inner nature, as development or discovery. The former sees it as certain base urges that need to be controlled, structured, and developed; the latter sees it as a cosmos-based set of dispositions that one needs to discover and cultivate. Westerners tend to understand inner nature in the first mode: weak and problematic, it is a reservoir of selfish and dangerous potentials that have to be harnessed, controlled, and trained, so that the person can cope with outside conditions. Daoists, on the other hand, tend to understand inner nature in the second sense as a link to the cosmos. Originally pristine and whole, however much covered by passions and ideas, it is the ultimate source of wisdom, the root of enlightenment, and the key to being as one is, never mind what the outside situation may be.[5]

The most detailed description in pre-Han China appears in the *Xing zi ming chu* (Inner Nature Comes from [Heaven's] Decree), a bamboo manuscript dated to around 300 BCE. It defines inner nature in terms of the energetic flow of the emotions, i.e., "dispositions and tendencies to react in certain ways. When stimulated by things, inner nature stirs, forming specific [emotional] reactions." In other words, it consists of vital energy flowing through the person. Although universally one, when stimulated by sensory data, it moves in specific, unique pathways that closely connect to the heart-mind. Giving rise to emotions that are unique to each individual, it thus determines the way the person reacts to reality and lives in the world.

The manuscript moves on to discuss inner nature as being modified by moving, enticing, restraining, or refining with the help of things, pleasure, deliberation, rightness as well as circumstances and practice. It then outlines a sequence of how best to deal with it. From becoming aware of how we react to and engage with outside things, we learn to restrain and fine-tune our ways. Once we have a certain degree of control, we can begin to draw it out, nourish, and grow it, moving ever closer to spiritual practice and Dao, and becoming more ourselves and more fulfilled in the process.[6]

The Confucian philosopher Mencius, too, proposes the cultivation of inner nature, which he defines in two dimensions. First, it is the seat of the "five dispositions," i.e., people's biological nature as expressed in unique reactions to data transmitted by the five senses. Second, it determines the inherent character of human beings and as such includes the sprouts of moral goodness. While the first should be harnessed and controlled, the latter should be uncovered and expanded.[7]

The Daoist thinker and *Zhuangzi* commentator Guo Xiang defines inner nature as the personal aspect, allotment, or share everyone has in Dao. Completely independent of the person's subjective wishes or concrete hopes, it orders personal existence from within. It is people's natural self-being, "what we rely on spontaneously without ever being conscious of it." The determinacy of any given moment, it is the way people are the way they are, independent of knowledge or conscious awareness. Firmly embedded in the individual's being, it cannot be altered, and any forced change to it means subjective suffering. However, with careful cultivation, it can be transcended. Inner nature is thus both limiting and liberating—limiting because it prevents people from reaching *any* goal they may set themselves; liberating because fulfilling *all* inborn gifts to the fullest brings perfect happiness. The trick is to realize which is which—inner strength or outer ideals—or, as the *Zhuangzi* has it, to "distinguish the heavenly from the human" (ch. 5).[8]

Determinism

The concept of inner nature is deterministic to a certain degree, since it demands that people fulfill their particular role in the greater universe as based on their unique inherent tendencies. Beyond that, however, people's life is also determined by the combined circumstances of their personal situation as embedded in material reality, geographical conditions, social forces, and overall cultural patterns. These factors determine what opportunities come into one's life, how much training is available, and what chances there are for performing to one's best abilities. As Malcolm Gladwell says in *Outliers*, "People don't rise from nothing … It makes a difference where and how we grew up. The culture we belong to and the legacies passed down by our forebears shape the patterns of our achievements."[9]

Daoists call this destiny (*ming*), a word that consist of the character for "decree," "command," or "mandate" combined with that for "mouth." It occurs first in the oracle bones, where it indicates a mission or gift granted by a higher authority to a lower person and, more specifically, the divine approval or command the Shang kings received from a high god or ancestor. Applied to individual lives in later centuries, the word came to mean that which is ordained, be it the duration of one's life on earth, a vocation to be fulfilled, or a particular role to play. Ordered and directed by heaven, destiny is thus a quasi-personified, impartial, and natural force.

Guo Xiang defines it as "that which one is given" and links it to cosmic principle, the structuring force of nature that makes everything be what it is. Originally showing the lines running through a piece of jade, the term indicates the natural structure of things, people, and events; by extension, it means any form of systematic pattern, rhythm, and order, including also the dynamics of experience. Guo Xiang applies this to human life as internal controlling principle. "Each individual has principle as much as each and every affair has what is appropriate to it," he says. "What is what it is without ever knowing why it is we call destiny. Thus, by giving up the very concept of destiny and letting it be as it is, destiny and principle are complete."[10]

This closely echoes the *Zhuangzi*, which states categorically, "Inner nature cannot be changed, destiny cannot be altered, time cannot be stopped, and Dao cannot be obstructed" (ch. 14). Destiny designates the factors of life: like inner nature, it is a contingency borrowed from heaven and earth.

> Life and death, existing and perishing, success and failure, wealth and poverty, worthiness and low status, praise and blame, hunger and thirst, heat and cold—all these change over time and are the workings of destiny. They come and go before us like day and night, and we can never understand their cause or beginning.
>
> (ch. 5)

The key to working with destiny, then, is to adapt to the inevitable progression of life and death, the unstoppable march of time. Time here is not "a continuous transformation of future into past," but a "sequence of extended phases of presence." On the one hand, it means a predictable temporal sequence, such as the cycle of the seasons or of day and night, life and death necessitating certain actions at specific times. Providing a sense of continuity, permanence, and inevitability, there is no point getting upset or disturbed by them. "Since life and death closely follow each other, why whine about either?" Zhuangzi says (ch. 22), and advises, "Connecting to the core of life, do not labor over what life cannot do" (ch. 19).

Yet, time also consists of discrete moments of presence, each constitutive element being strictly momentary, arising and passing in rapid succession, felt subjectively and relative to situations and attitudes. "Temporal change is permanent, while the temporal phases within this course are impermanent." To adjust to this, one must completely forget past and future. "Authenticity of existence" means living in "the immediate experience of time, in absorption in pure presence." Dealing with destiny, then, means to accept the ongoing change of everything in the flow of time with equanimity while being immediately present and vibrantly alive in every single moment as it comes and goes, expanding and fulfilling one's inner nature or inherent tendencies to the best of one's ability.[11]

Moving along with destiny, however, does not mean that one has no choice. Times change and life flows along, and within any situation people encounter, certain opportunities arise. Heaven not only sets limitations but also offers chances and new openings. "Reaching to destiny" as a result means "to grasp a great opportunity" (ch. 30). Seeing these chances, people make choices based on their inclinations and disinclinations that come from vital energy as it moves through them as inner nature. These choices create a new set of circumstances and they move along. At all times, the classical Daoist advice is: choose what is right for you. When you have a choice, follow your deepest yearnings and grow to be more and more truly yourself. When you have no choice (such as facing death), choose to remain whole within.

Multiple generations

While the classical philosophers describe human beings as embedded in the greater cosmos through inner nature and destiny, medieval and organized Daoists add another layer, connecting people not only to the supernatural administration but also to multiple generations—either in the form of ancestors or through transmigration and rebirth.

The connection to ancestors goes beyond the age-old understanding that deceased family members continue in spirit form and have an impact on the lives of their descendants. Asking the question why innocent babies die in the womb or in infancy, Daoists answer, "Because the sins of the ancestors and forebears bequeath calamities upon their descendants." The fourth-century *Baopuzi* lists fifteen good deeds to cultivate and seventy bad behaviors to avoid, stating that

> every one of these activities constitutes one sin, and according to its being either serious or light, the Director of Destiny (Siming) subtracts a unit of reckoning or a period [from the life expectancy]. When no more units remain, the person dies.

If units of bad behavior have not been accounted for, moreover, the bad fortune created is transmitted to family and descendants.

> Whenever you interfere with or steal from someone else, the gods may take into account [the life expectancy] of your wife, children, and other household members in order to compensate for it, causing them to die, if not immediately. Even if your evil behavior is not quite bad enough to bring death upon the members of your household, for a long time you will be plagued by floods, fires, burglaries, and other losses.
>
> (ch. 6)[12]

The same idea of inherited evil (*chengfu*), including also retribution for thoughts and attitudes, is further formulated in the *Taiping jing* of the Great Peace movement. It says that "when someone strives to be good but evil results, this is because he receives and transmits the mistakes men have formerly made." The concept here also extends to other social units beyond the family, such as the village or the groups of five families that had joint responsibility according to the legal codes, heightening the responsibility of the individual for his current and future social relations.[13]

Another dimension was added with the arrival of Buddhism and its doctrine of karma and reincarnation that became a mainstay of Chinese thought and practice and had a great impact on Daoism. Buddhists understand human life as the continuous succession of rebirth in six realms, two each on the level of heaven (gods, *asuras* or titans), humanity (people, animals), and the underworld (hungry ghosts, hell-dwellers). These are basically cosmological planes but they also indicate psychological patterns, so that each realm is associated with a particular attitude or emotion: gods are addicted to pleasure, titans like power, human beings are fundamentally ignorant, animals run on instinct, hungry ghosts are driven by greed and desire, and hell dwellers are full of anger and hatred. We all pass through these states variously in our lives, but some people are dominantly more in one mode than another and can be described as living in that particular realm.

The key factor that determines one's level is karma. A concept important in Indian religion since the Upanishads, it states that all actions have inevitable consequences and, after a period of maturation, revert to their perpetrator. As the individual's soul (*atman*) is the carrier of this load, it must continue to be embodied in physical form to receive the rewards and punishments necessitated by its former actions. Thus the notion of rebirth, including that in nonhuman and hellish states, became a close correlate to the idea of personally created and suffered-through karma. In Hinduism and Jainism karma was thought to be created predominantly through actions and imagined as an almost physical substance that clung to an eternal soul, but in Buddhism it was understood much less physically. Created primarily through good and bad intentions of the mind, it was transmitted in "consecutive moments of a psychic continuum," like the light of a candle, without the necessity of an eternal or substantial soul underlying the process of life. In all cases, however, karma was entirely centered within the individual and could be neither worsened nor improved by the actions of others.

This notion was later challenged by the Mahayana, whose followers claimed that good karma in the form of merit accumulated over long periods of time could not only serve as a positive inspiration to others but also be transferred to improve their lot. This gave rise to devotional cults toward savior figures or bodhisattvas, to rituals that would transfer merits for the sake of one's ancestors, and to the swearing of so-called bodhisattva vows. The latter placed the practitioner immediately on a high level of karmic attainment and gave him a "karmically protective coding," with whose help he or she could fulfill the spiritual goal of universal salvation and compassion for all that lives. Placing a strong emphasis on the community of all beings, Mahayana practitioners believed that the karmic activities of each being had an influence on all and that the country and even the world would benefit from the religious activities of the people. The king, therefore, participated to about one sixth in the merit or demerit created by all his subjects, and society as a whole became a forum for karmic and religious unfolding.[14]

Daoists adopted this vision, notably in the Numinous Treasure school, and expressed it variously, connecting rebirth in various animal forms to matching sins. To alleviate the karmic burden, they would perform various rituals, notably of repentance and penitence, and place their faith in savior figures, such as bodhisattvas, gods, and perfected, who would use their unlimited power and compassion to raise people from the worldly mire.

Among penitential rites, the so-called Purgation of Mud and Ashes stands out. Hoping to preempt punishments in the hells, devotees would smear yellow mud on their brows, undo their hair and tie it to the poles and railings of an altar erected on bare earth. Placing their hands behind their backs, they bound them together, then, with a jade disk in their mouths, they lay face down on the ground, spread their legs and struck their heads on the earth to seek forgiveness for sins. They did this for six hours facing west during the day and six hours facing north during the night, possibly as often as three times a year, vigorously placing themselves in the position of groveling supplicants, so that their misery and servility would evoke sympathy from the gods who would then grant them, their kinsmen, and their ancestors pardons for their transgressions.[15]

Some of the prime deities addressed in this fashion are the Ten Worthies Who Save From Suffering (Jiuku tianzun), an adaptation of the buddhas of the ten directions, in combination with savior bodhisattvas, such as Guanyin (Avalokitesvara), Dizang (Ksitigarbha), and Wenshu (Manjusri). In Daoism, they appear first in late sixth century with names still rather Buddhist in nature, including titles such as "Great Compassion," "Universal Rescue," and "Wisdom Transformation." Later, they are linked with the ten kings of hell and worshiped particularly in memorial services for the salvation of the dead from the karmic consequences of their evil deeds.

In addition, Daoists would also make sumptuous offerings to the Director of Destiny to help them bypass the underworld tortures or trick the administrators of the celestial ledgers into altering their preset course. Means here included a change of name and residence, the alteration of physical appearance, rituals to hide the soul, the feigning of death and planting of decoy corpses as well as the creation of a new spiritual embryo as an immortal alter ego.[16]

Notes

1 See Colavito 1992. For more philosophical sources, see Clack and Hower 2017.

2 On propensity, see Jullien 1995. For more on the human condition, see Kohn 2000.
3 Paul 1977, 172.
4 See Bodde and Morris 1973.
5 Kohn 2014, 102.
6 See Perkins 2010.
7 See Graham 1990.
8 Ziporyn 2003.
9 Gladwell 2008, 17.
10 See Kohn 2014, ch. 9.
11 On time, see Moeller 2004, 98–9. For more on destiny, see Lupke 2005.
12 Ware 1966, 118.
13 Kohn 2004, 18; Hendrischke 1991, 10–11.
14 See Mizuno 1987, 267–8.
15 Benn 2000; Hung 2019.
16 See the papers by Bokenkamp and Campany in Lupke 2005.

References

Benn, Charles. 2000. "Daoist Ordination and *Zhai* Rituals." In *Daoism Handbook*, edited by Livia Kohn, 309–38. Leiden: Brill.

Bodde, Derk, and Clarence Morris. 1973. *Law in Imperial China*. Philadelphia: University of Pennsylvania Press.

Clack, Brian R., and Tyler Hower. 2017. *Philosophy and the Human Condition: An Anthology*. New York, NY: Oxford University Press.

Colavito, Maria M. 1992. *The New Theogony: Mythology for the Real World*. Albany: State University of New York Press.

Gladwell, Malcolm. 2008. *Outliers: The Story of Success*. New York, NY: Little, Brown.

Graham, A. C. 1990. "The Background of the Mencian Theory of Human Nature." In *Studies in Chinese Philosophy and Philosophical Literature*, edited by A. C. Graham, 7–66. Albany: State University of New York Press.

Hendrischke, Barbara. 1991. "The Concept of Inherited Evil in the *Taiping Jing*." *East Asian History* 2:1–30.

Hung, Lichien. 2019. "Ritual Healing in Taiwan: The Rite for Concealing the Soul." *Journal of Daoist Studies* 12:120–38.

Jullien, François. 1995. *The Propensity of Things: Toward a History of Efficacy in China*. New York, NY: Zone Books.

Kohn, Livia. 2000. "Chinese Religion." In *The Human Condition: A Theory and Case-Study of the Comparison of Religious Ideas*, edited by Robert C. Neville, 21–47. Albany: State University of New York Press.

Kohn, Livia. 2004. *Cosmos and Community: The Ethical Dimension of Daoism*. Cambridge, MA: Three Pines Press.

Kohn, Livia. 2014. *Zhuangzi: Text and Context*. St. Petersburg, FL: Three Pines Press.

Lupke, Christopher. 2005. *The Magnitude of Ming: Command, Allotment, and Fate in Chinese Culture*. Honolulu: University of Hawaii Press.

Mizuno, Kogen. 1987. "Karman: Buddhist Concepts." In *Encyclopedia of Religion*, edited by Mircea Eliade, vol. 8, 266–8. New York, NY: Macmillan.

Moeller, Hans-Georg. 2004. *Daoism Explained: From the Dream of the Butterfly to the Fishnet Allegory*. La Salle, IL: Open Court Publishing.

Paul, Robert A. 1977. "The Place of Truth in Sherpa Law and Religion." *Journal of Anthropological Research* 33:167–84.

Perkins, Franklin. 2010. "Recontextualizing *Xing*: Self-Cultivation and Human Nature in the Guodian Texts." *Journal of Chinese Philosophy* 37.1:16–32.

Ware, James R. 1966. *Alchemy, Medicine and Religion in the China of AD 320.* Cambridge, MA: MIT Press.

Ziporyn, Brook. 2003. *The Penumbra Unbound: The Neo-Taoist Philosophy of Guo Xiang*. Albany: State University of New York Press.

Part III

Community

7 Forms of community

The earliest form of community goes back to the Paleolithic, when human beings formed bands, "small, politically autonomous groups of twenty to fifty people"—usually a few related extended families. Essentially egalitarian, bands were characterized by "fluid group organization, individual freedom of movement and group membership, immediate and relatively easy access to resources, simple division of labor, and relatively direct personal leverage on other individuals."[1] While they had some division of labor, guidance by a council of elders, and leadership by a headman, their community was simple, close to nature, and without centralized control.

As population increased, humans began to form tribes, defined as pyramids of social groups that traced descent to a common ancestor, often hypothetical or mythological. Increasingly sedentary after the end of the Paleolithic around 10,000 BCE, they lived in clan-based villages and were led by big men or chiefs, who tended to exercise influence rather than power and were responsible to a council of elders. Despite their larger numbers and increasing social structure, they showed little specialization and were still largely egalitarian. Linked by marriage, ceremonial interactions, and the sharing of resources, tribes constituted a powerful form of human networking.[2]

The next stage was that of chiefdom, a "multicommunity political unit" that "unites many thousands or tens of thousands of people under formal, full-time political leadership." Here society began to be stratified, divided into hereditary ranks or incipient social classes, notably rulers, warriors, and commoners. The chief was in charge of overall organization, controlling both the means of production and all economic surpluses; however, he did not have the pervasive power to coerce people into obedience.[3]

This changed with the next form of community: statehood. States "have a central government empowered to collect taxes, draft labor for public works or war, decree laws, and physically enforce them," wielding "centralized power in an order of socioeconomic stratification."[4] Community at this stage became complex, differentiating membership in five distinct ways: (1) segmentation by establishing parallel subgroups, (2) scheduling by creating temporal divisions, (3) specialization by dividing work according to specific tasks and spheres, (4) ranking by giving priority to individuals in certain spheres of action, and

(5) stratification by establishing preferred access to resources for elites. All these ways of differentiation serve to create order and reduce competition and conflict. "They accomplish by social separation what could no longer be reached by physical separation."[5]

Ideal vision

By the time the first Daoists appeared on the historical horizon, China had been a state with a highly complex society for several millennia, however, vague memories of happier and more egalitarian times remained. Based on this, Daoists envisioned an intricate combination of simplicity and complexity, egalitarianism and hierarchy, personal autonomy and autocracy, formulating their unique utopia, that is, "an imaginary society in which humankind's deepest yearnings, noblest dreams, and highest aspirations come to fulfillment, where all physical, social, and spiritual forces work together in harmony, to permit the attainment of everything people find necessary and desirable."[6]

The earliest formulation of a Daoist community vision appears in the *Daode jing*. Without rejecting leadership or favoring anarchism, it strongly advocates "naturalness" (*ziran*) and proposes that social leaders or "sages" should rest in nonaction (*wuwei*) and refrain from all overbearing behavior, never boasting, bragging, showing off, or in any way putting themselves forward (chs. 22, 24, 30). Accumulation of possessions creates problems, any show of superiority is harmful, and "to be proud of honor and wealth causes inevitable downfall" (ch. 9). The text decries any use of force and describes weapons as evil (chs. 29–31). It never tires to admonish its readers to "abandon sageliness and discard wisdom" (ch. 19), to get rid of all formality and contrived virtues. The ideal is to be simple and fluid like water (ch. 8), to behave in close alignment with heaven and earth (ch. 5), and to live in nonaction, letting all others and all beings do what comes naturally to them (ch. 64), so they can fulfill their inner nature and destiny.

The *Daode jing*, closely echoing early sedentary tribal organization, prefers communities to be small, the size of villages, so that all members are either closely related or friends. They collect their food and plant their gardens, growing all they need and, free from segmentation or specialization, locally produce their various utensils and necessities. They may have technology and weaponry, but never use them; they may know about the outside world, but never interact with it. Resting peacefully at home, relishing their tasks and their social life, they enjoy their days and pay more attention to living than to rising in a hierarchy or possessing great wealth (ch. 80).

Keeping their lives simple, ideal Daoists eschew overindulgence in information or sensory stimulation (ch. 12), never, as the *Zhuangzi* supplements, getting "confused by the five notes or bewitched by the six tones, by the sounds of gongs and chimes, strings and woodwinds" (ch. 8). Remaining true to themselves, they refuse to strive for anything outside life itself. Considering political leaders as "great thieves" (ch. 10), they never engage in the "crouching and bending of rites and music, the smiles and beaming looks of benevolence and righteousness," markers of complexity that only "destroy naturalness" (ch. 8). Nor do they interfere with nature, leaving all creatures just as they are. They never break in wild animals to bend them to their use—"singe them, shave them, pare them, brand them, bind them with martingale and crupper, tie them up in stable and stall" (ch. 9). Instead, they "stay home with no particular awareness of what they are doing, walk around with no particular awareness of where they are going. Their mouths crammed with food, they are merry; drumming on their bellies, they pass the time" (ch. 9). Like members of Paleolithic bands, they have plenty of leisure to engage in storytelling, dance, and song.

In later centuries, early organized Daoists described this vision in terms of Great Peace. An idea first documented in the third century BCE, it indicated a realm of total happiness and freedom, where justice prevailed, and all cosmic and social energies circulated in a continuous, smooth rhythm. A state of perfect order, Great Peace was affected by good government that satisfied not only the common people but also the forces of heaven and earth, thus leading to a state of blissful harmony that would find the natural forces always beneficent and never destructive and human community in perfect concord.

In its specifically Daoist understanding, as represented by the Great Peace movement of the second century CE and documented in the *Taiping jing*, it meant a community where everyone was closely connected to heaven and earth—everybody's father and mother—and each obtained the place that suited them perfectly to live in full accordance with inherent naturalness and work with ease in nonaction, i.e., by allowing the universal flow to move with and through them. In accordance with Han cosmology, this flow was seen as mediated through a variety of cosmological structures—starry constellations, numerological calculations, and *Yijing* hexagrams—while the individual was understood as a direct agent of the cosmos, entitled to receive necessities in food, education, and health care but in no way permitted to waste, hoard, slacken, or indulge in resentments and drunkenness.[7]

People in this ideal society were divided into nine categories, reaching from "divine men of pure formlessness consisting of *qi*" through various perfected and wise men, who govern perfectly according to yin and yang and the five phases, to the farming population in general and merchants and slaves at the bottom. While thus establishing hierarchy, Daoists yet also insisted on equality in the sense that all wealth had to be shared and each member, no matter of what status, had to fulfill a particular role for the greater good to prevent "deficiency, want, and worry in any one part of society that would certainly have an impact on the whole."[8] The key value in the *Taiping jing* accordingly is flow or circulation, its opposite being blockage or disruption. "On all levels—spiritual, material, economic, and physiological—things have to circulate: this is what Dao and life consist of." To ensure an active togetherness of people and the open interchange of information, all members were encouraged to write down observations of strange or calamitous phenomena that might indicate a disharmony of heaven or earth in so-called letters of good intention and drop them into suggestion boxes to be erected on the main roads to the capital. They should also present any ideas for improvement of social or production procedures to their elders, allowing sages to deliberate their practicality and adoption, thus creating an open forum of flow for the ultimate benefit of all.[9]

Communitas

Historically, Daoist communities saw themselves on the way toward these high-flying ideals, no longer fully part of normative society but not yet in a state of Great Peace, establishing what Victor Turner has called "communitas." This is a social organization of people in a state of liminality—of being betwixt and between, neither here nor there. Surrounded by complex society, communitas is characterized by simplicity and undifferentiation, and comradeship and egalitarianism prevail. A total institution, there are no distinctions, no favoritism, and no ranks; through it, the liminal state of "transition has become a permanent condition," which is nowhere "more clearly marked than in the monastic and mendicant states of the great world religions."[10]

Typical features of communitas include homogeneity and equality, anonymity, humility, and unselfishness; the absence of property, status, kinship rights and duties; sexual continence or community, disregard for personal appearance, total obedience to the leader; maximization of religious attitudes and behaviors, and acceptance of pain and suffering. In addition, they reject the divisions of mainstream culture and form open societies that cut across gender, ethnic, caste, and national divisions. Still, they are open only on the inside, while defining themselves on the outside through being on the margins of or beyond ordinary social structure, whose existence they need as a counterpoint to their own place and in whose juxtaposition they define themselves.[11]

The first formal Daoist organization, the Celestial Masters as founded by Zhang Daoling upon a revelation from Lord Lao in 142 CE, were in many respects a classical communitas. Their community rejected mainstream divisions: its members came from all walks of life and included many non-Chinese—notably Ba and Banshun Man—and women were highly valued and could attain leadership positions. Matching the ideal of Great Peace, they stressed open communication and easy transit, sponsoring a wide-ranging network of roads and maintaining so-called charity lodges, where travelers—both local and foreign—could stay on their journeys.[12]

They also defined both the individual and the community in close relation to heaven and earth: the physical health of the person as much as the functioning of the group depended on purity and proper behavior. If someone fell sick, it was because he had blocked his connection to Dao through moral failure and thus opened himself to a demonic attack; the remedy was confession and petition to the supernatural administration. By the same token, social harmony required the bodily activation of yin and yang, not only by making sure all members married and procreated, but through an initiatory practice known as the Harmonization of *Qi*. Formally choreographed intercourse between selected partners not married to each other, this was an elaborate ritual that also served as the main initiation rite into higher ritual—and thus administrative—ranks of the organization.[13]

The highest of these ranks was that of libationer, administrator of one of twenty-four districts and a direct representative of the Celestial Master. Below them, making up the bulk of the organization, were so-called register disciples, devotees in ritual training who received consecutively longer lists of spirit generals, complete with divine troops and supernatural clerks, for protection against demons. Their main unit of organization and center of production was the household, each working according to its abilities and resources, producing food or other necessities of daily living that were taxed flexibly without extortion. Resisting the stratification of mainstream society, Daoists relied on a domestic form of economy, where every single member had to be an expert, wielding (as well as repairing or even making) specific tools competently and efficiently.[14]

In addition, community life dominated the individual through sets of community rules. The earliest appears in the *Xiang'er* commentary to the *Daode jing*, associated with the grandson of the first Celestial Master. It guides followers to behave with obedience to the leaders and with reticence to their fellow members. They should not strive for positions beyond their status and abstain from sacrifices for popular gods. They must not to do evil, engage in warfare, accumulate riches, or praise themselves as great sages. On a more positive note, followers should develop a helpful and positive attitude within the community, controlling their senses and showing humility toward others. Advancing further, they should give active service to Dao, preserve living things, and live in accordance with the patterns of heaven and earth—never cutting down plants unnecessarily and especially not in spring time. The rewards are accordingly. Those who obey the highest rules become immortals, all other will extend their years and live happily ever after—surviving even cataclysmic changes prophesied to mark the impending end of the world.[15]

Occupying the fertile valleys of Sichuan and the plains of Hanzhong, the Celestial Masters established their own state, unimpeded by imperial or local control, which had largely broken down at the time. Aside from promising health and healing, they guaranteed safety from violent conflict and opened economic security by creating fluid and inclusive institutions, setting a low but attainable standard of living. Different from and marginal to normative society, their tight community cohesion and strict obedience, their insistence on equality of the sexes and ethnic groups, their orientation of life toward the divine, their sexual control, and their understanding of sickness as sin are typical of liminal communities, signifying a particular form of communal religious consciousness that sets believers apart and makes them special.

The very same characteristics, moreover, are present in the Daoist monastic institutions of the middle ages.

Monasteries

The first known Daoist monastery was Louguan, the "Lookout Tower" in the foothills of the Zhongnan range, established around 460. Here the border guard Yin Xi supposedly spotted the celestial signs of Laozi's emigration and convinced him to transmit the *Daode jing*. The institution grew in the wake of the Daoist theocracy under the Toba-Wei, when the state sponsored the New Celestial Masters under Kou Qianzhi (365–448) to administer the empire, establishing Daoist centers and ritual activities throughout, while demanding—under Buddhist influence—that the central officers lived in a celibate community in the capital. Following the Louguan model, in the sixth century, many important institutions developed that not only trained Daoist priests and leaders but also, notably under the Tang, became major centers of learning and economic and political power. Monasticism declined in the late middle ages to be revived again under the auspices of Chan Buddhism in the twelfth century, notably in the Daoist school of Complete Perfection, whose institutions still dominate Daoist monastic life today.[16]

To the present day, Daoist monastics live in fundamental equality. Both monks and nuns do the same work, fulfill the same functions, and equally perform rituals, but women wear more elaborate headdresses and officiate in twos rather than alone, matching the cosmic distinction of yin and yang. All limit possessions and keep free from accumulation. They typically own only two sets of clothing—for daily life and ceremonial occasions—have a set of personal dishes for food, and keep cell furnishings to a minimum, conscientiously practicing the Daoist principle of sufficiency.[17]

Their life is centered on heaven, realizing naturalness and nonaction. Matching their overall goal of ascension to the immortals, both through physical longevity practices and spiritual meditations that activate altered states of consciousness, their physical setting is designed to create a celestial space on earth. Monasteries, commonly located on mountainsides or surrounded by parks if in cities, form a home for the immortals, where celestials come to sojourn and practitioners can be as immortal as possible within the confines of this world. Humans imitate the structures found in the high heavens to set up numinous monasteries over here, creating auspicious places and residences fit for immortals.

Their institutions are inclusive, geared to benefit all: everyone receives according to his need and contributes according to his abilities. There is specialization, since some are more adapt at certain skills—scripture studies, ritual performance, herbal remedies, alchemical elixirs, or meditative trance. Still, training is flexible and the lifestyle fluid. "Monastics are free to do their readings and self-cultivation practices as they want." They can travel to study with masters at other institutions and even leave the organization to return to

lay life if they so desire.[18] While in residence, all work equally in the maintenance of community life, spending a few hours each day to keep their facility
in good shape and take care of basic needs. The vast majority of their time
they practice self-cultivation and interact with others—fellow monastics, lay
followers, and visitors.

Their food is simple and vegetarian, but presented formally and accompanied by ritual, usually involving incantations, prayers, bows, and stylized
movements. Physical behavior in general is highly formalized to the point
where their entire life is choreographed by the rules of the order, every detail
being prescribed so that a heightened consciousness of everyday motions
and thoughts becomes a transforming mental discipline. All movements of
the body here are a form of diffuse prayer, raising ordinary activities to a
higher, more cosmic level. This is most obvious in the chants monastics recite
as they undertake ordinary daily tasks, such as washing their face, cleaning
their teeth, and donning their vestments—in each case offering prayers for all
humanity and connecting to heaven and earth.[19]

Closely linked to nature, the daily schedule of Daoist monasteries matches
the rising and setting of the sun and changes with the seasons, and even today
they eschew the use of artificial light. They divide time according to divine
patterns. Just as the Celestial Masters scheduled their major annual festivals
to coincide with administrative events in the heavens, so monasteries arrange
their annual cycles in accordance with nature and the gods and also follow
a daily schedule determined by ritual. Adopted from Buddhism, their day
divides into six periods of worship—at midnight, cockcrow, dawn, noon,
dusk, and early evening. Each is marked with a ritual observance that consists
of prostrations and incense burning, as well as the chanting of scriptures and
incantations. After a minor rite at cock crow, the morning audience follows
at dawn, a formal assembly of all monastics in honor of the deities, complete
with hymns, prostrations, incense burning, and scripture reading. Breakfast is
served afterward, then there was unscheduled time until noon.

The noon meal is served around 11 am. It is a major ceremony involving
offerings, prayers, praises, and chants of repentance. Its timing matches that
of the feeding of the heavenly sages in order to secure the greatest benefit
for human practitioners. The afternoon is free, a time for personal cultivation, followed by the evening audience at dusk and another, lesser rite in mid-
evening. A sixth period of worship is scheduled around midnight. All around
the clock, therefore, in addition to the high holidays throughout the year,
Daoists follow the heavenly patterns and arrange their lives in service of the
divine.[20]

Food and sex, moreover, are tightly controlled, again continuing the tradition of the Celestial Masters and matching the monastic institutions of other
religions. Wine, meat, and the five strong vegetables (scallions, leeks, onions,
garlic, and ginger) are eschewed completely, their consumption seen as having
a potentially negative effect on the flow of cosmic energies, both in the body
and the greater universe. Similarly celibacy is predicated on the retention,

internal circulation, and refinement of sexual energy known as "essence" (*jing*), a key practice of monastic meditation. Any form of uncontrolled and sinful behavior offends the celestial officers, sickens the spirit and material souls, brings about nightmares and bad fortune, and leads to bad karma and unfavorable rebirth.[21] To prevent all this, monks and nuns, although they may be living together in the same institutions, are encouraged to remain segregated and avoid close contact. However, monastics are allowed to assist members of the opposite sex in emergencies and, if necessary, support family members in distress. Unlike in other traditions, Daoist monks and nuns retain their family name and stay in some contact with civil life, maintaining filial piety as a key virtue. "Leaving the family" in Daoism thus does not mean the complete severance of all worldly ties, but rather indicates the serious dedication to the attainment of Dao and the ultimate transformation of the world toward a state of Great Peace.

Joining nature

A yet different form of Daoist community emerges in the more specialized pursuit of individual seekers who leave society altogether to undertake ascetic practices for spiritual freedom and join nature and the cosmos as their prime community. They wander about the land, through mountains and rivers, communing with divine forces, concocting elixirs, or exploring the teachings of various masters. Without a settled abode, they are mendicants or mountain dwellers; begging or foraging in the woods, they rely entirely on their surroundings for survival. Intimately connecting to nature, they are exposed to the elements and open to cosmic flow; independent of cultural and social constraints, they find equality, freedom, and fulfillment.

Chinese culture has long embraced this ideal in the figure of the hermit or recluse, who leaves society to espouse solitary isolation in the wilderness where wild beasts and indigenous tribes roam, to follow simpler, even animal ways of life. Striving to maintain moral integrity, hermits were moral heroes, sage figures in the Confucian tradition. The earliest known examples are Boyi and Shuqi, who opposed the Zhou conquest and their father's inheritance decision and starved themselves to death rather than give in to moral depravity. Others were more fortunate and blossomed in the clean living of the mountains. Thus Shan Bao, as the *Zhuangzi* notes, "lived among the cliffs, drank only water, and didn't go after gain like other people. He went along like that for seventy years and still had the complexion of a young child" (ch. 19). Choosing a life outside of society for personal rather than moral reasons, they also included longevity masters along the lines of the long-lived Pengzu (ch. 15).[22]

Later Daoists expanded this ideal and connected it with the goal of immortality. Like hermits living in the wilderness and longevity masters cultivating health and spiritual enhancement, immortals fast by living on pure *qi*, eat raw food they find in the woods, and make themselves garments of leaves or deer skins. The very word for "immortal," *xian*, consists of a graph that shows a man next to a mountain. It associates them with the untamed and threatening parts of nature that civilized men stay away from. Pure men of spirit, they are immune to human needs, increasingly associated with birds in the lightness of their bodies and their ability to fly.

In medieval Daoism, practitioners living in the wilderness tended to be alchemists, striving to concoct an elixir to gain ascension into the Heaven of Great Clarity—also the name of their Daoist school. Working in small groups, often only consisting of a master and a few acolytes, alchemists needed to have exactly the right ingredients, typically found only after extensive wanderings through many parts of the country. Concoction itself had to be completely secluded, because the slightest contact with a nonbeliever could ruin the entire process.[23]

Complete Perfection Daoism continued the ancient hermit tradition in yet another way in that it required novices to spend time moving about the countryside while "wandering like the clouds." As the founder, Wang Chongyang, describes it in his *Lijiao shiwu lun* (Fifteen Articles on Establishing the Teaching, DZ 1233), this is

> to pursue inner nature and destiny in search of mystery and wonder [Dao]. One who wanders like this climbs into high mountains over dangerous passes and visits enlightened teachers without tiring. He crosses distant streams with turbulent waters and inquires for Dao without slackening.[24]

Practitioners moved about in small groups, always at least having one companion who would help out in emergencies, but avoided getting deeply attached to each other. They would beg for their food or forage in the mountains, also collecting herbs to enhance their *qi*.

Their possessions were strictly limited. As the seventeenth-century manual *Guiju xuzhi* (Rules to Know) says, wandering monks should have:

1   a rush mat, to keep free from demons on the outside;
2   a quilted robe, to cover heart and inner nature;
3   a single calabash, to contain the food and drink of the wise;
4   a palm-leaf hat, to keep off wind and rain, frost and snow;
5   a palm-leaf fan, to brush off dust from things;
6   a pure satchel, to carry and hold the sacred scriptures;
7   a flat staff, to point to the great Dao, pure wind, and bright moon.[25]

This enforced simplicity and exposure to nature serves to strengthen the inner resolve and positive connection to nature within the practitioner. The psychological mechanism is not complex: like in survival training today, the physical hardship creates new challenges, sets clear goals, and reduces inessentials. As Mihalyi Csikszentmihalyi points out, "many individuals who have suffered harshly end up not only surviving but do so thoroughly enjoying their lives." They grow in elementary "courage or what in earlier times was known simply as 'virtue'—a term derived from the Latin word *vir*, or man." Daoists in this context, too, speak of virtue (*de*), the quality of Dao that resides deep within the person and can be described as inner potency. Appearing first on the oracle bones as a character that shows seeing a path and walking on it, *de* referred to proceeding correctly and not straying from the path; later, when character for "heart" was added, it came to mean to maintain correctness within and thus grew to have the sense of virtue, morality, and goodness. Daoists as much as modern thinkers see it as involving qualities of "resilience, perseverance, mature defense, and transformational coping." Still today, people intentionally separate from society and eschew material comfort to find their own inner truth as hermits, vagrants, prophets, or wanderers. An example is Reyad, an Egyptian who decided to walk to Western Europe and continued his wanderings for over twenty years. His reflections echo Daoist ascetic endeavors,

> During my journey I have seen hunger, war, death, and poverty. Now through prayer I have begun to hear myself, I have returned toward my center, I have achieved concentration, and I have understood that the world has no value … If I am to live like a free man who does not depend on anyone, I can afford to go slowly; if I don't earn anything today, it does not matter. It means that this happens to be my destiny.[26]

No matter what happens, ascetic practitioners in search of immortality grow strong in inner potency and can cope with life under all different circumstances, flowing along with whatever happens while resting in unselfconscious self-assurance and finding sufficient resources for their simple needs. They become one with Dao on an elementary level, creating community with nature and the cosmos. No longer seeing themselves in opposition to Dao, life, others, or the natural environment nor as individuals who insist that their goals and their intention take precedent over everything else, they become part of whatever goes on around them, enhancing the cosmic dimension of Dao as manifest in nature and fulfilling in a personal way the ideal of Great Peace.

Notes

1 Citing Keeley 1996, 26; Cohen 1985, 99–100.
2 Service 1971, 111.
3 Carneiro 1990, 190; Service 1971, 143.
4 Keeley 1996, 27; Haas 1982, 142.
5 Cohen 1985, 109–10.
6 Kanter 1972, 1. For more, see Kohn 2017.
7 Kaltenmark 1979, 22, 30; Hendrischke 2006, 14, 70.
8 Hendrischke 2006, 14, 49, 52–3, 244–58; Kaltenmark 1979, 33–4.
9 Kaltenmark 1979, 35, 27–8.

10 Turner 1969, 107.
11 Turner 1969, 111–12, 127.
12 Kleeman 1998, 70–4; 2016, 353.
13 On these practices, see Kleeman 2016, 158–74; Raz 2008.
14 Kleeman 1998, 68–9, 2016, 5.
15 Bokenkamp 1997, 50–1.
16 On Daoist monasticism, see Kohn 2003a.
17 For contemporary monastics, see Herrou 2013.
18 Herrou 2013, 68, 142.
19 Kohn 2003a, 116–18.
20 Kohn 2003a, 175.
21 Kohn 2003a, 120–1.
22 Vervoorn 1990, 27, 35–7; Berkowitz 2010, 298.
23 For asceticism, see Eskildsen 1998. On alchemy, see Pregadio 2006.
24 Komjathy 2008.
25 Kohn 2003b, 385.
26 These citations are from Csikszentmihalyi 1990, 193, 200–2, 196–7, respectively.

References

Berkowitz, Alan. 2010. "Social and Cultural Dimensions of Reclusion in Early Medieval China." In *Philosophy and Religion in Early Medieval China*, edited by Alan Chan and Yuet-Keung Lo, 291–318. Albany: State University of New York Press.

Bokenkamp, Stephen R. 1997. Early Daoist Scriptures. With a conâtribution by Peter Nickerson. Berkeley, CA: University of California Press.

Carneiro, Robert L. 1990. "Chiefdom-Level Warfare as Exemplified in Fiji and the Cauca Valley." In *The Anthropology of War*, edited by Jonathan Haas, 190–211. Cambridge: Cambridge University Press.

Cohen, Mark Nathan. 1985. "Prehistoric Hunter-Gatherers: The Meaning of Social Complexity." In *Prehistoric Hunter-Gatherers: The Emergence of Cultural Complexity*, edited by T. Douglas Price and James A. Brown, 99–119. New York, NY: Academic Press.

Csikszentmihalyi, Mihaly. 1990. *Flow: The Psychology of Optimal Experience*. New York, NY: Harper & Row.

Eskildsen, Stephen. 1998. *Asceticism in Early Taoist Religion*. Albany: State University of New York Press.

Haas, Jonathan. 1982. *The Evolution of the Prehistoric State*. New York, NY: Columbia University Press.

Hendrischke, Barbara. 2006. *The Scripture on Great Peace: The Taiping Jing and the Beginnings of Daoism*. Berkeley, CA: University of California Press.

Herrou, Adeline. 2013. *A World of Their Own: Monastics and Their Community in Contemporary China*. St. Petersburg, FL: Three Pines Press.

Kaltenmark, Max. 1979. "The Ideology of the *T'ai-p'ing-ching*." In *Facets of Taoism*, edited by Holmes Welch and Anna Seidel, 19–52. New Haven, CT: Yale University Press.

Kanter, Rosabeth Moss. 1972. *Commitment and Community: Communes and Utopias in Sociological Perspective*. Cambridge, MA: Harvard University Press.

Keeley, Lawrence H. 1996. *War before Civilization*. New York, NY: Oxford University Press.

Kleeman, Terry F. 1998. *Great Perfection: Religion and Ethnicity in a Chinese Millenarian Kingdom*. Honolulu: University of Hawaii Press.

Kleeman, Terry F. 2016. *Celestial Masters: History and Ritual in Early Daoist Communities*. Cambridge, MA: Harvard-Yenching Institute.

Kohn, Livia. 2003a. *Monastic Life in Medieval Daoism: A Cross-Cultural Perspective*. Honolulu: University of Hawaii Press.

Kohn, Livia. 2003b. "Monastic Rules in Quanzhen Daoism: As Collected by Heinrich Hackmann." *Monumenta Serica* 51:367–97.

Kohn, Livia. 2017. *Pristine Affluence: Daoist Roots in the Stone Age*. St. Petersburg, FL: Three Pines Press.

Komjathy, Louis. 2008. *Handbooks for Daoist Practice*. Hong Kong: Yuen Yuen Institute.

Pregadio, Fabrizio. 2006. *Great Clarity: Daoism and Alchemy in Early Medieval China*. Stanford, CA: Stanford University Press.

Raz, Gil. 2008. "The Way of the Yellow and the Red: Re-examining the Sexual Initiation Rite of Celestial Master Daoism." *Nannü: Men, Women and Gender in China* 10:86–120.

Service, Elman R. 1971. *Primitive Social Organization: An Evolutionary Perspective*. New York, NY: Random House.

Turner, Victor W. 1969. *The Ritual Process: Structure and Anti-Structure*. Chicago, IL: Aldine.

Vervoorn, Aat Emile. 1990. *Men of the Cliffs and Caves: The Development of the Chinese Eremitic Tradition to the End of the Han Dynasty*. Hong Kong: Chinese University Press.

8   Women and the family

Ever since the beginning of patriarchy in the Neolithic—due to the testosterone-induced urge for dominance in massively increased numbers of surviving males—the major cultures of the world have been rather misogynistic. Women, of the same physical height and social rights as men in the Paleolithic, were shrinking physically due to lower-quality food and placed in the depth of the household as male chattels. Sedentary life making it possible to give birth close to every year rather than every four or five, they were allocated certain technologies that lend themselves to domestic practice, notably weaving, cooking, and pottery making.[1]

Going far beyond the biological differences between male and female, this meant the development of gender roles and stereotypes—socially determined and systematically learned ways of being masculine or feminine according to the norms of a particular culture. Gender is a process that creates social and symbolic metaphors for the particular complementarity between variously sexed people necessary for the functioning of a given society. Rather than a fact or an essence, it consists of a systematically reinforced set of acts, a process of repeat performances or mode of social habitus that produces stereotyped patterns and thus structures culture from within.[2]

Soon this gender division gave rise to myths, justifying it as divinely intended. Thus, according to Genesis, the first woman Eve was created from Adam's rib, thereby defined as his appendage and property. The ancient Greeks understood all humans to be part of a single sex, from which adult males developed due to a greater level of heat, making women the same as young boys. As a result, "free" women in classical Greece were lifelong legal minors who were mostly forbidden to leave their homes and who were not even their husbands' preferred sexual partners. Most cultures saw women as the "weaker" sex and attributed particular feminine virtues to them, including chastity, modesty, meekness, softness, passivity, humility, and the like. Creating a straitjacket that denies the inherent complexity and growth potential of human beings, then and now, "a strong conception of femininity not only encourages sexism, it also encourages racism and classism."[3]

Women in traditional cultures were defined entirely through the men in their lives, appreciated for their role as daughter, wife, or mother and given accolades in accordance with the perceived virtue of that status. Mothers in particular were highly valued, notably if they had produced a male heir and thus perpetuated the family line. Family in this context came less in its nuclear than extended form, including members of multiple generation as well as brothers and sisters, aunts, uncles, and cousins. In addition, ancestors played a strong role, people defining themselves through their patrilineal bloodline. In addition, the structure of the family corresponded to that of the state, usually an authoritarian-led kingdom, consisting of a single absolute ruler, a few ministers, and the host of subjects. While as mothers, women might rise to some influence, for the most part they were one step above servants and slaves, bound by rules of filial piety to their males, who in turn owed loyalty to their lords.[4]

The power of yin

Daoists have always lived in a highly gendered society, Chinese mainstream culture codifying life in terms of yin and yang and thus placing females in a position of weakness and inferiority. Understood to be natural and inescapable, the yin-yang dichotomy associates action, movement, transformation, and expansion with yang, and structure, quietude, stability, and contraction with yin. In terms of values, yang equals valor, courage, hardness, initiative, and the giving of orders, while yin finds expression in humility, letting go, softness, submissiveness, and obedience.

Ancient Daoists in many ways supported this vision, emphasizing feminine values as defined by mainstream culture, unquestioningly seeing the female as possessing softer, gentler characteristics, secondary to the outgoing, active male. However, they also counterbalanced this by extolling yin-type values and forms of behavior. Thus, the *Daode jing* represents Dao as the great mother, the essential element of water that nurtures all, possessed of feminine qualities such as softness and weakness. Dao as mother is where all beings come from and to which they all return, the invisible, deep, dark, and mysterious (female) source of the universe, the all-embracing and nurturing core at the root of all. The womb of the cosmos that brings forth and nurtures all, it is a single, integrated organism. People who attain Dao consequently have total trust in it as their universal mother. They allow all changes and transformations—even death—to happen naturally and place themselves in the mother's position at the mysterious center.[5]

Besides the strong emphasis on motherhood, the *Daode jing* also links Dao with female animals (chs. 6, 10, 28, 61) and uses various symbols that indicate containing and latency—such as the empty vessel (ch. 4), the bellows (ch. 5), the dark unborn (ch. 1), water (chs. 6, 78), and the valley (chs. 6, 28, 32). It also emphasizes that Dao embraces all (chs. 27, 32), evenly spreads its goodness (ch. 32), and cherishes all beings with motherly love (ch. 67). It notes that the female overcomes the male by its quality of stillness (ch. 61) and that in order to attain union with Dao one should abide by the female (ch.

28), cultivating the qualities of weakness and softness. In addition to giving and nurturing, Dao is yin in that it manifests as stillness, passivity, darkness, emptiness, and withdrawal. In contrast to mainstream culture, the *Daode jing* exalts this shadowy, submissive side of the female as a way to overcome and balance the dominant yang mode of the world.[6]

In later organized religion, the power of yin finds its most vivid expression in the Queen Mother of the West, an originally shamanic deity who resides on the central world mountain of Kunlun and reigns over all the immortals, on occasion descending to the human realm and sharing her secrets. Unlike women in real life, the Queen Mother not only works but serves as the key administrator of the universe. As her standard hagiography by Du Guangting (850–933) says,

> She controls and summons the myriad spirit forces of heaven and earth, assembles and gathers the perfected and the sages of the world, oversees all covenants and examines the people's quality of faith. She presides over all formal observances in the various heavens as well as over all audiences and banquets held by the celestial worthies and supreme sages. In addition, it is her duty to supervise the correcting and editing of the sacred scriptures in heaven, to reflect divine light on the proceedings. Her responsibility covers all the treasured scriptures of Highest Clarity, the jade writs of the Three Caverns, as well as the sacred texts that are bestowed at ordination.[7]

Fulfilling this role, the Queen Mother documents in a mythical way the potential of women to run important aspects of life—such as households and palaces—with competent management and full responsibility. In addition, women are empowered by the goddess because she creates a representation of femininity that involves superior ability and eminent leadership. There is nothing timid or hesitant about this goddess—she provides a model of feminine authority and assertiveness. Just as the image of the goddess encourages women to emulate this part of their inherent potential, so it reminds men of women's competence and inherent power.

Beyond this, the Queen Mother also serves as a positive representative of female sexuality, going beyond the dominant notion that women are mere vessels for men to harvest life force to increase health and longevity. As described in the Tang text *Yufang bijue* (Secret Instructions of the Jade Chamber), she is a strong woman who dominates the power exchange, using men—preferably young—to acquire their seminal essence and revert it to nourish her own longevity. It says, "If a woman is able to master this method and has frequent intercourse with men, she can avoid all grain for nine days without getting hungry."[8] Not only embracing her sexuality, the goddess in this role uses it in an aggressive, exploitative way to enhance her inner essences and thus increase her potential for health, beauty, and vitality. She dedicates herself selfishly to the attainment of pleasure and power, using enchantment to realize her sexuality and giving free reign to what mainstream society would consider shameful and dangerous.

Intentional ungendering

Activating this alternative understanding of women, organized Daoists both placed women in an elevated position and pursued active ungendering, that is, overcoming the gender division in favor of an androgynous ideal. Thus, among the early Celestial Masters, all members, independent of sex, from early childhood on underwent formal initiations at regular intervals, receiving registers of spirit generals for protection against demons—reaching 75 for an unmarried person and 150 for a married couple.

Among adults, moreover, some of these initiations took the form of the Harmonization of *Qi*, involving intercourse between selected non-married partners in an elaborate ritual that enacted the cosmic matching of yin and yang and thus contributed to greater universal harmony. Each partner performed a particular role, none less important or active than the other. The complex ceremony joined male (yellow) and female (red) sexual energy in accord with cosmic forces. Held in a sacred space, it consisted of slow, formal movements accompanied by meditations to establish harmony both in bodies and universe.[9]

In ordinary life, too, women functioned as equal partners. They were valued as important members of the community and carried their fair share of responsibility and benefits, active in the domestic mode of production. They had access to all leadership positions up to the rank of libationer, and also functioned as "female masters" in charge of teaching and ritual supervision.

Women would also perfect their personal cultivation. For example, Wei Huacun (251–334) was originally the daughter of a high official and an adept of the Celestial Masters. Married to a leading religious officer and the mother of two sons, she retired to a separate part of the family compound and devoted herself to self-cultivation. In 299, upon visions of perfected beings who presented her with sacred scriptures and oral instruction, she became a libationer with ritual powers and administrative duties. During the war that led to the rise of the Eastern Jin in 317, her family fled to Jiankang (modern Nanjing), after which she spent much of her life in seclusion, receiving further visits from celestial perfected of high rank. Eventually she attained Dao on the holy mountain of the south in Hunan, ascended into heaven, and became a key revealing deity of Highest Clarity.[10]

Inheriting the early community spirit, Daoist monastics, go beyond even gender neutrality and the elevation of yin qualities to engage in an active program of ungendering. They no longer think of themselves as men and women, instead calling themselves "Heaven Dao" (*qiandao*) and "Earth Dao" (*kundao*), adopting terms from the Y*ijing*. In their community living, they make no difference among male and female ranks, activities, or clothing. Both historically and today, men and women pursue the same goals, undergo the same training and ordination, participate equally in community tasks, and attain the same status.[11]

To ungender personal perception, monastics work with the methods of internal alchemy. They merge yin and yang internally in self-cultivation and invert the process of cosmic unfolding. To refine their sexual essences such as seminal fluid and menstrual blood, they begin with sex-specific techniques, then equally circulate the purified energy throughout the body to sublimate it into pure spirit. Eventually they store this in the lower elixir field beneath the navel and there grow their spiritual alter ego, the immortal embryo. The process is thought to be easier for women, since they are naturally set up for gestation. Over time, due to hormonal modifications, it leads to a reduction in sexual characteristics: women stop menstruating and their breasts shrink while men experience a retraction of the penis and shrinking of testicles.[12]

Becoming physically more alike, all Daoists wear their hair tied up in a top-knot and don the same vestments: a dark-blue robe of thick fabric crossed in front, combined with loose pants, held below the knee by white puttees, with their feet clad in black cloth shoes. Not differentiated in garb or status, or even in the lines of teaching, they all receive the same monthly stipend and do the same jobs. Nor are there special quarters for either of them: monks and nuns live in individual cells scattered throughout the temple territory. Having single rooms avoids problems possibly caused by too much closeness and facilitates ascetic practice. The administrators assign rooms as they become available, to no particular scheme or layout.

Both monks and nuns take on domestic and community chores, each working according to their skill and expertise. Unlike in mainstream society, monks frequently clean vegetables, cook, or wash linens, while nuns carry heavy loads, push transport carts, or work in construction. In ritual activities, too, Daoists pursue ungendering: all serve in the same roles, all officiate at various ceremonies—funerary, healing, celebratory, or inaugurational—and all work in administration, when needed even taking on the post of honorary abbot.[13]

Overall, they strive to fulfill an androgynous ideal already expressed in the *Daode jing*, which understands the realization of the sage in the world as lying in the reconciliation of all opposites and the attainment of life as a consummate person who is neither feminine nor masculine. They also follow the age-old ideal of immortals, already in Han tomb reliefs depicted as androgynous beings. Going beyond gender and sex, they create a completely new level of being fully human, an identity that surpasses all established social characteristics, goes beyond situational flexibility, transcends sex roles, and renders cultural patterns irrelevant in favor of fluid, integrated wholeness. Involving the deconstruction of all binary opposites in combination with new ways of processing cognitive data, the free expression of unique personality traits, and the activation of an unchartered repertoire of social behavior, this androgyny is both the primal and ultimate stage of human development.[14]

Intentional ungendering, therefore, represents yet another way Daoists enhance and strengthen women within their communities.

The family

Despite all this, Daoists yet remain connected to the family in various ways. For one, monastics think of themselves as an integrated family: organized around a joint residence and common property, they live together like a domestic group. Within a system of family-style relationships, their relative rank is determined by the master's generation and the chronological order of entry. Using ungendered male-based kinship terminology, those ordained later become "sons" and "younger brothers," regardless of biological sex and age. The duties of disciples toward their master resemble those of sons toward their father; following the rules of filial piety, they practice obedience toward their seniors and care toward their juniors. Even what little personal possessions they have are handed down along these family lines. "Disciples generally inherit jointly from their master; the eldest or sometimes a chosen one succeeds the abbot as head of the temple."

They also behave like parents when it comes to major life events. For example, at New Year's, when ordinary people crowd the trains to return to their old home and visit their parents, young monks studying at the Daoist Academy travel to their home temple to pay respects to their master. Like ordinary people, they have a strong sense of generational continuity and spiritual lineage, beginning with the founder of their order. Following the model of the "family poem" that serves as a generational marker in kinship groups of civil society, every Daoist order has its own sacred "lineage poem," a character of which forms part of the personal name of all members of the same generation. Receiving a religious name marks the entry into the Daoist family: it comes with the obligation of worshiping the "ancestors," all the way back to Wang Chongyang, the founder of Complete Perfection, and Zhang Daoling, the first Celestial Master.[15]

Another way in which Daoists remain family oriented is that, even though they have "left the family" (*chujia*), the technical term for joining a monastic order, they still retain their original family name—unlike Buddhists who all take the family name of the Buddha, Shi, short for Shakyamuni—and continue to have contact and certain obligations. Thus, the very first precept they take, already documented in the medieval text *Chuzhen shijie wen* (Ten Precepts of Initial Perfection, DZ 180), says: "Do not be disloyal or unfilial, without benevolence or good faith. Always exhaust your allegiance to your lord and family, be sincere in your relation to the myriad beings." To enter successfully into the spiritual realm and attain immortality, good relationships with the family are essential. Lack of filial piety is understood as producing karma that will cause suffering in hell, bad rebirth, loneliness, and the inability to reach spiritual purity. The clearest formulation of this view is found in the

Shier shangpin quanjie (The Twelve Highest Precepts with Explanation, DZ 182), a text associated with the Numinous Treasure school.

> The Eleventh Precept: Do Not Fail in Filial Piety
>   The Heavenly Worthy said: Being students of Dao, once you have received the precepts of the perfected, you must not lack in filial piety, be disobedient in your heart, or go against the wishes of your parents. Never fail to give them your proper respect and love, never turn your back upon your ancestors and kin. Never fail to think of them with loving care and gratitude, nor fail to develop proper feelings of shame.[16]

As in mainstream society, Daoists are to appreciate the hardships that parents, and especially mothers, undergo in carrying and raising their children. Neglecting one's parents, therefore, is an offense on the same level as insulting senior recluses or slandering the Three Treasures of Dao, scriptures, and teachers. However, going beyond ordinary family obligation, the understanding here is that it is the foremost act of filial piety to repay one's parents by saving them from otherworldly suffering. Rather than providing for the parents in their old age and continuing the family line, Daoists pray and make offerings for them to enhance their spiritual standing while alive and conduct rituals that transfer them from the underworld into the heavens of the immortals after death.

In a yet different permutation, there are also Daoists who never leave ordinary society but remain householders, so-called fire-dwellers. They serve as priests of the Celestial Masters, today a non-monastic organization, where ritual expertise and temple property are transmitted from father to son. Ever since the early movements, these priestly Daoists have placed a strong value on intergenerational integrity. One of the earliest surviving codes of the Celestial Masters, for example, is the *Laojun shuo yibai bashi jie* (180 Precepts Revealed by Lord Lao, in DZ 786). It does not address issues of filial piety *per se*, but emphasizes that followers should respect the harmony of others, never "causing a rift in other people's families," spying on their privacy, ignoring their taboos, or wrongly venerating their ancestors. Moreover, they should not "form a party or clique on the basis of their own families" (no. 61), but instead burn incense and pray "for the good of the myriad families and the establishment of Great Peace on earth" (no. 152).[17]

Along similar lines, the medieval *Dajie wen* (The Great Precepts, DZ 1364) emphasizes that Daoists should not live separate from their families or form a clique on their basis. They must not encourage others to leave home, plot against their elders or parents, or generally behave in an unfilial manner. In more concrete terms, the *Nüqing guilü* (Nüqing's Statutes Against Demons, DZ 790) of the fourth century says that lack of filial piety, bad family relations, or living in separation from one's parents or children causes the subtraction of 180 days from one's life expectancy. Irresolute behavior and disrespect toward one's own or others' families, moreover, will bring the loss of 3,000 days and bad fortune for one's descendants for seven generations. Filial piety, therefore, is not only a virtue in current relationships but a behavior with long-term consequences for one's own life and that of others.[18]

Universal kin

The emphasis on cosmic consequences and wider social impact, then, is the feature where the Daoist understanding of both family and filial piety diverges most from mainstream society. As noted earlier, Daoists think globally and cosmically, their main concern being their relationship to heaven and earth with the underlying assumption that everything else flows from there and rights itself accordingly. Thus, family thinking and virtues of filial piety serve the transformation of the cosmos at large, the universal salvation of the world

One way this is expressed appears in the Tang code *Qianzhen ke* (Rules for the Thousand Perfected, DZ 1410). Echoing the ancient Confucian treatise *Daxue* (Great Learning), it sees positive value by teaching filial piety and other classical virtues first on a personal level, then expanding them to involve care and compassion for all beings. Beginning with the family, practitioners learn to develop empathy for all and grow into cosmic rather than merely personal or social beings. As the text says,

> Recluses should at all times have a loyal and upright demeanor.
> Whether coming or going, moving or staying,
> Always strive to set all things and people right.
> First, set yourself right.
> Second, set your disciples right.
> Third, set both the local leaders both lofty and lowly right.
> Fourth, set the distant followers of the divine law right.
> Fifth, set the obstinate ordinary people right.
> Doing the first, you serve as a model for others.
> Doing the second, you help to imbue all with righteousness.
> Doing the third, you create respect among both noble and humble.
> Doing the fourth, you help spread the righteousness of the divine law.
> Doing the fifth, you widely increase wisdom and purity.
> Only one who can act like this truly deserves to be called a Daoist.[19]

Here Daoists are no longer concerned only with the attainment of immortality for themselves and the benefit of their personal relations, but have become responsible for the transformation of the world at large into a realm of goodness and morality. If they do not set themselves right, they cause disrespect for themselves and by extension lack of filial piety and propriety among the wider populace. The responsibility for the moral salvation of the entire world is thus placed on their shoulders.

This enormous burden is justified in the *Fengdao kejie* (Rules and Precepts for Worshiping the Dao, DZ 1125), a manual of monastic Daoism of the early seventh century. It attributes great responsibility to monks and nuns because of their particular karmic standing.

> Whoever, in the seventh generation [over seven lives], rejoices in the Dao, honors the precepts, and recites the scriptures, gives freely in charity and aids the poor, prays for the living and helps save the dead, always acts with compassion and sympathy, and presents offerings to the Three Treasures without being slack or lazy, will be born in the body of an ordained monk or nun.[20]

By inversion this means that only those who already involved with Dao over many lifetimes or generations are monks or nuns today. They should have the corresponding karmic strength and moral mettle to serve as social models. Accordingly, only people with a strong Daoist background are considered candidates for successful ordination. The *Fengdao kejie* specifies a total of twenty-five kinds of people who "can be caused to become ordained monks or nuns." The first five are:

1 those whose families have worshiped Dao for generations and who believe and delight in the divine law of the scriptures;
2 those who themselves over several lives have worshiped Dao and who believe and delight in the divine law of the scriptures;
3 those who in this life actively worship Dao and believe and delight in the divine law of the scriptures;
4 those whose families have been pure and good for generations and have believed and worshiped the perfection of the right path;
5 those who themselves over several lives have been pure and good.[21]

The merits accumulated in this life are thus similar to those gained over several previous lives and match those created by one's family. The Daoist monastic is the carrier of cosmic power by virtue of his or her good karmic deeds, which are enhanced by those in former lives as well as created by the ancestors. The individual thus never stands alone, but is part of a larger unit, be it the continuity over lifetimes or the connectedness with the family. Only when the person is morally strong within this expanded context, can he or she be a true moral catalyst and guide the world toward greater harmony and the practice of perfect filial piety.

Filial benefits for generations to come, moreover, are also closely linked with support for Daoist institutions and recluses. Venerating the Three Treasures will create filial sons and grandsons, while copying the scriptures will cause one's descendants to be wise and sagely. Similarly, donating facilities for meditation and retreats brings nobility upon one's descendants, while providing incense and fragrant oils will cause one to have handsome sons and grandsons. Assisting others in becoming Daoist masters will cause one's descendants to attain rebirth in the Middle Kingdom, and practicing Daoist rites will cause them to flourish and to have ancestors that are well satisfied and bring good fortune.

All these various activities are not ultimately geared toward creating a better fortune for individual families, although the enticement is certainly there. The overarching vision is the cosmic transformation or universal salvation of the world at large. Ultimately, filial piety as a virtue directed toward one's own family must be superseded by the awareness of the karmic interconnectedness of all—family must be everybody's family, children must be everybody's children. As a set of resolutions in the *Dajie wen* has,

> May I regard the parents of others like my own.
> May I regard the children of others like my own.
> May I regard the self of others more importantly than my own.
> May I regard the wounds and pains of others more importantly than
> my own.
> May I regard the shame and evil of others more importantly than
> my own.[22]

In other words, the ultimate realization of filial piety, family relations, and community connections is to transcend personal thinking and individual being in favor or a greater and higher state of universal salvation, a time of Great Peace where everyone is fully responsible not only for the realization of their own inner nature and destiny but also for the greater good of other people, all beings, and the cosmos at large.

Notes

1 Kohn 2017, 137.
2 Eller 2000, 75; Wright 1996, 85.
3 Eller 2000, 68; Joyce 2008, 92.
4 See Rosenberg 1978.
5 Chen 1974, 57. See also Despeux and Kohn 2003, 7.
6 Chen 1974, 51–3.
7 Cahill 1993, 104.
8 Furth 1994, 134; Despeux and Kohn 2003, 38–9.
9 Despeux and Kohn 2003, 11–12, 106–7; Bumbacher 2012, 86–8.
10 Despeux and Kohn 2003, 19.
11 Herrou 2013, 66, 180.
12 Ho 2018, 105–6.
13 Herrou 2013, 231–2.
14 Cook 1985, 23, 40–6. On androgyny in the *Daode jing*, see Ames 1981.
15 Herrou 2013, 217.
16 Kohn 2004a, 97.
17 Hendrischke and Penny 1996.

18 Kohn 2004a, 95.
19 Kohn 2004a, 103.
20 Kohn 2004b, 83.
21 Kohn 2004b, 106.
22 Kohn 2004a, 102.

References

Ames, Roger T. 1981. "Taoism and the Androgynous Ideal." In *Women in China: Current Directions in Historical Scholarship*, edited by Richard W. Guisso and Stanley Johannesen, 21–45. Lewiston, NY: Edwin Mellen Press.

Bumbacher, Stephan-Peter. 2012. *Empowered Writing: Exorcistic and Apotropaic Rituals in Medieval China*. St. Petersburg, FL: Three Pines Press.

Cahill, Suzanne. 1993. *Transcendence and Divine Passion: The Queen Mother of the West in Medieval China*. Stanford, CA: Stanford University Press.

Chen, Ellen Marie. 1974. "Tao as the Great Mother and the Influence of Motherly Love in the Shaping of Chinese Philosophy." *History of Religions* 14.1:51–64.

Cook, Ellen Piel. 1985. *Psychological Androgyny*. New York, NY: Pergamon Press.

Despeux, Catherine, and Livia Kohn. 2003. *Women in Daoism*. Cambridge, MA: Three Pines Press.

Eller, Cynthia. 2000. *The Myth of Matriarchal Prehistory: Why an Invented Past Won't Give Women a Future*. Boston Beacon Press.

Furth, Charlotte. 1994. "Rethinking Van Gulik: Sexuality and Reproduction in Traditional Chinese Medicine." In *Engendering China*, edited by Christina Gilmartin et al., 125–46. Cambridge, MA: Harvard University Press.

Hendrischke, Barbara, and Benjamin Penny. 1996. "*The 180 Precepts Spoken by Lord Lao*: A Translation and Textual Study." *Taoist Resources* 6.2:17–29.

Herrou, Adeline. 2013. *A World of Their Own: Monastics and Their Community in Contemporary China*. St. Petersburg, FL: Three Pines Press.

Ho, Chung-tao. 2018. *Internal Alchemy for Everyone*. St. Petersburg, FL: Three Pines Press.

Joyce, Rosemary A. 2008. *Ancient Bodies, Ancient Lives: Sex, Gender, and Archaeology*. London: Thames & Hudson.

Kohn, Livia. 2004a. "Immortal Parents and Universal Kin: Family Values in Medieval Daoism." In *Filial Piety and Chinese Culture*, edited by Alan Chan, 91–109. London: RoutledgeCurzon.

Kohn, Livia. 2004b. *The Daoist Monastic Manual: A Translation of the Fengdao kejie*. New York, NY: Oxford University Press.

Kohn, Livia. 2017. *Pristine Affluence: Daoist Roots in the Stone Age*. St. Petersburg, FL: Three Pines Press.

Rosenberg, Charles E. 1978. *Family in History*. Philadelphia: University of Pennsylvania Press.

Wright, Rita P. 1996. "Technology, Gender, and Class: Worlds of Difference in Ur III Mesopotamia." In *Gender and Archaeology*, edited by Rita P. Wright, 79–110. Philadelphia: University of Pennsylvania Press.

9   Leadership

All communities, however cosmic, come with some form of leadership, defined as the "process whereby an individual influences a group to achieve a common goal, … the ability to frame and define the reality and conduct of others."[1] Always involving a principal and several subalterns, leadership is the capacity to control, channel, or restrict the choice that followers are able to make: the tighter this restriction, the greater the power of the leader. In the course of history, as community evolved toward increasing complexity, leadership moved from authority to authoritarianism, from consensus to control. Power came to derive socially from influencing kinship and community networks, economically from possession of the means of production and supervision of the exchange of goods, and militarily from coercing compliance with superior strength.[2] Over time, the latter increasingly also extended to civil society, so that authoritarian leaders would resort to violence, i.e., controlling, dominating, subduing, coercing, or even killing others by direct assault with brute force. Eventually this led to the phenomenon of war, defined as the sustained, coordinated violence between political organizations—the ultimate arena of power.

Philosophically, leadership can be understood in the two dimensions of sanction and function, that is, answering the fundamental questions of where power comes from and how one should best exercise it. Sanction, thus, means the legitimation of a given position or individual ruler in terms of the dominant belief system of the culture. Traditionally, it often involved divine support, positive omens, rituals of coronation, and the like. Thus, rulers of republican Rome were sanctioned by the electoral process in combination with propitious auspices and proper ritual procedures; in the European middle ages, they were seen as anointed by God and crowned through the authority of the church; in Buddhist countries, they were understood as *chakravarti*, movers of the dharma wheel, the secular counterpart of the Buddha exercising both temporal and spiritual kingship.

Function indicates the actual performance of leadership, the ideals and guidelines leaders follow in the execution of their tasks. The dominant Western view goes back to the Italian statesman Niccolo Machiavelli (1469–1527), who in his work, *The Prince*, outlines five principles of successful leadership, defined as the exercise of complete power with a minimum of opposition. These combine an inherent ruthlessness (better to be feared than loved; the end justifies the means) with sharp wits (act with cunning) and the appearance of respectability (vie for the support of the people; always appear capable and faithful).[3]

Today, leadership discussions have expanded from the political arena to the realm of business. Function is accordingly seen increasingly in terms of "leadership agility," the ability to deal with issues flexibly and lead by inspiration and cooperation rather than coercion and trickery, to the benefit of all rather than just the ruling group or the leader himself. Agile leaders are open to others' viewpoints, able to zoom attention in or out as needed, and constantly self-reflecting, even in tight situations. Rather than equating the exercise of power with self-interest and seeing themselves in opposition to their subordinates, they empower everyone and stimulate things to evolve in new ways. Plugging into the larger social, even global context, they strive to develop organizations animated by a shared purpose. Their vision is expansive, their purpose reaches far beyond themselves to the greater good of all. Always highly creative and imaginative, moving ever more from "I" to "us," their leadership is as intangible as it is pervasive.[4]

Types of leaders

Daoists were very aware of the potentials and pitfalls of leadership. Thus, the *Daode jing* distinguishes four types of leaders:

> The highest—you don't even know they're there.
> The next—you love and praise them.
> The next—you fear them.
> The lowest—you despise them.

(ch. 17)

The lower three are all authoritarian and Machiavellian in nature, exercising forceful mastery over others to benefit mainly themselves and their peers, but to a different degree. The least invasive can be described as chiefs who get their power from networking and military ability. Supported by, and often chosen from, a council of elders, they depend heavily on the cooperation of the tribe as a whole, whose members, moreover, are all armed and dangerous. Understanding that they are nothing without the group, they work for the greater good of all and accordingly deserve love and praise.

The ones to be feared, next, are kings or other central rulers of fully developed states. In addition to power through networking, they also have control, that is, the ability to restrain access to resources and especially arms. Rather than directly sanctioned by the populace, their rule is mediated by a hierarchy of feudal followers, a tightly structured bureaucracy, and fully controlled military. Their reign still works to benefit the entire group, however, here the goals justify the means: people are coerced into following and come to dread their rulers. The lowest of the lot, moreover, are highly authoritarian figures best described as tyrants. They rule with brute force and exclusively to their own personal benefit. Deriving political clout from police brutality, blood sacrifices, systematic warfare, and other forms of sanctioned violence, they are despised and viewed with contempt.[5]

In contrast, the highest form of leadership in the *Daode jing* is consensual, highly fluid, and flexible. Matching the agile leaders of today as well as the strongmen in small, egalitarian bands—often appointed for particular projects based on their unique skills—they focus entirely on the well-being of the group as a whole. Competent, intelligent, strong, and healthy, such leaders receive deference and make decisions, yet they remain in the background, so that, as the *Daode jing* has it, "the people say they did it all themselves" (ch. 17). Without force or coercion, they have authority, i.e., recognized and accepted capabilities, to which followers respond with respect and willing obedience, and thereby "sustain the smooth operation of their society."[6]

Abraham Maslow calls this "Being-leadership," reflecting a way of life that focuses on Being rather than Deficiency, on the present rather than the future, the well-being of all rather than the might of a few. He observed it in action among Native Americans:

> The Blackfoot Indians tended not to have general leaders with general power but ... different leaders for different functions ... The leader had absolutely no power whatsoever that wasn't deliberately and voluntarily given to him *ad hoc* by the particular people in the particular situation. That is to say, he didn't really influence anyone or order anyone about.[7]

Leaders in Daoism are not necessarily members of the aristocracy or specially trained agents, but individuals of any social background who embody Dao and best serve their communities. They never engage in self-justification or strut in the limelight, remaining consistently without pride, possessiveness, and personal acclaim (ch. 22). They may act in the world, but "withdraw as soon as the work is done" (ch. 9), recognizing the underlying spiritual dimension of reality and respecting all beings for what they are. Possessing the relevant knowledge, skills, and expertise for their tasks, they have a clear mission yet remain free from personal desires and never take interfering action. Without exerting force or control, they inspire people to do their best, closely matching nature and the continuously changing circumstances of life. As a result, leaders work with efficacy rather than for effect, blending energies as they serve as facilitators, communicators, and team builders.[8] Exerting only a minimal influence on the lives of followers, employing soft tactics, such as persuasion, empowerment, modeling, collaboration, and service, and never resorting to force or violence, they encourage followers to take ownership of and responsibility for their tasks.

Personal virtues

The overarching goal of Daoist leaders is the establishment of Great Peace in their community, which means they promote harmony with nature and with people, whom they empower to the best of their ability. The vision behind this is the understanding that Dao is fundamentally good, and each individual has his or her own unique talents, abilities, and inclinations that allow him to make the best possible contribution to the benefit of all. The more people are able to fulfill their inner nature and destiny, the happier they are and the better society functions. This means that, in modern business terms, ideal Daoist leaders possess the key characteristics of vision, insight, responsibility, adjustment, initiative, tolerance, competence, and integrity. In terms of leadership types, they are democratic as opposed to autocratic, laissez-faire as opposed to coercive, service-oriented as opposed to domineering, and charismatic as opposed to bureaucratic.[9]

The *Daode jing* says, "The best person is like water; water is good: it benefits all beings and does not compete" (ch. 8). Like water, which is shapeless and only takes form through its container, leaders should be imbued with flexibility, transparency, honesty, and gentle persistence. Living in fulfillment of the virtues of kindness, faithfulness, order, timeliness, and competence (ch. 8), "they place themselves in the background, put themselves away, and have no personal interests" (ch. 7).[10] Demonstrating creativity and flexibility, they live a life of service rather than rulership and embrace the virtues of simplicity, humility, and altruism.

More specifically, simplicity or sufficiency is the absence of luxury, pretentiousness, and extraneous ornaments combined with a freedom from deceit and guile, the practice of plainness and clarity. Daoists overall advocate a life of flow and are centrally concerned with health and harmony. Thus, they emphasize nonaction as a way of being (ch. 43), prefer "feminine" qualities of tranquility and steadiness (ch. 61), discard "the extreme, the extravagant, and the excessive" (ch. 29), and in general place peace above possessions.

Humility, next, involves an accurate assessment of one's own characteristics and abilities, clear insights in to one's inner nature, thus admitting limitations without downplaying oneself and relishing the ability to just be. It is a way of self-definition that is internally centered and based on a connection to destiny and the universe rather than socially determined status. It means being open-minded to new ideas and advice, tentative of one's own beliefs, free from self-focus or self-preoccupation, and generally non-competitive.

Altruism, moreover, is "the willingness to act in consideration of the interests of other persons, without the need of ulterior motives." It, too, involves a way of looking at the world as an integrated organism, regarding oneself as an essential part of a group, a member among others, and finding identity as part of a larger whole. More easily activated in smaller communities, it means seeing others as fellow travelers instead of as strangers or potential threats. As a result, altruists typically state that their unselfish actions are entirely natural and that they do not have a choice over whether or not to help someone. They have a strong will to give and a vivid sense of social interconnectedness.[11]

The *Daode jing* in addition emphasizes the personal realization of what it calls "the three treasures" of caring or fundamental kindness, thriftiness or frugality, and "not daring to be ahead of the world" (ch. 67). These three incorporate a fundamental principle, a basic attitude, and way of being, linking material simplicity with altruism in contrast to social complexity and competition. The text further notes,

> Do not exalt the worthy, and the people will not compete.
> Do not value rare goods, and the people will not steal.
> Do not display desirable objects,
> and the people's hearts will not be troubled.
>
> (ch. 3)

"Not daring to be ahead of the world," moreover, means embracing a stance of non-competition even in the face of social inequality and authoritarian hierarchies, placing oneself below and behind others (ch. 22), never allowing to be in a state of strife with the world (ch. 68), and remaining entirely free from all "desire to display one's excellence" (ch. 77). The main virtue here is to remain withdrawing, always be useful to the group and true to oneself without boast or brag, ambition or competition (ch. 8). These values, moreover, have continued to play a key role in the religion, and later leaders and community rules never tire to emphasize the importance of caring and remaining free from competition.

Daoists, therefore, understand that while there may be competition and conflict in the world, their forms vary, and there is no need to develop a competitive mindset. They propose a life in accordance with the fundamental laws of nature, honoring heaven and earth while decrying both aggressive acquisition and destructive subjugation. Sharing resources rather than hoarding them, Daoists value all beings equally and consistently honor expertise over rank. It is thus no accident that the figures with the greatest knack, the most admired characters of great accomplishment in the *Zhuangzi* and later Daoism are not of high social rank. Doing quite ordinary things with extraordinary skill, they are low-class: woodcarver, cicada catcher, ferryman, butcher, and so on.[12].

The sage

Any of these figures can be a sage, the ideal human being and perfect leader. The character *sheng* consists of the words for "king," "ear," and "mouth," indicating that the sage is the master of hearing and speaking. His senses perfectly attuned to the movements of the cosmos, he can recognize and understand signs that others hardly notice. Not only can the sage hear the inaudible sounds of the depth of the universe, he can also know its intimate indications. As the third-century BCE *Lüshi chunqiu* (Spring and Autumn Annals of Mr. Lü) has it, "The knowledge of the sage reaches for millennia into the past and the future—he is not guessing at things; he always has reasons for what he says."

In ancient Chinese thought, the sage is the ideal ruler, the key mediator between heaven and humanity, the bringer of order in the world. Putting his duties before any personal needs, he may appear harsh or inhuman in his actions yet ultimately works for the greater good. A classic example is the sage-king Yu, famous for taming the great flood. Working with a large crew around the country, chiseling through mountains and plains to allow the billows to flow off into the ocean, he passed his own home three times: the first time he heard his infant son cry, newly born during his absence; the second time he saw him play in the mud; the third time he spoke to him, now ten years old, refusing his wish to join his father. All three times, Yu passed but did not stop, being aware of his personal concerns but not giving in to them and behaving with impersonal distance even to his dearest. Apparently uncaring and even immoral, he was yet true to himself as part of the larger workings of the cosmos in his great task of controlling the flood. While he had become almost inhuman to the people around him, he was yet the representative of something higher and bigger, something that went beyond the moral or humane concerns of the world.[13]

The *Daode jing* expresses this as, "Heaven and earth are not humane, they treat the myriad beings like straw dogs [things without value]" (ch. 5). Similarly, the sage, although essentially virtuous, is not evaluated by normal standards or bound by established virtues and may appear to treat people roughly. The apogee of human relationships, he has developed the roots of cosmic goodness to their limits: he is thus moral in his basic attitude toward life but transmoral when it comes to the realization of his higher, cosmic purpose. Because the sage goes beyond ordinary morality, he is not bound by the rules of society. As the medieval thinker Sun Chuo (314–371) explains, the sage may even kill because his actions are performed in a state of oneness with the cosmos, i.e., without personal clinging or self-interested intention. Whatever a sage does will not leave the same violent impact that it would have if committed by a lesser man. His perfection of virtue is at the same time its complete obliteration.[14]

Most of the time, the sage is not called upon to take radical action but exerts a subtle impact on society and life. Resting in nonaction, he empowers all beings while remaining unobtrusive, subtle, and independent, free from all attachments and without formal programs or agendas. Matching the natural forces of heaven and earth, "the sage is whole" (ch. 22), while his accomplishments are thorough, have a deep, permanent effect. One such effect is that he inspires some of the same qualities in others, "causing them to be unknowing and free from desires, so that the smart ones will not dare to impose" (ch. 3).[15] He is "always there to help the people, rejecting no one and no creature" (chap. 27), never puts himself forward in any way yet finds himself a nucleus of social and cosmic activity. As the *Daode jing* has it,

> Not presenting himself, he is radiant.
> Not thinking himself right, he is famous.
> Not pushing himself forward, he is meritorious.
> Not pitying himself, he is eminent.
>
> (ch. 22)

Not only unobtrusive and withdrawing, the sage also has his particular transformative power because he refuses to make ordinary judgments, to classify things and people along common standards such as good and evil, virtuous or depraved. The goodness of the common people is not the same as that of the sage who goes beyond the standards of social existence, yet he embodies the basic laws of the cosmos observable by everyone. The more people are influenced by the sages among them and improve through their model of self-cultivation, the more the moral goodness of everyday life contributes to the greater goodness of the universe. The sage, himself beyond moral standards in his oneness with heaven and earth, nevertheless forms a strong pillar of morality within the world.

Although born with particular talents and tendencies, the sage attains oneness only through systematic self-cultivation, by driving out personal attachments and desires while holding on to Dao. As the Han-dynasty *Daode jing* commentary by Heshang gong (Master on the River) notes, not only essential to sagehood, this process of self-cultivation is also the same as ruling the country: the creation of political order is structurally isomorphic with the cultivation of physical integrity and mystical realization. Government, therefore, is an extended act of self-cultivation, reflecting the correspondences between the political and the physical organization of life: the ruler in his country functions exactly in the same way as the heart in the body, all other parts playing the role of subjects and administrators.

Legitimation

In historical reality, this vision of the ideal leader plays out variously. To begin, religious founders, masters, and patriarchs are seen as central agencies of the universe, functioning with and through Dao while sanctioned by the deities above. Thus, the first Celestial Master Zhang Daoling went into a deep trance, during which he encountered Lord Lao, the personified Dao. The god closed the Covenant of Orthodox Unity with Zhang and appointed him his representative on earth, giving him deep insights into the workings of the universe, leadership charisma, healing powers, as well as instruction in various ritual and personal techniques. Other leading Daoists had visions of sacred scriptures and talismans in caves; yet others ecstatically traveled to the otherworld and actively sought our major gods. In other words, in addition to strenuous self-cultivation and complete dedication, in religious Daoism, good leadership rests on the powers of Dao activated through a direct relationship with the divine, originally entered spontaneously, later formalized in initiation and ordination ceremonies.[16]

As for political rulers, the Chinese understood that a sage as ruler was too much to ask for. The next best thing was to provide the Son of Heaven with an imperial adviser who represented Dao and could guide with wisdom. This connects to the dominant vision of political legitimation as the bestowal of the so-called Mandate of Heaven (*tianming*). The idea was that heaven, a quasi-personified divine agent, manifest in the movements of the planets, the patterns of nature, and high moral principles, would direct the course of mundane events by giving a mandate to a certain figure as ruler. Usually it picked a morally upright person and empowered him to establish a dynasty. The new ruler would work hard to live up to the charge: as long as he was morally upright and strove for his own cultivation and the world's benefit, there was Great Peace. However, his successors would become increasingly depraved and government more corrupt, causing the cosmic order to be disturbed and the world subjected to increasingly violent calamities. These in due course lead to uprisings that would bring a new ruler to the fore. When that happened, auspicious signs appeared in the vicinity of a virtuous candidate, and sages came to serve as his adviser or founding saint.

The first such figure was Zhang Liang (ca. 250–189 BCE), an alleged ancestor of Zhang Daoling, who provided the key military expertise to the founder of the Han dynasty. Originally an ascetic practitioner of longevity and immortality techniques, he wandered around various mountains and once met an old man and representative of Dao, known as the Master of the Yellow Stone (Huangshi gong). Ordered to retrieve and put on his shoe for him, Zhang Liang complied without question and was rewarded with a scripture on warfare and a prediction that he would become the teacher of an emperor. The book, *Taigong bingfa* (Strategic Methods of Lord Tai), in due course became the decisive element in the military victory that established the dynasty.[17]

In the wake of this story, the idea was projected backward, so that rulers even of the Shang and Zhou dynasties had spiritual advisers behind their throne. Later famous examples include Wang Yuanzhi (d. 635), the tenth patriarch of Highest Clarity who met the founder of the Tang and predicted his rise to emperor; Chen Tuan (d. 989) who correctly identified the future Song ruler; and Zhang Sanfeng, the alleged creator of taijiquan, who served as the legitimizing sage of the Ming. Typically, imperial advisers as founding saints have two distinct characteristics. They are in an initial position of poverty or obscurity, simple and ordinary folk, often engaged in menial labor— representing the ubiquity, simplicity, and sufficiency of Dao; and they at first refuse the offer to rule and to rise in social status—symbolizing the sagely virtues of humility, integrity, and "not daring to be ahead of the world." In the end, however, the new ruler prevails, raises the lowly sage and with his help destroys the depraved tyrant. The sage accepts what he did not originally want; the tyrant is forced to give up what he originally enjoyed. The new ruler thus reestablishes harmony and balance in society, in many stories proving his own humility and integrity by trying to abdicate his rule to the sage.[18]

In addition, Lord Lao, the personified Dao, is stylized as the teacher of dynasties, representing the political charter of the religion. His presence, however subtle and vague, explains why the ruler governs in perfect harmony and also justifies the necessity of active Daoist practice either by a sage adviser or preferably by the ruler himself. It also establishes a reason for the existence of Daoist reign-titles, court rituals, and state-sponsored monasteries. Thus, rulers under Daoist auspices would adopt a new, more divine reign title, such as "True Ruler of Great Peace" used by Emperor Taiwu in the fifth century. They might also adopted Daoist liturgy for court purposes, bringing Daoist gods, astral constellations, talismans, and chants into the political realm. And, especially after the Sui dynasty in the later sixth century, they would establish imperial Daoist temples throughout the empire, creating a network of divinity within the realm.[19]

Lord Lao in his turn would bestow various kinds of miracles to document his approval and support, legitimizing rulers beyond the original dynastic founder through visible and tangible manifestations of auspicious heavenly signs. For example, in 741, a palace guard saw a purple cloud advancing from the northwest that contained Lord Lao on a white horse with two attendants. Coming closer, the deity addressed him, "Long ago, when I left with Yin Xi for the floating sands [in the west], I hid a golden casket with a numinous talisman at the old border post in Taolin district. Ask the emperor to retrieve it." The guard duly reported the incident and, together with several officers, was sent to the old border pass, now occupied by a Daoist monastery. There they indeed found a stone container with a golden box and several jade plates that were inscribed with red characters in old seal script. In response to this sign, the emperor changed his reign title to "Heavenly Treasure" and honored the monastery on the pass with an imperial stele and generous gifts.[20]

In times of political upheaval, moreover, the deity would support people encountering emergencies. A case in point is the story of a commoner living in Chang'an around 880, who never tired of worshiping Lord Lao and was duly rescued with his family from certain death at the hand of a rebel mob. Similarly, in 873, a fellow on his way to Luoyang saw an old man by the roadside. Like Zhang Liang in his encounter with the Master of the Yellow Stone, the old man made request, in this case a drink of water. The man complied and was rewarded with both a prophecy of great future unrest and the assurance that the deity would stand by to help. Once he had spoken, the old man vanished, confirming the supernatural nature of the encounter.[21]

Miraculous events like these, typically involving Lord Lao, a Daoist priest, a ritual occasion, or an institution, provided legitimation and Daoist sanction to a given ruler, enhancing his standing toward a more heavenly level and thus increasing his authority among the people. The basic qualities associated with perfect rulership continued, albeit in a more devotional and mythological form, all equally in service of an idealized harmonious society on its way to Great Peace.

Notes

1 Amaghlobeli and Celepli 2012, 47.
2 Earle 1997, 7; Wrong 1995, 2, 6.
3 Ledeen 1999.
4 Joiner and Josephs 2007, 111–15, 127; Amaghlobeli and Celepli 2012, 50.
5 Earle 1997, 4, 7; Wrong 1995, 41.
6 Earle 1997, 3; Wrong 1995, 35.
7 Maslow 1965, 123–4.
8 Heider 1985, 43; Amaghlobeli and Celepli 2012, 49.
9 Northouse 2001, 18; Amaghlobeli and Celepli 2012, 47.
10 Lee et al. 2008, 90.
11 Nagel 1970, 79, 82–3; Munroe 1996, 9–14, 197–216.
12 Graham 1981, 135–42.
13 Ching 1997, 56–62.
14 Kohn 2002, 192.
15 Ching 1997, 214–18.
16 Kohn 1998, 93.
17 See Bauer 1956.
18 Allan 1981, 45–6.
19 Kohn 1998, 323.
20 Kohn 1998, 50.
21 Verellen 1994, 130–1.

References

Allan, Sarah. 1981. *The Heir and the Sage: A Structural Analysis of Ancient Chinese Dynastic Legends*. San Francisco, CA: Chinese Materials Center.

Amaghlobeli, Givi, and Miray Celepli. 2012. "Understanding Taoist Leadership from a Western Perspective." *Journal of Business* 1.2:47–52.

Bauer, Wolfgang. 1956. "Der Herr vom gelben Stein." *Oriens Extremus* 3:137–52.

Ching, Julia. 1997. *Mysticism and Kingship in China*. Cambridge: Cambridge University Press.

Earle, Timothy. 1997. *How Chiefs Come to Power: The Political Economy in Prehistory*. Stanford, CA: Stanford University Press.

Graham, A. C. 1981. *Chuang-tzu: The Seven Inner Chapters and Other Writings from the Book of Chuang-tzu*. London: Allan & Unwin.

Heider, John. 1985. *Tao of Leadership: Lao Tzu's Tao Te Ching Adapted for a New Age*. Atlanta, GA: Humanics New Age.

Joiner, Bill, and Stephen Josephs. 2007. *Leadership Agility: Five Levels of Mastery for Anticipating and Initiating Change*. Hoboken, NJ: Wiley.

Kohn, Livia. 1998. *God of the Dao: Lord Lao in History and Myth*. University of Michigan, Center for Chinese Studies.

Kohn, Livia. 2002. "The Sage in the World, the Perfected Without Feelings: Mysticism and Moral Responsibility in Chinese Religion." In *Crossing Boundaries: Essays on the Ethical Status of Mysticism*, edited by G. William Barnard and Jeffrey J. Kripal, 188–206. New York, NY: Seven Bridges Press.

Ledeen, Michael Arthur. 1999. *Machiavelli on Modern Leadership*. New York, NY: Truman Tally Books.

Lee, Yueh-Ting, Ai-Guo Han, Tammy K. Byron, and Hong-Xia Fan. 2008. "Daoist Leadership: Theory and Application." In *Leadership and Management in China*, edited by Chao-Chuan Chen and Yueh-Ting Lee, 83–107. Cambridge: Cambridge University Press.

Maslow, Abraham H. 1965. *Eupsychian Management: A Journal*. Homewood, IL: Richard Irwin.

Munroe, Kristen Renwick. 1996. *The Heart of Altruism: Perceptions of a Common Humanity*. Princeton, NJ: Princeton University Press.

Nagel, Thomas. 1970. *The Possibility of Altruism*. Oxford: Clarendon Press.

Northouse, Peter G. 2001. *Leadership: Theory and Practice*. Thousand Oaks, CA: Sage.

Verellen, Franciscus. 1994. "A Forgotten T'ang Restoration: The Taoist Dispensation after Huang Ch'ao." *Asia Major* 7.1:107–53.

Wrong, Dennis H. 1995. *Power: Its Forms, Bases, and Uses*. New Brunswick: Transaction Publishers.

Part IV

Ethics

10 Daoist ethics

There are three major philosophical positions on ethics. First, the utilitarian or prudential conviction, also known as consequentialism, claims that people act morally because it is useful for them and for society. "Actions, institutions, and human characteristics should be judged by their tendency to maximize the highest good."[1] It is, by and large, advantageous to be a morally upright person and disadvantageous to be an immoral one. The cost for breaking rules and precepts, both on the psychological and social or material levels, being enormous, it is easier and more useful to comply. Modern penal codes and prison systems rely on this concept, imposing harsh punishments for misdeeds in the hope that people will see their futility.[2] Along similar lines, the ancient Buddhist propagation of the five precepts included a distinct set of benefits for laymen, such as wealth, good repute, self-confidence in public, an untroubled death, and rebirth in heaven.

Unlike this explanation of moral behavior, the deontological viewpoint, also known as ethics of duty or divine command morality, emphasizes the belief in a superior deity or law. As outlined by its most prominent champion, Immanuel Kant (1724–1804), people act morally not because it is useful or advantageous, but because a divine agency, a root power of the universe, has so decreed. The purpose of rules is beyond the limited faculties of human reason and perception to comprehend; the rewards of morality, despite all apparent futility on this earth, are of a higher nature. Problems with this particular approach arise when the deity demands actions that are not only incomprehensible but even cruel and repulsive. At this point the devotion to the divine has to be tempered with human reason and conflict arises.[3]

A third major position is that of virtue ethics. It engages the issue of a responsible self as the center of morality, asking "What is happening to me? What is most fitting for myself?" The responsible self, then, involves admirable attitudes enhancing human flourishing, described as specific virtues and character strengths. While the core virtues in classical Western ethics are temperance, fortitude, prudence, and justice,[4] recent psychological research, focusing on issues of authentic happiness and flourishing, has defined core values as six virtues in specific dimensions of life that give rise to twenty-four character strengths. They are:[5]

Virtues	Dimensions	Character Strengths
wisdom	cognitive	creativity, curiosity, open-mindedness, love of learning, perspective
courage	emotional	bravery, persistence, integrity, vitality
humanity	interpersonal	love, kindness, social intelligence
justice	civic	citizenship, fairness, leadership
temperance	protective	forgiveness, humility, prudence, self-regulation
transcendence	spiritual	appreciation of beauty and excellence, gratitude, hope, humor/ playfulness, faith/purpose

Covering the full spectrum of life, these virtues and character strengths provide the necessary backbone for individuals to fully flourish within their particular setting, protecting and enhancing their inborn gifts and allowing them to deal efficiently with social issues and situational obstacles.

Contemporary psychologists further determine the presence or absence of these traits with the help of a "Signature Strength" survey and other personality assessments that can be taken online ("Authentic Happiness," www.authentichappiness.sas.upenn.edu). They ask participants to find several top strengths and among them look for two or three of the following:

1. A sense of ownership ("This is the real me.").
2. A feeling of excitement when displaying it, especially at first.
3. A rapid learning curve as first practiced naturally.
4. A sense of continuous learning of new ways to use it.
5. A sense of yearning to use it.
6. A feeling of inevitability in using it ("Try to stop me").
7. A sense of invigoration rather than exhaustion when using it.
8. The creation and pursuit of projects that revolve around it.
9. Joy, zest, and enthusiasm, even ecstasy when using it.[6]

The inner sense of rightness, joy, and enthusiasm people find when engaging in their top strengths closely matches the flow experience of Mihalyi Csikszentmihalyi (1990). The more they excel at many or even all of these strengths, the more they realize their natural talents and can life their best life.

Uniqueness

Classical Daoist philosophy strongly matches the tenets of virtue ethics. Its fundamental concern being the full attainment of inner nature and destiny in close cooperation with social and cosmic harmony, the understanding is that, "if I personally have the chance to recognize my inborn inclinations, enhance my character strengths, train to the fullest, and apply my arts fruitfully in accordance with situational dynamics, the least I can do is respect and support the same in everybody else."[7] This means the recognition of individual uniqueness, which leads to an ethics of difference with two key demands: accepting everyone and everything as unique and acting for their good rather than for personal gain.

The *Zhuangzi* never tires to extol the variety of life on the planet and the importance of uniqueness. Thus thoroughbred horses may run fast, oxen may be big, but they cannot catch mice like cats or raccoon dogs; an owl may see perfectly well in the dark, while others see best during daylight (ch. 17). Some creatures live in marshes, but people would get sick doing so; others live on trees, but humans would get scared; they live in houses, which others would find constricting (ch. 2). A duck's legs are short while those of a crane are long, and any forceful attempt at changing that would only create hurt (ch. 8).[8]

In other words, nature knows what it is doing, the underlying blueprint of the universe arranges things to perfection, and we should not try to double-guess or change it. Just as the acceptance of ethical diversity is part of the larger acceptance of the richness and diversity of the world itself, people's job is to be open-minded, adaptable, tolerant, and flexible. They should cultivate reciprocal consideration of others, appreciation of variety, and respect for individual uniqueness.[9]

People must never interfere in the decisions and actions of others. If they see someone in difficult circumstances, no matter how certain they may be of what would be best for that person, they may make some suggestions but overall need to stay clear. Each and every one has to find what works best for their inherent tendencies, make their own mistakes, and find their own way. Interference, however well intentioned, is bound to cause harm. Classic examples in the *Zhuangzi* include the Lords of the North and the South drilling sensory openings into the shapeless yet kindly ruler of the center known as Hundun (Chaos) (ch. 7); the Marquis of Lu caging the rare seabird and honoring it with a feast (ch. 18); and Bo Le breaking horses to his will (ch. 9). They each cause the death of the subject they are hoping to honor. By the same token, although Lady Li ended up enjoying her time at the bar-barian court, it was wrong to abduct her, taking away her ability to make an autonomous decision on how to live (ch. 2).[10]

People have to realize that they can never see the complete picture, step into another's shoes, or second-guess the intentions of heaven. They have no firm grounds to value one thing over another as permanent standard. This is where relativism, skepticism, and perspectivism in the *Zhuangzi* play their role: not as philosophical positions in themselves but as tools toward ethical guidelines, as conscious, intellectual means of loosening the rigidity of pre-conceived thinking patterns, of the fixed mind.

Uniqueness also applies to specific times, places, and situations. The *Liezi* expresses this most clearly:

> Nowhere is there a principle which is right in all circumstances or an action that is wrong in all circumstances. The method we used yesterday

we may discard today and use again in the future. There is no fixed right and wrong to decide whether we use it or not. The capacity to pick times and snatch opportunities, never be at a loss to answer events, belongs to the wise. (ch. 8)[11]

Within the overall framework of virtue ethics, early Daoists thus not only espouse an ethics of difference but also a situational ethics, a heterogeneity of values, which requires that we forget standard approaches and established moral distinctions, seeing each situation afresh. "Right action is an occasional determination within a particular concrete circumstance rather than a matter of principles."[12] Like a carefree child, people should pay attention with ease and newness, acting within the parameters of the situation, never worried about it or trying to match it to established norms. The moral imperative is thus not the Golden Rule of the Confucians—also found in ancient Greece, Indian thought, and the Bible—to avoid doing to others what one would not want to have done to oneself. Rather, Daoists propose to "do for others in not doing for others," encouraging people to connect to heaven and earth in their own unique way, allowing them to be who and what they are without impositions. Alternatively, it means applying the Copper Rule: "Do unto others what they would have us do unto them," i.e., being gentle, kind, and tolerant toward nature and all beings.[13]

The ethical focus in this system is on the recipient of the action rather than the actor, the moral patient rather than the agent or appraiser. Any action is judged not by some general principle or the attitude of its initiator, but according to what it does to the recipient. A truly moral person is one who matches his or her tendencies with those of his social partners. Precluding any overarching or universal standard, it also implies an emphasis on equality, or at least equal opportunity. One should "treat all according to their natural tendencies, observe their inner nature." This also means that one cannot act on another unless one accepts that this person equally acts on oneself. At all times should people work to transform themselves first before even thinking of working on others. They must never intentionally harm another being yet come to accept death as part of the natural flow.[14]

Freedom from domination

On a wider social and political level, the ethical demand for personal self-realization translates into the ideal of freedom in three dimensions: freedom from external restraint and coercion on the part of others (negative); freedom to actively pursue one's goals (positive); and freedom as autonomy or mastery over oneself (liberty), which includes the right to disengage from society. This means both liberation from conventional values and the exercise of human rights.[15]

The main obstacle to freedom in any form is domination, the willful distortion of the inherent balance of life, the forceful twisting of individuals into directions not their own. This occurs most obviously through social and political dominance, the unmitigated power exercised by ruthless leaders. In the *Zhuangzi*, reflecting the harsh reality of the Warring States period, the human realm is dominated by power, leaving the people punished, intimidated, even mutilated. As the text says, "In the world today, the victims of the death penalty lie heaped together, the bearers of cangues tread on each other's heels, the sufferers of punishments are never out of each other's sight" (ch. 11).

Never tiring to point out the dangers of social and political domination, the text condemns violent excesses and, far from being passive and merely acknowledging the occurrence of atrocities, it encourages resistance against being pulled into political games. The more people are true to themselves and grow in their own unique way, the less they accept domination by others and, by extension, political terror. It thus praises masters who stay away from the lure of office and relax in their own so-being. In contrast, political power is a burden on self and society. As if following Lord Acton's (1834–1902) famous statement, "Power corrupts, and absolute power corrupts absolutely," Zhuangzi sees political power less in terms of concrete instances of domination than as a fundamental danger to integrity and self-realization. Those who carry it are either corrupted by it or find a way to free themselves from it.[16]

Political power as dominance is particularly insidious because it works stealthily by invading people's minds. Internalized as concern or worry, it appears in the petty ways of social coercion and attachment, in ordinary thinking that creates the rigid patterns of the fixed mind, in customary judgments and prejudices that justify the social order and make people strive for social recognition and external goals. Activated as consciously crafted, formal virtues, such as the classical Confucian values of loyalty and filial piety, this leads to feelings of shame or sin and makes people into "victims of their own willing, subjugated to their own intentionality"[17]—thus the text's injunction to practice mind-fasting, sit in oblivion, and forget morality.

The ideal social connection in early Daoism is accordingly that of friendship, the most equal and balanced among the five major relationships of Confucianism—the others being ruler and minister, father and son, husband and wife, plus older and younger brother. Friendship lies between the direct, close reciprocity of kinship and the more complex, indirect reciprocity of acquaintances and strangers, allowing for intimacy without inescapable obligation or the codification of social norms. In friendship, which requires radical surrender, "two individuals engage in a common project of mutual self-realization," respecting each other fully as ends-in-themselves, in mutual recognition and acceptance.[18]

Friends come together on the basis of common convictions and goals. In ancient Daoism, this is the focus on realizing Dao, the shared commitment to the project of Daoist flourishing. It also involves the ability to "pay no attention to proper behavior, disregard personal appearance and, without so much as changing facial expression, sing in the presence of a corpse" (*Zhuangzi*, ch. 6). As the text says,

Who can join with others without joining with others? Who can do with others without doing with others? Who can climb up to heaven and wander in the mists, roam the infinite, and forget life forever and forever? Who can look upon nonbeing as his head, on life as his back, and on death as his rump? Who knows that life and death, existence and annihilation, are all a single body? I will be his friend!

(ch. 6)[19]

Rather than being defined by social roles and conventional patterns, ancient Daoists are "friends in virtue" (ch. 5), individuals who come together not for calculated rewards or special benefits, conscious designs or planned expectations, but in intrinsic joyfulness, forgetting self and other in ecstatic oneness. Being both with and not with each other, they disregard personal shortcomings—"The Master and I have been friends for nineteen years and he's never once let on that he's aware I'm missing a foot" (ch. 5)—and always look out for each other, taking them food when needed (ch. 6) and offering them a lavish welcome when visiting (ch. 20). The ideal community, then, is small—all members know and relate to each other in reciprocal altruism, easily keeping track of others' reputations and exchanged favors, matching the ideal formulated in the *Daode jing* and representing an organic way of human congregation, free from imposed social rules, political dominance, and contrived moral reasoning.

Religious ethics

Later Daoists continue these fundamental tenets and establish rules and precepts to create an attitude that realizes both personal uniqueness and universal interconnectedness. At the same time, their thinking takes on a distinctly utilitarian thrust in that it postulates the immediate and extensive effect of moral actions. Thus, Daoists acknowledge that while the cooperation of all things and beings in the universe constitutes its perfection and is its ultimate and most natural state, any particular individual or entity can realize its pure Dao-nature to a greater or lesser degree, causing good or bad consequences not only for himself and his family but for the country, the natural environment, and the world at large.

Daoists living in harmony who have realized their inner nature to the utmost and are spontaneously who they were meant to be have excellent health and create good fortune for their families while spreading the purity of underlying goodness all around them. Through their purity and harmony with Dao, others too come to attain a higher degree of peace and personal realization, even without consciously wishing or noticing it. On the other hand, people who have not realized their true potential have become removed from the inherent harmony of Dao, developing patterns of disharmony and an inclination toward immoral and harmful actions. Their health declines, they come to live in conflict and trouble, and negatively affect the world around them.

As outlined in the *Chisongzi zhongjie jing* (Essential Precepts of Master Redpine, DZ 185) of the fifth century, these effects not only manifest due to people's overt and open actions but also involve their thoughts and intentions. They all have an immediate effect, so that "when the people of the world commit violations, bad actions, or faults, or speak contrary words, heaven's way is no longer smooth and even but is distorted and loses its naturalness." All bad deeds, all vicious thoughts, all cursing and scolding upset the greater universe and create cosmic imbalance. So does the suffering that people undergo as a result of their bad deeds. Even worse, heaven is strongly discomfited when people afterwards try to implore it and garner favor. The text says:

> Getting imprisoned and locked into the cangue upsets heaven. Being hungry and poor, ill and sick upsets heaven. Unseasonable cold and heat, frost and snow upset heaven. Irregularities in the length of day and night upset heaven. It upsets heaven even more when people do evil then come to pray and besiege it [for help]. Or go against the four seasons, disobey the five phases, expose their naked body to the Three Luminants [sun, moon, planets], and then come to request a benefit at a shrine or temple of the Three Luminants or the various stars and constellations.[20]

People cause cosmic disharmony by not having respect for heaven and earth, the demons and spirits, by cursing the wind and the rain, by denigrating the sages and the scriptural teachings, and by desecrating shrines and temples. Not only religious and cosmic violations, but all manner of social harm disturbs the cosmos: being unfilial toward father and mother; digging up tombs to steal the valuables of the dead; cheating the blind, the deaf, and the dumb; throwing impure substances into food and drink; killing other beings; accusing and slandering others or spying on their affairs; obstructing roads and letting drains be blocked; stealing and cheating, destroying nature's riches, and in other ways harming society and life. All these acts cause heaven and earth to be upset and imbalanced. They in turn do not keep their displeasure to themselves but give human beings ample warning that something is amiss, causing all manner of natural irregularities and disasters, including "landslides and earthquakes, hurricanes and tornadoes, sandstorms and flying stones, floods and locust plagues, famines and droughts, epidemics and more."

Daoist ethics thus place a heavy burden of cosmic responsibility on the individual while making it prudent to stick to the rules to prevent harm to self, others, and society. The underlying argument is that, as people realize the fact that they ultimately are at the root of heaven and earth and have the power to make the cosmos move in harmony or go awry, they act more and more in goodness—a moral goodness that abstains from harmful actions and supports the community of all life. They replace negative and destructive attitudes with supportive and helpful ones. For example, as the *Chisongzi zhongjie jing* outlines, instead of "when burdened by debt, they wish that the money-lender may die and the debt expire," they now strive to pay back the money. "When they see someone who in the past was in debt to them run afoul of the officials, they develop an intention of helpfulness and support." Or again, when they see someone blessed with beautiful wives and concubines, instead of developing an intent toward adultery, they now count their blessings and "realize that their own partner does not create quarrels or upheaval." Starting with an elementary observation of precepts and prohibitions, they gradually develop a greater awareness of heaven and earth and come to create good fortune for themselves, the society around them, and the world at large.[21]

Notes

1   Van Norden 2007, 30.
2   Mabbott 1969, 15–30.
3   See Idziak 1980.
4   Duncan 1995, 75–88; Van Norden 2007, 37–9.
5   Peterson and Seligman 2004.
6   See Seligman 2002.
7   Kohn 2004, 238.
8   Huang 2010a, 77.
9   Fraser 2009, 439, 453.
10   Citations from Huang 2010a, 89, 74; examples from *ibid.*, 75–6, 87.
11   Cua 1977, 312.
12   Cua 1977, 313; also Huang 2010b, 1057.
13   Huang 2005, 394; 2010b, 1060.
14   Huang 2010a, 72–3; 2010b, 1059; Cua 1977, 318.
15   Duncan 1995, 17; also Lee 2014.
16   Møllgaard 2003, 348, 358–59.
17   Møllgaard 2003, 360; Van Norden 1999, 191–2.
18   Citation from Duncan 1995, 30. See also Blakeley 2008, 320–1; Kohn 2004, 241–2; Lee 2014, ch. 3.
19   Blakeley 2008, 318–19, 325. See also Galvany 2009.
20   Kohn 2004, 14.
21   Kohn 2004, 15.

References

Blakeley, Donald N. 2008. "Hearts in Agreement: Zhuangzi on Dao Adept Friendship." *Philosophy East and West* 58.3:318–36.
Csikszentmihalyi, Mihaly. 1990. *Flow: The Psychology of Optimal Experience.* New York, NY: Harper & Row.
Cua, Antonio S. 1977. "Forgetting Morality: Reflections on a Theme in the *Chuang-tzu.*" *Journal of Chinese Philosophy* 4.4:305–28.
Duncan, Steven M. 1995. *A Primer of Modern Virtue Ethics.* New York, NY: University Press of America.

Fraser, Chris. 2009. "Skepticism and Value in the *Zhuangzi.*" *International Philosophical Quarterly* 49.4:439–57.

Galvany, Albert. 2009. "Distorting the Rule of Seriousness: Laughter, Death, and Friendship in the *Zhuangzi.*" *Dao: A Journal of Comparative Philosophy* 8.1:49–59.

Huang, Yong. 2005. "A Copper Rule versus the Golden Rule: A Daoist-Confucian Proposal for Global Ethics." *Philosophy East and West* 55.3:394–425

Huang, Yong. 2010a. "The Ethics of Difference in the *Zhuangzi.*" *Journal of the American Academy of Religion* 78.1:65–99.

Huang, Yong. 2010b. "Respecting Different Ways of Life: A Daoist Ethics of Virtue in the *Zhuangzi.*" *Journal of Asian Studies* 69.4:1049–69.

Kohn, Livia. 2004. *Cosmos and Community: The Ethical Dimension of Daoism.* Cambridge, MA: Three Pines Press.

Idziak, Janine Marie. 1980. *Divine Command Morality.* Lewiston, NY: Edwin Mellen Press.

Lee, Jung H. 2014. *The Ethical Foundations of Daoism: Zhuangzi's Unique Moral Vision.* New York, NY: Palgrave-McMillan.

Mabbott, J. D. 1969. *An Introduction to Ethics.* Garden City, NJ: Anchor Books.

Møllgaard, Eske. 2003. "Zhuangzi's Religious Ethics." *Journal of the American Academy of Religion* 71.2:347–70.

Peterson, Christopher, and Martin E. P. Seligman. 2004. *Character Strengths and Virtues: A Handbook and Classification.* Oxford: Oxford University Press.

Seligman, Martin E. P. 2002. *Authentic Happiness: Using the New Positive Psychology to Realize Your Potential for Lasting Fulfillment.* New York, NY: Free Press.

Van Norden, Bryan W. 2007. *Virtue Ethics and Consequentialism in Early Chinese Philosophy.* Cambridge: Cambridge University Press.

11   The nature of evil

In most cultures, evil is described as arising only after the creation of human beings, who start out pure and as an integral part of the primordial unity of the natural life. Then, however, something happens, and human beings set themselves apart, rupture the cosmic and communal coherence, and no longer acting with but in opposition to nature, the universe, and God. At this time good and evil first appear, often starting with human knowledge and from there evolving unto the world.

The decisive event that separates the primordial from the conscious world is commonly called "the fall." The fall describes the transition of primordial humanity to its present state of strife, the change from timelessness to time and history. It signifies the mutation of an entirely harmonious world into one of good and evil, the development of culture from the simple to the complex, the beginning of disharmony and strife. A gradual emergence of more intricate forms of living, it is felt as the irreparable loss of the pristine state of the golden age and often described as a single traumatic event. Thus, it can be the fall of the One into the many, the emergence of the physical universe out of a transcendent God, the fall of the soul into time, the entrapment of an angelic soul into the body of primitive man, or the fall of an unconditioned consciousness beyond subject and object into the syntax of thought pounded into form by each heartbeat.[1]

In whichever way the fall is described, be it the expulsion from the Garden of Eden, the betrayal of a brother, the battle between light and darkness, the loss of unified consciousness, or the derailing of enlightened government, it is always about cultural progress, the ongoing transformation of the world into more complex forms, the diversification of society into various segments, and the production of more intricate living conditions. All these are seen with a sense of great regret, so that, as Douglas Adams says in *The Hitchhiker's Guide to the Galaxy*, people came to feel that "they'd all made a big mistake in coming down from the trees in the first place. And some said that even the trees had been a bad move, and that no one should ever have left the oceans."[2]

Inherent and created evil

The Chinese cosmos, emerging naturally from the depth of chaos, in inherently good and harmonious, pervasively ordered by Dao, *qi*, and the regular cycles of yin-yang and the five phases. Evil in this context is understood on two levels: as an inherent part of the natural processes, the necessary yin to every yang, and second as "the result of man's temporary distortion of universal harmony."[3] Evil is thus a natural part of life, just as without the shady part of the mountain there can be no sunny side. Similarly, without an appreciation of evil there can be no valuing good, without suffering some toils there can be no enjoyment. The world exists in human consciousness through the continued alternation of complementary opposites, the elimination of one of which also means the end of the other. To be at ease and delight in the world, one has to have a certainty amount of hardship and toil, suffering and evil are thus necessary aspects of life as a human being.

On the other hand, evil also occurs in the distortion of primordial harmony, as a break from the inherent goodness and purity of Dao and its manifestation in worldly rhythms. This kind of evil is not necessary and seen as a hostile force, a powerful infringement on cosmic harmony. As such it is mythologized as demons, a horde of nasty creatures that lurk at the borders of human society, ready to pounce on unsuspecting creatures.

The same dichotomy is also evident in Chinese medicine. Sickness is, on the one hand, a temporary weakness of the body, a response of the physical system to changes in the outside world. As such it is nothing irregular but part of the natural process, a necessary correlate to health and strength, a phase among others in the continuously changing universe. On the other hand, disease can be caused by an active break with the patterns of nature, which weakens the physical system and allows demonic or infectious forces to enter.

In Daoism, there is, therefore, first of all natural or inherent evil, a negative force that yet forms part of life and which one has to accept and accommodate. To avoid it, people should behave as much as possible in accordance with their own inner nature and destiny as well as with the seasons and the rhythms of the world, adapting to changes as they come. Second, and more potently, there is created evil, caused by an active distortion of primordial harmony, which may well lead to a massive attack by demonic forces. This evil has to be fought with all means, using medical cures, repentance, prayers, exorcism, and more. Both types, moreover, are intimately connected, created evil developing only on the basis of inherent evil, often beginning as a resistance to, or displeasure with, a difficult phase or state, and manifest in the same concrete phenomena—sickness, poverty, pain. To prevent created evil, one therefore must accept inherent evil as part of life, bearing one's lot with patience and never opening the doors to the demons.[4]

Souls and body gods

In medieval Daoism, both the inherent and created forms of evil appear as spiritual entities that live within the person: souls of yin and yang, on the one hand, and bodily demons and gods, on the other. The two souls, called spirit and material (*hun/po*, see Chapter 5), are essential for the existence and survival of the individual. Human beings cannot live without them, yet they pull them into different directions: the yang souls toward purity, cultural refinement, and virtue; the yin souls toward defilement, social rapaciousness, and evil. Rather than consisting of only one entity each, as they do in classical thought and medicine, moreover, there are now three spirit and seven material souls.

The Tang-dynasty *Baosheng jing* (Scripture of Preserving Life, DZ 871) describes the spirit souls as looking like human beings and gives them the names Spiritual Guidance, Inner Radiance, and Mysterious Essence. An illustration shows them human in shape, noble in appearance, and dressed in courtly garb. Their positive impact should be supported with prayers, chants, and visualizations.

The material souls, on the contrary, are nasty creatures; bent on survival, they are prone to fear, worry, and other negative emotions. "They can make a person commit deadly evils, be stingy and greedy, jealous and full of envy. They give people bad dreams and make them clench their teeth, incite them to say 'right' when they think 'wrong'." Far from looking like human beings, they are strangely formed devils, having birds' heads, only one leg, tails, abominable outgrowth, and the like. Their names are accordingly Corpse Dog, Arrow in Ambush, Bird Darkness, Devouring Robber, Flying Poison, Massive Pollution, and Stinky Lungs.[5]

Evil here is part of being human: we all have survival instincts and feel threatened on occasion, giving rise to strong emotions that in turn may cause negative thoughts and harmful actions. Evil thus created in due course leads to suffering through loss of vital energy, illness, and death. Inherent and natural, this can only be alleviated by circumspect action, by the active subduing of survival urges and nurturing the call of the higher souls.

Also built in but less inevitable in their effect and therefore representatives of created evil are the supernatural entities residing in the human body. They, too, divide into yin and yang.

On the yang side, there are first the Three Ones, pure deities of Dao who are inherently present in the three elixir fields as the immediate manifestation of pure primordial *qi*. Representatives of the divine and utterly pure ground of being and life as such, they are the Celestial Emperor in the head, the Cinnabar Sovereign in the heart, and the Primordial King in the abdomen, each commanding a force of a thousand chariots and ten thousand horsemen. Originally residents of the higher heavens, people can call them down and activate them within through prayers and visualizations. Powerful good forces of Dao, divine powers of longevity, good fortune, and immortality, they help in all that is good and holy and assist the practitioner both in navigating life and in his ascent to the divine.

Their yin counterparts are correspondingly evil. The "three deathbringers," also called the three worms or three corpses, are a cross between demons and souls, who reside in the head, torso and lower body of the individual and incite people to commit transgressions and fall ill. After the death of their host, when the various souls have returned to heaven and earth, these noxious parasites remain with the corpse and gorge themselves on its blood, bones, and muscles. Having partaken of the human body, they are able to assume its former intact shape and appear as ghosts, feasting further on the offerings laid out for the ancestors. They have thus a vested interest in bringing a person to death quickly and without mercy. Each of the three has a distinct personality and role. As the *Baosheng jing* describes them,

> The upper deathbringer is called Peng Ju, also known as Shouter. He sits in the head and attacks the elixir field in the Niwan Palace [center of the head]. He causes people's heads to be heavy, their eyesight blurred, their tears cold. He makes mucus assemble in their noses and their ears go deaf. Because of him, people's teeth fall out, their mouths rot, and their faces shrink in wrinkles. He deludes people so that they desire carriages and horses and crave for fancy sounds and sights …
>
> The middle deathbringer is called Peng Zhi, also known as Maker. He enjoys deluding people with the five tastes and makes them greedy for the five colors. He lives in the human heart and stomach and attacks the Scarlet Palace [in the heart] together with its Central Heater. He causes people's minds to be confused and forgetful, so that they are full of troubles, dry in saliva and low in energy …
>
> The lower deathbringer is called Peng Qiao, also known as Junior. He lives in people's stomachs and legs and attacks the lower parts of the body. He makes energy leak [through the genitals] from the Ocean of *Qi* and thereby invites a multiplicity of ills. Attracting the robbers of human intention, he makes people hanker after women and sex.[6]

These divine-demonic agents are further assisted by the "nine worms," purely organic entities that look like ordinary worms or bugs, some long and slithering, others round with little leg-like extensions, yet others spongy or crab-like. They are physical parasites, bacteria that cause illnesses, and serve as the minions of the three deathbringers, who themselves are the managers of evil and suffering.

Measures against them are, first of all, virtuous behavior in accordance with the precepts and the continued meditation on the Three Ones, who ideally come to replace the three deathbringers in the major energy centers of the body. For those who lack such saintly virtue and power of concentration, there are more physical countermeasures, prominent in medieval China and still practiced in Japan as part of the so-called Kōshin cult. They include most importantly a vigil on the night of *gengshen* (Jap. *kōshin*), the 57th day of the 60-day cycle, when the three have to ascend to the heavens to make their report to the celestial administration. They can only leave the body when the person is asleep and, without proper directives for destruction from above, they will be helpless and disoriented. After seven successful vigils, they will be so emaciated that they die altogether.

For those who cannot stay awake long enough or lack the moral purity required for this vigil, various drugs and medicines as well as specific temporal and spatial taboos keep the three deathbringers from doing too much harm. While these remedies will not eradicate them and people may still die from their activities, they at least hamper them in their evil ways, and one can breathe a little easier.[7]

The Daoist vision of created evil is therefore quite parallel to its understanding of inherent evil. Both good and evil forces in the universe can be called upon and followed by the individual. Behaving virtuously and meditating with dedication will cause inherent good forces to develop and good deities to descend, thus gradually diminishing the power of both inherent and demonic evil. Being egoistic and greedy or committing acts of disharmony, on the contrary, will open the gates wide for nasty specters and demons to invade and grow strong. They will delude the person's mind and devour his vital energy, leading him further into evil and causing both physical and spiritual suffering. Once a breach has occurred, rituals, repentance, prayers, and medicines will help, but ultimately only the full restoration of primordial cosmic harmony and its continued maintenance will guarantee liberation.

Social dimensions

From a more social perspective, as shown by Paul Ricoeur, evil evolved in the three stages of defilement, sin, and guilt. Defilement, typical for the world of primitive cultures, centers on the relation between the individual and the cosmos, manifesting in "a dread of the impure and rites of purification."[8] All evil here is externalized in nature: heaven and the gods are doing evil to people by visiting them with natural catastrophes, fires, droughts, famines, and disease. Evil and misfortune are not separate in this world; purity, moral good, and good fortune are one and the same.

> In such a universe, the elemental forces are seen as linked so closely to individual human beings that we can hardly speak of an external, physical environment. Each individual carries within himself such close links with the universe that he is like the center of a magnetic field of force. Events can be explained in terms of his being what he is and doing what he has done.[9]

The answer to evil as defilement is a detailed system of taboos and interdicts, minute prescriptions in domains that for us are often ethically neutral, as well as by ritual cycles of purification and sacrifices. Over both stretches the shadow of vengeance to be paid if the proper order is violated. The power of the interdict, the need to reaffirm life in rituals and sacrifices, is ubiquitous: its anticipatory fear is the prime root for human thought and action, and evil as defilement is essentially exorcised.

With increasing complexity, a more diversified environment develops. Societies begin to concentrate on themselves and less on their relationship with the cosmos, so that defilement is replaced by sin, defined by Paul Ricoeur as the "violation of a personal bond." Sin is a religious and social dimension of evil: it signifies the development of a higher individual awareness while defining the individual as a predominantly social being. Accordingly, during the stage of sin, behavioral rules and social regulations emerge, "elaborated ritual, penal, civil, and political codes to regulate conduct."[10]

Evil at this stage is a transgression against one's fellow human beings and the dreaded punishment is social chaos or expulsion, or—in the Jewish context—the wrath of God. The most serious transgressions are injustice, adultery, arrogance, and disobedience, that is, anything that disrupts interpersonal relationships. Recovery is found through redemption, the return to the fold, the reestablishment of social harmony. At this stage, there is no distinction between sickness and fault. Whereas the primitives identify any form of disaster as personal misfortune, people in more developed societies recognize their personal involvement in events. Yet the separation of the independent self from nature and others is not complete.

This only happens in the third stage of guilt, which comes with the recognition of personal responsibility for one's own intentions and actions, the acceptance of an inner rather than a cosmic or social control of impulses. Redemption, too, is internalized as the unadulterated feeling that one deserves punishment and the powerful anxiety that comes with its anticipation. "Guilt is the achieved internality of sin."[11] The multiple prohibitions of the cosmos, the various codes of society are internalized and placed in a position of the absolute, symbolizing a moral perfection that can never be reached. Guilt in its fully developed form is the eternal strife for altruistic perfection, the never-ending fight against egoistic impulses—a strife that can never be won, a fight that is eternally lost. Guilt is the full recognition of the potentially evil nature of the individual, by himself, for himself, and through himself. Guilt can be expiated through penance, confessions, and altruistic good deeds. But just as guilt becomes a basic fact of existence, so the expiation of guilt has to be a continuous process.

In the Western tradition, the emerging consciousness of guilt led into three directions. First it brought about the ethico-judicial experience, where the individual was judged not only according to his or her actions but also according to his intentions and where guilt was allotted in varying degrees. This experience, in turn, allowed for true tragedy in the Greek sense, the possibility of a fatal but fundamentally innocent error that caused major transgressions but was not culpable in itself. It also brought about the internal conflict within the individual between the feeling of guilt and the necessity to be active in the world.

In a second direction, guilt in the West led to an extreme scrupulousness of conscience. To make the guilt bearable, the individual subjected himself to voluntary heteronomy under the sway of detailed rules and regulations. This experience taken to its extreme led to the hypocrisy and self-righteousness associated with the Pharisees in the Jewish tradition.

Third, the fully developed stage led to an "impasse of guilt," recognized most powerfully by St. Paul. An ever-increasing number of laws and regulations caused a commitment of ever new sins and offenses. These, in turn, created a bottomless pit of guilt, a vicious circle of law and offense. Rules and transgressions developed a "deadly circularity," from which only the powerful grace of God could liberate.[12]

The Chinese development

The oldest evidence on Chinese beliefs and ritual practices clearly indicates the presence of a cosmos-centered vision typical for primitive cultures and the stage of defilement. In the Shang dynasty (1554–1028 BCE), the individual human being was linked closely with the cosmos, and the various activities of nature were considered as indicating good and bad fortune. Heaven and the gods, mediated by the ancestors, were willful, purposeful agents; all human activity had to be properly aligned with them to prevent disasters.[13]

Evil was bad fortune and defilement. It could be prevented through taboos and regular ancestral sacrifices, propitiation of the gods and service to the spirits of the dead. Under the Shang, everything from political problems through family issues to bodily symptoms was thought to be caused by the "curse of an ancestor," the willful interference in human affairs by a super-natural agent. Poor harvests, natural disasters, and other misfortunes were laid at the same door and seen as signs of universal disease. The character for "sickness" (*ji*) that developed at this time consisted of the image of a bed and an arrow, showing how evil was understood as "an injury caused by the evil action of a third party."[14] Purity, the ideal state of harmony of the various cosmic and earthly forces, was beset by dangers; the world, however unified in its patterns, was in constant jeopardy through defilement.

Widely present in popular religion to the present day, this thinking in Daoism appears most clearly among the early Celestial Masters who under-stood disease as caused by demons, able to infiltrate a person's defenses if and when they had been careless and committed a moral or ritual offense. As a result, all healing was undertaken through ritual and magic; acupuncture, herbs, and other medical treatments were expressly prohibited. First the sick person was isolated in a so-called quiet chamber or oratory, an adaptation of a Han institution for punishing wayward officials involving solitary con-finement. There they had to think of their sins going all the way back to their birth to try and find an explanation for the illness.

Once certain causes of defilement had been identified, a senior master would come to write them down—in triplicate and together with a formal petition for their eradication from the person's divine record. The three copies would then, in a formal ceremony, be transmitted to the realms of heaven (by burning), earth (by burying), and water (by casting into a river), whose officials ideally set the record straight and restored the person's good health. Additional measures of purification involved the ingestion of "talisman water"—the ashes of a talisman dissolved in water—healing exercises, and meditative reflections.[15]

Classical philosophy of the Warring States period, especially Confucian thought, is the prime source for the understanding of socially defined evil during the stage of sin. For early thinkers, the highest arbiter of moral judgment was no longer the cosmos at large although that dimension was never fully lost. Of more immediate importance was the social community and kinship group, and all reward and punishment, good and bad fortune were defined socially: living in harmony, having plenty of descendants, gaining status and wealth as opposed to social unrest and strife, childlessness and bodily harm, poverty, and dishonor. The reality of the social life came to the foreground, and with it a set of moral rules and intricate codes that emphasized the restraint of individual in favor or the group.

Social harmony was the main goal of the Confucian rules, related immediately to a personal integrity within and a larger-scale cosmic state of peace without. A strictly hierarchical system, society placed each and everyone into positions of senior or junior, making sure that they all knew which role to play under which circumstances and followed the correct patterns of behavior. Before, the individual human being had been submerged in the group of humans vis-à-vis heaven and earth; now he or she became part of a subtly interwoven social pattern, fulfilling a role, corresponding to the cues of a part. What had been taboos and interdicts became rules directed against any excesses of temperament and personal inclination that could propel people to leave their social niche and cause disharmony: sex, aggression, greed. What had been punishment from heaven because of ritual impurity now became shame and a sense of separation from the group. Where the myths had been concerned with the phenomena of nature and the positions of the ancestors, they now dealt with the perfection of the golden age and the harmonious delights of sage government.[16] This dimension of evil today continues in the ubiquitous veneration of the family described earlier, and in Daoism informs the identity of the individual as a member of the religious community or the monastery.

The rejection of guilt

China never developed an indigenous stage of guilt but retained the cosmic and social dimensions of evil throughout, becoming a culture centered on shame and seeing evil as combination of defilement and sin, described dominantly in terms of disharmony.

This is evident variously. Philosophically it appears in the absence of a notion of self in the sense of a complex, fully individualized, autonomous—guilt-centered—personality. There is neither the concept of critical self-reflection nor the true tragedy of an individual caught in an inescapable dilemma. In literature, second, there is no quest for self-knowledge, extended self-pity or self-mortification. Rather than facing severe moral choices, the protagonist of traditional fiction only follows the lessons of the ancients and obeys the demands of his particular social situation, which inevitably prescribes the only possible mode of action. Autobiography, too, although an ancient and varied genre, does not contain critical self-questioning or self-analysis. The individual emerges only as the conglomerate of different standardized patterns and critical evaluations or questioning searches of the self do not appear before the contact with Western culture.[17]

Chinese traditional law, third, similarly denies an autonomous self. Serving to restore social harmony after a breach, it determines punishment entirely on the basis of the severity of the disruption, disregarding whether the deed was done with or without harmful intention. The individual does not count; only his or her impact on the whole of society. No guilt in Ricoeur's sense, therefore, means that in traditional China there were neither the extreme scrupulousness of individual conscience nor the impasse of guilt with its sense of utter helplessness and individual aloneness.

Still, the Chinese had to confront the notion of personal guilt when Buddhism appeared on the horizon in the first century CE. Buddhism with its elaborate moral rules and monastic precepts, its detailed doctrines of karma and retribution, placed the responsibility for evil firmly in the individual, where it appeared as ignorance, desire, and aggression. All circumstances of life and being were entirely due to one's personal conduct and intentions, and the way out lay in a massive development of voluntary heteronomy, the strict obedience to the numerous rules and regulations of the religious codes and the severe suppression of egoism and a personal will. Any violation was not only punished by immediate pain but also in bad future rebirths and tortures in the hells.

The Chinese fought the acceptance of Buddhist doctrines and practices. Not surprisingly, the argument made most frequently against them was the destruction they would wreak on the social institutions and inner harmony of the Chinese oikumene. While this was certainly true—people leaving the family and setting up independent institutions did disrupt the social coherence—it also expressed the rejection of a guilt-dominated culture, the panic in the face of a truly autonomous individual.

Over the centuries, Buddhism was integrated and still plays an important role today, having molded much of Chinese culture, provided Daoism with many of its institutions and doctrines, and exerted a great impact on later Confucian thinking. In the process of integration, however, the Buddhist teaching also underwent radical changes. The culture of guilt it represented was gradually reinterpreted in the light of sin and defilement: the Chinese went back to the earliest stage just as they absorbed the last.

Ignorance, for example, in early Indian Buddhism had been placed strictly within the individual. It emerged as a fully independent cosmic force in the apocryphal Chinese work *Dacheng qixin lun* (Awakening of Faith in the Mahayana) of the 6th century, having moved far beyond the limitations of personal responsibility. Buddhist moral rules, although originally centered on the individual, were similarly reinterpreted in a cosmic framework. Their observance or breach was seen parallel to, and interactive with, planetary movements and bodily processes. Any action in line with or against the rules immediately resonated within the entire cosmic system and could cause bodily, social, and universal disruption.[18]

Karma and retribution, the core doctrines of the religion, did not stay the same either. Punishments in the hells became part of Chinese popular religion, but at the same time the Buddhist teaching was expanded to allow the possibility of either suffering due to transgressions of one's kin or alleviating the ancestors' plight by performing efficacious rituals. No longer carrying only his own fate, the individual was again firmly embedded in social and cosmic structures.

The understanding of evil in Daoism is, therefore, both similar and different from its Western counterpart—allowing both for a natural and a created dimension and moving socially from defilement through sin to disharmony. Its rejection of guilt was intentional and consistent and cannot be considered a failure. Thus, after the advent of Buddhism, "patterns entered consciousness that were recognized as leading to a possible individualization and therefore deviation. They were banished quickly with the help of a new emphasis on depersonalization."[19] Throughout history, Daoists have enhanced the universal dimensions of thinking and being, recovering cosmic defilement and preserving social sin in the continued use of disharmony as their most potent symbol of evil. Again and again, they have placed evil unmistakably outside of the individual and pursued personal security in taboos, regulations, and prohibitions.

Notes

1 Thompson 1981, 9–10.
2 Cited in Girardot 1985, 77.
3 Bodde 1981, 287.
4 Kohn 1998, 93.
5 Kohn 1998, 95.
6 Kohn 1998, 104.
7 See Kohn 2015.
8 Ricoeur 1967, 25.
9 Douglas 1966, 81.
10 Ricoeur 1967, 52–3.
11 Ricoeur 1967, 100, 103.
12 See Ricoeur 1967, 108–18, 119–38, 139–50.
13 Keightley 1978, 38.
14 Unschuld 1985, 19–20.
15 Kobayashi 1992, 22–3.

16 See Eno 1990.
17 Lau 1985, 363; Bauer 1964, 12.
18 On the Buddhist reception in China, see Ch'en 1973.
19 Kubin 1990, 101.

References

Bauer, Wolfgang. 1964. "Icherleben und Autobiographie im älteren China." *Heidelberger Jahrbücher* 8:12–40.

Bodde, Derk. 1981. "Harmony and Conflict in Chinese Philosophy." In *Essays on Chinese Civilization*, edited by Charles Le Blanc and Dorothy Borei, 237–96. Princeton, NJ: Princeton University Press.

Ch'en, Kenneth. 1973. *The Chinese Transformation of Buddhism*. Princeton, NJ: Princeton University Press.

Douglas, Mary. 1966. *Purity and Danger: An Analysis of Concepts of Pollution and Taboo*. London: Routledge and Kegan Paul.

Eno, Robert. 1990. *The Confucian Creation of Heaven: Philosophy and the Defense of Ritual Mastery*. Albany: State University of New York Press.

Girardot, Norman. 1985. "Behaving Cosmogonically in Early Taoism." In *Cosmogony and Ethical Order: New Studies in Comparative Ethics*, edited by Robin W. Lovin and Frank E. Reynolds, 67–97. Chicago: University of Chicago Press.

Keightley, David N. 1978. "The Religious Commitment: Shang Theology and the Genesis of Chinese Political Culture." *History of Religions* 17:211–25.

Kobayashi, Masayoshi. 1992. "The Celestial Masters Under the Eastern Jin and Liu-Song Dynasties." *Taoist Resources* 3.2:17–45.

Kohn, Livia. 1998. "Yin and Yang: The Natural Dimension of Evil." In *Philosophies of Nature: The Human Dimension*, edited by Robert S. Cohen and Alfred I. Tauber, 91–105. Lancaster: Kluwer Academic Publishers.

Kohn, Livia. 2015. "Kōshin: Expelling Taoist Demons with Buddhist Means." In *Daoism in Japan: Chinese Traditions and Their Influence on Japanese Religious Culture*, edited by Jeffrey L. Richey, 148–76. New York, NY: Routledge.

Kubin, Wolfgang. 1990. "Der unstete Affe: Zum Problem des Selbst im Konfuzianismus." In *Konfuzianismus und die Modernisierung Chinas*, edited by Silke Krieger and Rolf Trauzettel, 80–113. Mainz: Hase und Köhler.

Lau, Joseph S. M. 1985. "Duty, Reputation, and Selfhood in Traditional Chinese Narratives." In *Expressions of Self in Chinese Literature*, edited by Robert E. Hegel, 363–83. New York, NY: Columbia University Press.

Ricoeur, Paul. 1967. *The Symbolism of Evil*. Boston, MA: Beacon Press.

Thompson, William Irwin. 1981. *The Time Falling Bodies Take to Light: Mythology, Sexuality, and the Origins of Culture*. New York, NY: St. Martin's Press.

Unschuld, Paul U. 1985. *Medicine in China: A History of Ideas*. Berkeley: University of California Press.

12 Religious precepts

Matching the different dimensions of evil and its symbolism, religions have created a variety of rules and precepts. The earliest, matching the stage of defilement, are taboos, cosmically defined prohibitions that center on space and time, preventing people from stepping into certain areas, eating certain foods, offending divine powers such as stars and planets, or committing acts considered inauspicious. Any of these would bring people into close contact with supernatural or high-energy forces considered extremely potent and thus dangerous if encountered without protection. The violation or breach of a taboo accordingly creates a form of cosmic pollution, which is resolved with various methods that range from procedures of ritual purification through temporary exile from the tribe to ritual killing. If undiscovered and unresolved, the defiance of a taboo can lead to natural catastrophes and epidemics sent by the gods.

Next is the level of sin, where people define themselves socially rather than cosmically. Here precepts come in three distinct forms. The first is a set of four fundamental behavioral restrictions that are universal, often described as the "great moral rules." Prohibiting major social infringements such as killing, stealing, lying, and sexual misconduct, they appear in all great religions, from the Ten Commandments of the Old Testament through the Buddhist and Yogic precepts to Chinese adaptations. Studied cross-culturally by moral philosophers and scholars of religion, they are considered essentially rational, non-religious rules that are geared to the individual, essential to civilization, and beyond the limitations of particular societies or cosmologies. They are so basic that, even if formulated in a specific social and historical context, they are not primarily social or cultural, but formulations of an absolute morality that is valid for all and based on being essentially human.[1]

A second kind of precepts in sin-based societies consists of prohibitions of specific social actions and attitudes that are considered detrimental to the group and may lead to the disruption of social bonds and the destruction of integration and harmony. Formulated in "elaborate ritual, penal, civil, and political codes" that differ depending on the specific culture, they are generally geared toward the upholding of propriety and social order, controlling sex, aggression, greed, and other potentially harmful tendencies. People at

this stage recognize their personal involvement in events but do not fully separate the independent self from nature and others and accordingly make no
distinction between sickness and fault. What they experience within is linked
to events without; sickness is the punishment for sin and misfortune is the
result of evil intentions. Beyond this, violations are punished by preventing
people from attaining the established social goals of long life, prosperity,
respect, and well-being. They often come with shunning, imprisonment, exile,
or other forms of removal from the group.[2]

The third type of precepts here are admonitions or "supererogatory" rules,
a term that literally means "paying out more than required." Admonitions
encourage positive behavior, actions that go beyond the call of duty and are
of special value. They can be acts of heroism, beneficence, kindness, or forgiveness, and always carry an extra level of goodness. Supererogation creates
merit and enhances virtue as a moral quality. Rules of this type are formulated
as "should" rather than "don't," indicating a preferred course of action, "what
one should do if one desires to achieve moral perfection."[3]

Going beyond these, there are also rules specifically geared to enhance
the individual's awareness of what is right and redirect thinking toward a
more moral outlook. They prescribe sets of internal affirmations, personal
prayers, subjective resolutions, and memorized statements. Unlike all other
rules, which are formulated as imperatives, these are phrased in the first
person. Declarations of positive intent, they provide personal guidelines
for developing particular attitudes and ways of thinking. They go beyond
even supererogatory rules in that they focus on the welfare of all beings and
engage practitioners increasingly in universal ethics. Creating a culture of
pure altruism, affirmations and positive resolutions guide people to feel benevolence, sympathy, love, and compassion. They purify consciousness and
enhance goodness, supporting an increasingly non-ego-centered approach
to the world that encompasses positive attitudes that are not reciprocal but
one-sided in that they teach one to do good without expecting anything in
return.[4]

Taboos

The primary form of taboo in traditional Daoism is temporal. The annual
cycle, for example, is divided into the so-called eight nodes—two solstices,
two equinoxes, and four seasons' beginnings (between the solstices and
equinoxes)—and twenty-four solar periods of about two weeks each, named
after weather patterns such as "great heat," "slight cold," "great rain," and
"slight snow," but also include the solstices and equinoxes.

In matching activities to the seasonal cycle, Daoists follow the rules of
antiquity. First documented in the chapter "Monthly Commandments" of
the *Liji* (Book of Rites) of the fourth century BCE, one of the six classics
of Confucian orthodoxy, seasonal taboos have played an important role in
traditional Chinese culture and politics. Serving to create cosmic harmony

through correct seasonal behavior, they prohibited not only the commission but even the watching of impure activities and prevented all close contact among unrelated members of the opposite sex. In addition, they also guarded against the taking of improper foods that would violate the harmony of yin and yang, the balance among the food groups, and the law of moderation.[5] For example, since heaven and earth make the myriad creatures blossom in spring, one should in that season sleep early and rise at dawn, dress in the color green or blue, eat fresh, leafy things, and allow all beings to live, abstaining from killing. Spring was a time of giving and not of taking, of growth rather than decline, reward rather than punishment. All executions had to wait until the fall, and slaughter and hunting were severely limited, lest the cosmic powers be offended and send down disasters and calamities.

Beyond observing these seasonal taboos, medieval Daoists also performed regular rituals to enhance positive energy. Thus, as described in the *Zhaijie lu* (Record of Purgations and Precepts, DZ 464), they held major ceremonies or purgations at the eight nodes, in each case establishing cosmic patterns of goodness and clarity, thereby to extend good fortune, enhance well-being, create luminosity, prolong life, and bring about wide blessings.

In terms of particular days, the *Lingshu ziwen xianji* (Immortals' Taboos According to the Purple Texts Inscribed by the Spirits, DZ 179), a Highest Clarity document of the fifth century, outlines taboos regarding the proper conduct of aspiring immortals, focusing on the avoidance of certain foods.

> Do not eat the flesh of animals associated with the day of your parent's birth.
> Do not eat the flesh of animals associated with the day of your own birth.
> Do not eat the meat of armored [shell] animals like turtles or dragons on *jia* ["armored"] days.
> Do not eat pheasant on *bingwu* days.
> Do not eat the meat of black animals on *bingzi* days.
> Do not take alcohol on *yimao* [confusion] days.[6]

In each case, the taboo relates either to a birthday or to a day defined by a specific name. The names of the days (and also of years, months, and hours) go back to the Shang dynasty. They come in pairs of characters representing twelve stems of heaven and ten branches of earth. The twelve stems designate the stations of Jupiter, which revolves around the sun once in twelve years; they each come with a cyclical character and a zodiac animal (e.g., rat, ox, hare). The ten branches go back to the names of the ten days of the Shang week and are represented with another set of nominal characters that yet also have specific meanings. Thus, for example, "armored" animals such as shell fish or turtles should not be consumed on days that have the word "armor" in their name, alcohol should be avoided on days that spell "confusion," and sexual intercourse is highly recommended on days that contain the word for "increased reproduction."

After listing the taboos, the text also emphasizes that each violation has a direct effect on the physical well-being of the person, leading to nightmares and the appearance of specters, and causing "essence and body fluids to become coarse and violent, spirits and body gods to turn crazy and confused."

On a yet different levels, temporal taboos apply to the use of daily rhythms. Practically every Daoist text, from antiquity to today, states firmly that "from midnight to noon is the time of life-*qi*; from noon to midnight is the time of death-*qi*. Always practice during the time of life-*qi*."[7] Adepts accordingly are admonished to practice after midnight or in the early morning—a tendency still common among taijiquan and qigong followers today—avoiding the afternoons and early evenings because the *qi* is of yin quality.

In terms of space, Daoist taboos have mostly to do with the proper use of the natural environment and a respectful attitude toward the stars. Thus, the communal code of the early Celestial Masters, the *Laojun shuo yibai bashi jie*, contains over twenty rules that limit the use of natural resources. Members must avoid cutting trees, picking flowers, startling birds and beasts, disturbing worms and insects, and burning fields or forests without a good reason and proper ceremonial precautions. They must not expose their bodies to the natural forces, bathe in the nude, or urinate facing north, lest they offend the powers of heaven and earth.

Generally, they should live in a low-impact manner, be conservative in their use of food and drink, keep the roads and wells free from obstructions, and abstain from throwing harmful substances into public supplies of water and food. Their building of houses, graves, and roads should match the *qi* of the natural surroundings, and they should respect natural marshes and waterways, only minimally interfering with the topography of the land. Often the rules prohibit the "wanton" taking or despoiling of natural things, thus leaving the possibility open to use these resources as and when necessary, with respect and consideration. As Kristofer Schipper points out, the main theme of the rules is "that of respect, not only for nature, but for all men, women, and children, their ways of life, customs, and culture."[8]

The five precepts

Precepts form part of the culture of sin, where rules focus on social context and the group predominates. In China, this is borne out by the very word for "precept" (*jie*): its radical is the character for "spear" or "lance," next to the word "together," which represents the image of joined hands. The picture of the entire graph, thus, shows a phalanx of people with spears in hand guarding something or warning someone off.

The core precepts in Daoism come in a group of five, matching the four great moral rules against killing, stealing, lying, and sexual misconduct, with intoxication as a fifth. They occur in all major collections of Daoist rules, sometimes as a block, sometimes scattered in the larger context. Clearly present in Daoist texts from the fifth century onward, they closely imitate the five abstentions (*pañca sīla*) of Buddhism, which in turn go back to the five basic prohibitions for Brahmanic priests already used in Vedic times. They first appear as part of the *Pratimokṣa*, whose 250 rules the monks recited on each new and full moon as a formal declaration of intent and communal commitment. Here they feature right at the beginning: known as the four *pārājika* rules, they are punished by excommunication and expulsion from the order.[9]

Later the five precepts became also the foundation for lay practice. Any lay devotee had to observe them since they were the beginning of Buddhist cultivation and the outward sign that one strove to care for others, support the community of monks, and pursue the Eightfold Path to enlightenment. More than just prohibitions of bad conduct, they provided guidelines for good behavior, means to raise the conscience of practitioners to honor and cherish all that lives. Only a householder who based his behavior on them could ever hope to be a good Buddhist. The constitution of community, from an oral declaration of faith had shifted to the performance of morally impeccable behavior.

The most detailed outline of the five precepts appears in the *Taishang Laojun jiejing* (The Precepts of the Highest Lord Lao, DZ 784), which claims that they were revealed as part of the transmission of the *Daode jing* to the border guard Yin Xi. After a three-stanza poem in which Lord Lao encourages Yin Xi to follow Dao with his whole heart, the text gives a short list of the basic precepts, followed by an explanation that places them into a wider cosmological context. He says,

> Heaven has the five planets that keep it on its course. Earth has the five sacred mountains to provide stability. The seasons function according to the five phases, which stabilize their rhythm. The state has the five sage emperors who set up proper culture. And human beings have the five inner organs to keep them supplied with *qi*.

The implication is that the precepts in human behavior are as essential and as stabilizing as the different cosmological agents in the greater universe and form part of the cosmos as it functions in perfect harmony. More specifically, it links the five precepts with the five directions and the five inner organs, establishing a direct connection between moral failure and health.

> The precept to abstain from killing belongs to the east. It embodies the energy of Germinating Life and honors natural growth. People who harm and kill living beings will receive corresponding harm in their livers.
>
> The precept to abstain from stealing belongs to the north. It embodies the essence of Great Yin and presides over the resting and storing of nature. People who steal will receive corresponding calamities in their kidneys.

The precept to abstain from licentiousness belongs to the west. It embodies the material power of Lesser Yin and preserves the purity and strength of men and women. People who delight in licentiousness will receive corresponding foulness in their lungs.

The precept to abstain from intoxication belongs to the south and the phase fire. It embodies the energy of Great Yang and supports all beings in their full growth. People who indulge in drink will receive corresponding poison in their hearts.

The precept to abstain from lying belongs to the center and the phase earth; its virtue is faithfulness. People who lie will receive corresponding shame in their spleens.[10]

In each case, sickness and physical decline appear in the organ that matches the phase and direction of the precept violated, placing physical well-being in an immediate relationship to the moral quality of thoughts and actions. Just as the human body is part of the greater universe and matches heaven and earth in its constitution and functioning, so all activities undertaken in and through it have a direct impact on the cosmic pattern and reverberate back to take their toll or give their benefits. The body becomes the central agency in the understanding of the close connection between morality and well-being. It is an essential indicator of moral standing and the key vehicle for transformation, purified not only through proper insights and dedicated self-cultivation, but in the moral purity of everyday activities and thoughts.

Prohibitions and admonitions

The earliest systematic admonitions appear in the precepts associated with the *Xiang'er* commentary to the *Daode jing* of the third century. It presents nine rules outlining positive attitudes based on philosophical concepts, such as nonaction, desirelessness, nonaggression, weakness, and softness. The practice of these, too, was seen as closely related to physiological cultivation. Thus, "embracing clarity and stillness is a practice of *qi*-ingestion that serves to return human energy to its root and thus create a more stable sense of being in the world." Along similar lines, nonaction was an admonition for concrete behavior, intending that people should act without artifice and in a way that was not contrived or willful. It involved a quiet mind, a laying-to-rest of the passions, and a sense of moving along with the Dao.[11]

A combination of admonitions and prohibitions features in the Ten Precepts of Initial Perfection, first outlined in a medieval text of the same title (*Chuzhen shijie wen*) and to the present day the basic set of rules any Daoist receives. They include the five precepts as well as prohibitions of disloyal and unfilial behavior, ruining others for gain, slandering religious worthies, interacting with impure folk, and speaking carelessly or frivolously, in each case combined with a positive admonition. They are:

1. Do not be disloyal or unfilial, without benevolence or good faith. Always exhaust your allegiance to your lord and family. Be sincere in your relation to the myriad beings.
2. Do not secretly steal things, harbor hidden plots, or harm others in order to profit yourself. Always practice hidden virtue and widely aid the host of living beings.
3. Do not kill or harm anything that lives in order to satisfy your own appetites. Always behave with compassion and grace to all, even insects and worms.
4. Do not be lascivious or lose perfection, defile or insult the numinous energy. Always guard perfection and integrity, and remain without shortcomings or violations.
5. Do not ruin others to create gains for yourself or leave your own flesh and blood. Always work with Dao to help others and make sure that the nine family members all live in harmony.
6. Do not slander or defame the wise and good or exhibit your skill and elevate yourself. Always praise the beauty and goodness of others and never be contentious about your own merit and ability.
7. Do not drink wine beyond measure or eat meat in violation of the prohibitions. Always maintain a harmonious energy and peaceful nature, focusing on your duty in purity and emptiness.
8. Do not be greedy and acquisitive without ever being satisfied or accumulate wealth without giving some to others. Always practice moderation in all things and show grace and sympathy to the poor and destitute.
9. Do not have any relations or exchange with the unwise or live among the mixed and defiled. Always strive to control yourself; in your living assemble purity and emptiness.
10. Do not speak or laugh lightly or carelessly, increasing agitation and denigrating perfection. Always maintain seriousness and speak humble words, making Dao and virtue your main concern.[12]

More detailed and more specific prohibitions, moreover, make up the vast majority of the 180 precepts of the early Celestial Masters as well as of the more advanced rules of Complete Perfection still in use today. They tend to cover all contingencies of community life, from interaction among members through the consumption and treatment of food to personal integrity and spiritual propriety. They prohibit abortion and musical entertainment, the forming of cliques and political parties, ownership of slaves and cruelty to animals. They also pay close attention to personal interaction. For example, members must not spy into the affairs of others, use fancy or ambiguous language, scold others in anger, discuss the faults of others, criticize the teachers, claim great merit and virtue, or use words in other unseemly ways.[13]

Later monastic codes, in addition, contain practical injunctions and dignified observances, prescribing in detail how and when to perform a certain action. Injunctions regulate every aspect of life and physical activity, causing the submission of the individual to the communal pattern and enabling the complete transformation of personal reality toward a celestial level. Dignified observances, in addition, prescribe proper ritual behavior, such as how far to bow to whom and for how many times.

Thus, as outlined in the Complete Perfection manual *Qinggui xuanmiao* (Pure Rules, Mysterious and Marvelous, ZW 361),[14] monks and nuns are supposed to stand erect and straight, not leaning on one foot. They are to stand up whenever they face a master or a guest and when performing a rite. Even then, the movement should not be abrupt and they should not lean toward the master or infringe on his space. They are to sit with their backs straight, mostly kneeling on their heels but also using the cross-legged posture, especially for meditation exercises (being careful not to touch their neighbors' knees or elbows).

The sleeping posture, too, is prescribed: on one's side with the legs bent. One must not sleep in the nude, even during the heat of summer, and during sleep periods must refrain from talking. One must never lie down on the same mat or even in the same room as one's master, and one cannot retire before the master does so himself. It is also prohibited to lie down during the day, after a meal, or with one's head towards the fire. In getting up, monks—belonging to cosmic yang energy—should place their left foot down first, while nuns move first on the right.

All movements are to be executed gingerly and consciously, with a constant awareness of all body parts and all social situations. Monks or nuns must not step in front of someone reciting a scripture or bowing in prayer; they should tread carefully in all areas that house sacred activities. Never run or walk in haste, swing the arms wildly, walk about with lay followers, or go near socially suspect people.

The senses, too, are monitored. Monks must not look at unwholesome or sensually stimulating sights nor read improper texts, those of lay origin or representing other teachings. When walking inside monastic buildings or hallways, guard the eyes by looking only straight ahead, neither right nor left. When walking in the outside world, never look at pleasant sites and landscapes, entertainments and amusements, girls and colorful folk. Guard the ears and never listen to news or gossip, jokes or chatter, music or drama. Guard speech by avoiding loud or boisterous vocalization as much as gossip and idle chatter. Speak calmly and quietly, and never discuss the faults and mistakes of others, the affairs of state and the common world, matters of women and marriage, jokes and fictional stories, as well as secret techniques, secret talismans, magical spells, and the practices of other religious groups. Sleep periods, meals, and hours of rest are times of complete silence, and only words of prayer and recitation are to be uttered in the halls of worship. The master has to be addressed with utmost softness and politeness, and only in words suitable to the holy and honorable occasion.[15]

Resolutions

To ensure that these various rules do not just remain on the surface but form part of the depth of the Daoist's thinking and intention, they also use internal affirmations and resolutions. Accessible to both lay and monastic practitioners, these reorient thinking away from personal, ordinary concerns and toward oneness with Dao through the establishment of a heightened awareness of personal activities combined with a strong desire for universal salvation.

Unlike other rules, resolutions are formulated in the first person. They plant good fortune for self and others through the right attitude and are expressed as good intentions, positive prayers, and vows in one's heart. The key term here is *yuan*, literally "wish" or "pray," and also the translation of the Buddhist *pranidhāna*, that it, the bodhisattva vow: to be resolute in seeking liberation and assist all beings in their spiritual efforts.

The earliest Daoist set is found in the *Taiqing wushiba yuanwen* (Fifty-Eight Prayers of Great Clarity, DZ 187). The rules specify various situations, turning them into opportunities for strong communal and spiritual intent. For example,

1. When I encounter wives and children living in their homes, I shall pray that all may soon emerge from their prison of love, concentrate their intention, and observe the precepts.
2. When I encounter people drinking wine, I shall pray that all may control their gates of destiny and be far removed from bad fortune and disorder.
3. When I encounter young girls, I shall pray that all may guard their passions, restrain their sensuality, and set their wills and wishes on becoming wise.
4. When I encounter people engaging in licentiousness, I shall pray that all may get rid of their depraved thoughts and elevate their minds to the level of the prohibitions and precepts.[16]

The text continues by going through a whole gamut of possible types of people one may encounter: perfected and ordinary folk, good and bad, poor and rich, noble and humble, and those of numerous different ranks, from the emperor and his lords to the wise, recluses, and others. Having exhausted this, it moves on to different places: large states and small countries, busy marketplaces and quiet cottages, or high mountains and wide oceans, as well as to different activities people undertake. They could be performing religious observances, wandering about, talking to others, or eating and drinking. They could be hunting and fishing, ailing and growing old, or singing and dancing. Then again, there could be various natural phenomena one may encounter, such as snow and rain, wind and sunshine, or star light and rivers. All different situations trigger thoughts of universal salvation and good wishes for all beings. Adepts transform mentally to become as pure as the driven snow and as nurturing as the pouring rain, while their desires and sensory pleasures are scattered as if before a hard-blowing wind.

Resolutions further come in the form of daily verses, mental affirmations that raise the awareness of ordinary functions. For example, the Tang code *Daoxue keyi* (Rules and Observances for Students of the Dao, DZ 1126) prescribes that Daoist when they first wake up should think: "I pray that all living beings leave the path of error and enter awakening, bright and open like this bright morning." Upon hearing the bell that orders them to rise, they reflect: "May the great sound of the bell wake all to truth and perfection!" Verses like these echo Buddhist practices as outlined in the *Vinaya*, materials found in the *Huayan jing* (*Avatamsaka sutra*; Flower Garland Sutra), translated in the early fifth century, and are still used in Zen today.[17] They accompany all daily activities of Daoists, creating a sense of cosmic connection and universal well-wishing even during the most mundane of acts. Thus, when brushing the teeth, they are to mentally recite:

> The great yang [of the sun] harmonizes its energy
> To let spring arise and make the willow grow.
> Breaking a branch, I take it firmly
> So I can clean my body and my mouth.
> Studying Dao and cultivating perfection,
> May all go beyond the Three Worlds of existence!
> Swiftly, swiftly, in accordance with the statutes and ordinances![18]

Similarly, when combing their hair and tying their topknot, Daoists implore various deities of the hair and head to give them protection. Following ancient Chinese models, which saw hair as an expression of the person's essence and placed special significance on its grooming, the chant invokes first the Emperor of Heaven and the Five Elders, deities associated with the five phases in the five directions, to create a general cosmic connection. It then turns to the god of the Niwan Palace, who represents the center of the head and resides in the upper elixir field, as well as the Lord of Mysterious Florescence, a deity more specifically associated with hair.

The chant was sung while using a special comb known as the Comb of Mysterious Florescence when adepts groomed their hair at cock crow each morning. They took the comb out of its special box and ran it through their hair while facing north. Grooming properly was very important since, as the *Daoxue keyi* points out, a disheveled look made one appear like a commoner in grief, a sick or suffering person, someone poor and destitute, or just lazy and wayward. Daoist nuns, moreover, should avoid putting their hair up in the fashion of the world and should not use ornaments from precious metals. Also, any hair combed out should be kept in a clean place and burned in secret within nine days of the combing.[19]

Among more recent chants as found in the *Zhongji jie* (Precepts of Medium Ultimate, ZW 405), containing precepts for the second level of Complete Perfection ordination, there are several regarding the sacred robes, tablet, shoes, and headdress. To give one example, the chant for vestments runs,

> The scarlet robes of the precepts
> Are my body's ornaments.
> Cloudy skirts save from distress,
> Auroral pendants lift coveting inclinations.

All hundred limbs fully covered,
Never dare I not behave with gravity.[20]

Here vestments are described as divine agents of protection against distress and signs of the formal dignity of Daoists. Symbolizing the precepts and the importance of their mission in the world, the robes encourage the strong determination to maintain seriousness and always behave with gravity. Similarly, the ritual tablet is described as symbolic of Daoist dignity and propriety, encouraging reverence and deep respect, while the shoes become the central focus of various protective deities who stand by them and walk everywhere with them, creating good fortune and spreading positive energy into the world, thus making it a better place.

Notes

1 Gert 1970, 60–9; Green 1987, 94–6.
2 Ricoeur 1967, 53.
3 Heyd 1982, 182; Kant 1948, 57–8.
4 See Nagel 1970; Munroe 1996.
5 Emmrich 1992, 52, 72, 93–9.
6 Bokenkamp 1997, 365.
7 Kohn 2012, 75.
8 Schipper 2001, 84.
9 For the *Pratimokṣa*, see Prebish 1975. For its impact on Daoism, see Penny 1996.
10 Kohn 1994, 204–5.
11 Bokenkamp 1997, 51–2.
12 Kohn 2004, 255–6.
13 See Penny 1996.
14 ZW stands for *Zangwai daoshu* (Daoist Texts Outside the Canon), a mid-twentieth-century collection of Daoist materials. The number follows Komjathy 2002.
15 Kohn 2003; 2004, 97.
16 Kohn 2004, 104.
17 See Horner 1992, 2:391; Clearly 1984, 318; Kennett 1976, 302.
18 Kohn 2004, 106.
19 Kohn 2004, 107.
20 Hackmann 1931; Horner 1936.

References

Bokenkamp, Stephen R. 1997. *Early Daoist Scriptures*. Berkeley: University of California Press.
Clearly, Thomas. 1984. *The Flower Ornament Scripture*. Boston, MA: Shambhala.
Emmrich, Thomas. 1992. *Tabu und Meidung im antiken China: Aspekte des Verpönten*. Bad Honnef: Bock + Herchen.
Gert, Bernard. 1970. *The Moral Rules*. New York, NY: Harper & Row.
Green, Ronald M. 1987. "Morality and Religion." In *Encyclopedia of Religion*, edited by Mircea Eliade, 10:92–106. New York, NY: Macmillan.

Hackmann, Heinrich. 1931. *Die dreihundert Mönchsgebote des chinesischen Taoismus.* Amsterdam: Koninklijke Akademie van Wetenshapen.

Heyd, David. 1982. *Supererogation: Its Status in Ethical Theory.* Cambridge: Cambridge University Press.

Horner, I. B. 1936. *The Early Buddhist Theory of Man Perfected.* London: Williams and Norgate.

Horner, I. B. 1992 [1938]. *The Book of the Discipline.* 6 vols. Oxford: The Pali Text Society, Translation Series. Reprinted by Routledge and Kegan Paul.

Kant, Immanuel. 1948. *Fundamental Principles of the Metaphysics of Morals.* Edited by J. Paton. London: Hutchinson.

Kennett, Jiyu. 1976. *Zen Is Eternal Life.* Emeryville, CA: Dharma Publishing.

Kohn, Livia. 1994. "The Five Precepts of the Venerable Lord." *Monumenta Serica* 42:171–215.

Kohn, Livia. 2003. "Monastic Rules in Quanzhen Daoism: As Collected by Heinrich Hackmann." *Monumenta Serica* 51:367–97.

Kohn, Livia. 2004. *Cosmos and Community: The Ethical Dimension of Daoism.* Cambridge, MA: Three Pines Press.

Kohn, Livia. 2012. *A Source Book in Chinese Longevity.* St. Petersburg, FL: Three Pines Press.

Komjathy, Louis. 2002. *Title Index to Daoist Collections.* Cambridge, MA: Three Pines Press.

Munroe, Kristen Renwick. 1996. *The Heart of Altruism: Perceptions of a Common Humanity.* Princeton, NJ: Princeton University Press.

Nagel, Thomas. 1970. *The Possibility of Altruism.* Oxford: Clarendon Press.

Penny, Benjamin. 1996. "Buddhism and Daoism in *the 180 Precepts Spoken by Lord Lao.*" *Taoist Resources* 6.2:1–16.

Prebish, Charles S. 1975. *Buddhist Monastic Discipline: The Sanskrit Pratimoksha Sutras of the Mahasamghikas and Mulasarvastivadins.* University Park: Pennsylvania State University Press.

Ricoeur, Paul. 1967. *The Symbolism of Evil.* Boston, MA: Beacon Press.

Schipper, Kristofer M. 2001. "Daoist Ecology: The Inner Transformation. A Study of the Precepts of the Early Daoist Ecclesia." In *Daoism and Ecology: Ways within a Cosmic Landscape,* edited by Norman Girardot, James Miller, and Liu Xiaogan, 79–94. Cambridge, MA: Harvard University Press, Center for the Study of World Religions.

13 Karmic consequences

Taking all these various features of Daoist ethics together—the emphasis on virtue ethics, the organic and social understanding of evil, and the various forms of precepts—the structure underlying the entire system can be described as a form of moral determinism. Daoist as much as Buddhist ethical thinking assumes that the life and good fortune of the individual are determined by his or her moral actions, that there is "a law of just recompense in the world," which will make sure one reaps exactly as one sows. This viewpoint stands in contrast to materialistic accidentalism, according to which everything happens at random and is due entirely to chance; it is also significantly different from divine election or fatalism, which maintains that decisions about one's life and fate are made on a supernatural plane and have nothing to do with one's actions or intentions. Moral determinism takes into account three factors: the motivation or intention for one's action, the practical steps taken to carry it out, and the consequences resulting from it. Aside from providing a reasonable answer to the fundamental questions of fate and good fortune, it also encourages social conservatism—since social status is due to previously gained merit—and a certain degree of individualism since one is largely responsible oneself.[1]

While Daoists place great emphasis on inner nature and destiny as well as on the conditions and tendencies inherited from the ancestors, they also follow Buddhist thinking in considering intention as the central factor for all actions—mental, vocal, and physical. "By the law of karma, every intention good or bad will eventually be awarded or punished," often independent of the actual outcome of any given deed—or vice versa, the same outcome will be treated differently depending on the original intention of the perpetrator. A classic example is the case of the masturbating monk contrasted with one who has seminal emission during a dream. The former is guilty and punishable according to the *Vinaya*, the latter is not.[2] The goal of the path of self-cultivation with all its disciplines and meditations accordingly is to create a "choosing will" that is based on right knowledge and will always opt for actions in accordance with the best intention and the purest mind. "One wills to act because his actions are in conformity with his own inward state that has been cultured by awareness derived from right knowledge."[3] It is the purity of mind and moral quality of intention that brings about the desired soterio-logical results, i.e., improvement of karma and the eventual complete release from the chains of conditioned existence. However, on the path there, the religion also defines very specific rewards and punishments, relating deeds to effects and emphasizing the accumulative effect of persistent behavior—both negative and positive.

Moral rectitude

Creating the right mindset is the key factor in Daoist ethics, and one that has immediate reverberations for the person as well as consequences in his surroundings. As the *Chisongzi zhongjie jing* says:

> All human practice of good and commitment of evil begin with the mind. The mind is the seed of the five robbers and the root of the myriad evils. When the human mind intends to perform a good deed, then even before it is done, the good spirits already respond to it. In the same way, when it intends to commit a bad deed, even before that manifests, all the inauspicious spirits already know about it.[4]

The retribution for good and evil as they sprout in the human mind is thus immediate and irrevocable, an automatic process of energies of the same kind attracting and multiplying each other. This matches the overall structure of the cosmos, as outlined earlier, which works in a pattern of impulse and response, heaven reacting to living beings "like a shadow following its object" and earth responding to human actions "like an echo following a sound." These larger cosmic forces make their will known through signs. Heaven "brings forth thunder and lightning, rain and snow, intertwining rainbows, eclipses of the sun and the moon;" earth shows its displeasure by making "rivers and streams dry up and creating landslides and earthquakes, hurricanes and tornadoes, sandstorms and moving stones, floods and locust plagues, famines and droughts, epidemics and other disasters." In the same manner, on the individual level, good and evil spirits and energies attach themselves to the person and cause good or bad fortune in accordance with his or her intentions.

These intentions are rooted in the human mind and come in sets of five robbers and virtues that match each other. Greed and envy, the first robber, thus matches the virtue of benevolence or compassion, a sense of communion with others rather than one of opposition. Killing and murder, the second, are countered by righteousness or social responsibility, a feeling of personal involvement with the community rather than an egoistic urge. Violence and disorder, third, are alleviated by propriety or social awareness, the inherent code of behavior that keeps society functioning smoothly. Cheating and betrayal, fourth, connect to wisdom or fundamental honesty, a sense of personal worth and understanding that makes dishonesty unnecessary. And deception and flattery, the fifth robber, are held in check by trust or trust-worthiness, the feeling of mutual integrity and personal reliance on others. Thus, the five basic Confucian virtues, thus, form the fundamental basis for good moral behavior, each holding a particular form of evil in check and supporting the attainment of goodness in this world and salvation in the next.

In addition, the *Chisongzi zhongjie jing* specifies nine basic ways of thinking that will either create evil or enhance goodness. The nine thoughts of evil typically are directed toward the destruction or acquisition of someone else's property, such as his gold stash, high rank, beautiful wife, or big home. In case one is in debt to someone, a negative hope would be for the moneylender's death and the expiration of the debt. The worst possible thought of this sort, moreover, is the wish that one's parents may die early so that one can get one's hands on their estate.[5]

Where bad thoughts thus increase acquisitiveness and aggression, good thoughts encourage an attitude of humility and compassion, recognizing one's own limitations and wishing for the good of others. Highly practical and oriented toward this world, these thoughts yet follow the same line of reasoning and have a similar goal. Thus seeing someone prosper, one should realize that one's own good fortune still needs developing; seeing someone pile his rice in one storehouse after another, one should realize that one has not worked hard enough oneself; seeing another's big house, one should think that one can also be content in a small and humble cottage. In addition, in case of debt, whether one owns it or owes it, one should think only the best of people and value their efforts on one's behalf. Most of all, one should always remain conscious that one can never repay the kindness of the parents.

Thoughts like these are the foundation of wisdom, which will lead to personal contentment and material prosperity, and from here extend to personal success and the flourishing of family and descendants. Wisdom, moreover, comes in three forms: high, medium, and low, depending on one's inborn aptitudes. People of high wisdom have a spontaneous understanding of heaven and earth, knowing without being taught what the proper way of the universe is at any given moment. As a result, as the text has it,

> their hearts are full of love and compassion, and they do not take other people lightly. They know success and failure, understand when to advance and withdraw, distinguish life and death. People like these, although they may be poor, will in the end be rich; although they may be humble for a time, they will in the end be noble.[6]

People of medium wisdom are book learners, those who garner insight from the study of the scriptures. They follow the rules of ritual propriety, are filial and loyal, and never speak a harsh word. In their behavior, "they are always humble and withdrawing, warm and modest. Even if they do not study too much, they yet find awakening in the end; although they do not stand out, they will eventually arrive." People of low wisdom, finally, are devout believers. They follow the rules outlined in the codes and never take anything that is not freely offered. They tread carefully, realizing the dangers of the world, and try to protect their lives and bodies as best as they can. "Like this making continuous efforts, they never undergo loss or failure, never meet with obstructions or misfortune," as the text says.

This tripartite division into spontaneous knowers, book learners, and devout believers recalls the division in the *Lunyu* (Analects) of Confucius into four types of people:

> Those who are born with the possession of knowledge are the highest class of men. Those who learn and so, readily, get the possession of knowledge are the next. Those who are dull and stupid and yet endeavor to learn are the third. Those who are dull and stupid and yet do not learn—they are the lowest of people.[7]

Both ancient Confucians and medieval Daoists use this division to encourage learning and moral awareness toward the creation of an ideal society. Daoists in addition apply it in a more cosmic dimension as leading to perfection and even immortality while also providing detailed information about just what to expect from what kind of learning and moral activity, integrating Buddhist notions of karma and rebirth.

Rebirth patterns

The main Daoist text discussing these issues is the *Yinyuan jing* (Scripture of Karmic Retribution, DZ 336) of the sixth century. It closely matches information in Chinese Buddhist sources, such as the *Baoying jing* (Sutra on Retribution, T. 747), translated by Gunabhadra (394–468), a Brahmin from India who arrived in Guangdong in 435 and settled in Jiankang in 443.[8] These, in turn, go back to Indian Buddhist sources found in the Pali canon, notably the *Majjhima Nikaya* (Middle Length Sayings). The latter, for example, says,

> A person who refrains from taking life tends to be long-lived. A person who harms living creatures tends to be sickly; someone who refrains from harming living creatures tends to be healthy. A person who is irritable tends to be ugly; someone who is not irritable tends to be handsome.
>
> A person who is jealous tends to be weak; someone who is not jealous tends to be powerful. A person who is miserly tends to be poor; someone who is liberal tends to be rich. A person who is humble tends to be reborn in a good family; someone who is haughty tends to be reborn in an evil family. A person who does not consult the religious teachers for advice on what is good and bad tends to be ignorant; someone who does so tends to have great wisdom.[9]

Great wisdom, then, means the proper understanding of karmic patterns and ongoing efforts toward improvement.

The main difference between Buddhist and Daoist works is that the former describe behavior patterns within the larger realm of society, whereas the latter focus strongly on people's behavior toward religious institutions. Still, they all rest on the understanding that specific modes of behavior result in particular forms of rebirth and, vice versa, that one's present state of life comes from certain thoughts and actions in a former existence. Thus, killing leads to a period in hell and a short life during rebirth, while slander of the Three Treasures (Dao, scriptures, and masters or Buddha, sutras, and monks) results in dumbness and the inability to speak. Willful ignorance of moral rules and the divine law causes blindness in both eyes. Leprosy is a typical punishment for lack of faith in, or desecration of, the Three Treasures, while being born as a pig or other excrement eater comes from having engaged in gluttony and lasciviousness. Beyond this, coming to life in an ugly body is the result of lacking respect for the teaching; insanity is caused by an addiction to alcohol before. Enslavement, poverty, or low status come from stealing, a prison sentence from cruelty, a big belly and thin neck from pilfering food, and a lascivious nature and foul habits from having been a pig or dog in the past.[10]

In terms of positive effects, nobility comes from faith in the Three Treasures, long life from compassion and observance of the precepts, wealth from generous donations, brightness from devotion to the scriptures, a handsome and clean body from not drinking alcohol or eating smelly food, and a melodic voice from avid chanting of the holy texts. Vice versa, these various moral and devotional activities will result in good karma and a noble, prosperous, and happy rebirth in a future incarnation.

There is, moreover, a continuing cycle of karmic cause and effect. For example, someone who supports monasteries and is charitable over many lifetimes eventually ends up being born as an emperor. After death, he goes to heaven as an immortal, from where he may be reborn again as a sage, thus giving more support and charity to the religion and quite possibly becoming an emperor yet again. In a less fortunate case, someone may desecrate a temple or statue, as a result of which he falls into hell and is eventually reborn as a leper. Being an outcast and disgusting to others, he may develop anger and again come to desecrate a holy object, which causes him to enter the same cycle over and over again. Similarly, lack of respect for the scriptures causes one to be reborn as a fish. Fish, as everyone knows, drink, so one comes back into the world as an alcoholic. This alcoholism leads to insanity and a rebirth in mud and filth, as a result of which one may again show disrespect for the scriptures and come back once more as a fish. Stealing the goods of the Three Treasures, in an analogous cycle, one is reborn in a state of abject poverty or as a slave. Being destitute already, one is yet subject to robbery by brigands, thus driven to further extremes, one may well again steal from the opulent tables of the religious institution.[11]

In other words, the karmic pattern in many ways is a vicious circle, in which the "where to" becomes time and again the "where from," where cause and effect interact in continuous mutual dependence. The continued invocation of cycles, such as stealing→enslavement→hunger→stealing or no faith→madness→no faith, presents a terrifying picture of the endlessness of the karmic law. It is intended to give people strong motivation to kick their bad habits and overcome their sinful tendencies, to actively support and generously give to the religious institutions.

In addition, in terms of typical connections established, the obverse of the Golden Rule applies: what you do to another in one lifetime will be done to you the next! Thus people who kill, cutting short the life of others, will themselves be punished with a short life; those who steal, taking away the nourishment of others, will themselves be short of supplies; those who despise others will be short of stature, while those who respect their fellow beings will be tall and upright. Similarly, typical characteristics of animals are associated with particular forms of human behavior ever since the ancient Buddhist canon, creating a sense life's continuity throughout the different types and species of existence. Pigs and dogs are thus linked with lasciviousness and gluttony, foulness and excrement; wild beasts with hunger and cruelty; deer with fear and terror; and insects with the darkness of prison and the helplessness of disasters.[12]

In some cases, the punishment is not a continuation of the excessive behavior in a more lowly life form but a way of making restitution. Thus, for example, lasciviousness and debauchery may lead to rebirth as a duck, an animal known for its fidelity, while the inclination to pick marital fights may bring a new life as a pigeon or dove, a symbol of calmness and peace. Coveting the strength of others may lead to rebirth as an elephant, while the ruthless exploitation wreaked by an official on the people may cause him to be reborn as a water buffalo, pulled along by a ring in his nose and beaten with a stick. Other examples include rebirth in a crippled body due to cruelty to animals, failure to have children due to killing animal pups, and the loss of teeth due to taking delight in eating meat.[13] In other words, one either comes to embody the positive counterpart to one's evil actions or is forced to suffer from the very deeds one inflicted upon others. Caught in this unrelenting cycle, with potential pitfalls lurking everywhere, not to mention the possibility of falling into the hells or the realm of hungry ghosts, people come to see human birth as a precious commodity that must not be squandered with sensual pleasures or addictions to lust and drink but used to enhance learning, knowledge, and wisdom and reach for higher, subtler, and more morally upright levels of being.

Accounting of deeds

Unlike in India, where the execution of karmic rewards and punishments is part of a universal law and happens automatically, in China it is administered by celestial officials. From the very beginning of Chinese history, the otherworld was run bureaucratically, first by an "elaborate hierarchy of ancestors, each with his specific jurisdiction," later by various celestial administrators, such as the Director of Destiny who, as already noted in the *Shujing* (Book of History), kept "a record of the moral behavior of men and bestowed upon them either a long or a short life."[14] Bureaucrats and their offices are predictable and reliable, they record all deeds and intentions carefully and systematically, then issue the appropriate rewards and punishments. More than that, the ratio of deed to fate is known as recorded in systematic lists.

Thus, as the *Chisongzi zhongjie jing* outlines, one good deed makes spirit and intention calm and at peace, ten give the person strong physical energy, twenty keep the body free from affliction, thirty ensure that all one's goals are achieved as planned, and so on, until hundreds of good deeds will make certain that one's family brings forth noble, prosperous, and well honored people, if not actually sages and immortals. In reverse, one bad deeds makes one restless and nervous, ten cause one's energy to decline, twenty cause physical afflictions, thirty prevent one's plans from being realized, forty will put one in constant difficulties, and so on, until a hundred bad deeds see one in prison and even suffering execution and several hundred cause one's family to decline, become lowly, destitute, and criminal. In each case, good deeds accumulated result in the emergence of nobles, sages, or immortals in later generations, while

> "the misfortune that comes from accumulating evil overflows and causes calamities to strike for many generations to come. First the Director of Destiny subtracts time from the sinner's life expectancy, then the star that connects him to heaven tumbles and his body dies, then his soul is captured in the dark realm of Fengdu, and finally the misfortune hits his descendants of later generations.[15]

In a less mythological description, the effect of increasing numbers of good or bad deeds can be said to move parallel and expand in concentric circles. Beginning with influencing the person's mind and attitude toward life, they cause changes in his or her physical well-being, which in turn leads to a tendency to succeed or fail in one's ventures. This next leads to an increase or reduction in social standing, which in turn influences first the prosperity of the immediate family, then the rank and power of later generations. Looked at from this perspective, the system, although formulated in rigid lists and explained in mythological terms, has a certain psychological and sociological logic, through which it provides a framework for understanding one's present situation and shows a possible way out of the predicament.

The same list reappears three times in Daoist literature, expanding the system to widening circles of followers. Thus, the *Xuandu lüwen* (Rules of Mystery Metropolis, DZ 188) of the sixth century is a compilation of for the Celestial Masters community and concerns primarily lay followers of an organized group. The *Zhiyan zong* (Comprehensive Perfect Words, DZ 1033), a ninth-century compilation of Daoist practices of longevity and visualization, is a manual for individual practitioners, many of whom were aristocrats hoping to enhance their destiny. The *Ganying pian* (On Impulse and Response, DZ 1167), third, is an illustrative guide to moral merit and retribution from the Song dynasty. Compiled by a Confucian official, the text was printed first in 1164 and distributed by the emperor to convey the message that good and bad fortune do not come without reason. Reprinted many times and still popular today, it addresses a much wider circle of popular followers interested in improving their lives.[16]

Moving on, the exact listing and calculated accounting of deeds became part of popular culture, finding its way into the so-called morality books (*shanshu*), religious treatises for the general populace, often channeled by spirit mediums and ritual masters in direct contact with deities in charge of rewards and punishments. They were based on Confucian ethics mixed with the popular Buddhist concept of karma and Daoist beliefs in longevity and immortality. While Song works tended to emphasize compassion and piety, texts published since the Ming have placed an increasing emphasis on practical moral teachings. Inspired by these, people began to keep ledgers of merit and demerit (*gongguo ge*), recording each good or bad deed in an assigned place and thus keeping track of where exactly they stood in the greater scheme of karmic consequences. More specifically, 3,000 good deeds were believed to grant one a son, while 10,000 would allow one to pass the imperial examination that served as the gateway to higher office. Anyone could become a virtuous sage if he or she followed this practical science of moral cultivation. While for individuals these morality books and ledgers of merit were a concrete way of clarifying moral obligations and of calculating progress in moral cultivation, for the court printing them, they served not only to accumulate merits but also to reinforce values that maintained societal stability under imperial rule.[17]

Another way of accounting for deeds involves the attachment of precise numerical values to specific deeds. This rests on the calculation that 120 years, the biological human life span and ideal life expectancy in ancient China, comes to 43,800 days. From this, then, either a unit or a period of reckoning are subtracted for each bad deed: the unit being one or three days of life while the period ranges from 100 to 300 days. While most deductions match the crime, especially among the monastic codes as documented in the Tang work *Fengdao kejie*, certain offenses we would describe as highly disparate in nature are punished with the same severity.

For example, the highest subtraction of twelve periods or 3,600 days is imposed on failure to observe the proper order of rank or ritual, a rather serious infringement on community harmony, but also on the wearing the wrong type of underwear. Similarly placing adornments on one's shoes is punished with almost the same subtraction as not following the proper ritual procedures during the noon meal. Not folding one's vestments properly is on the same level as not staying within the proper order of ritual rank. Physical actions and details of daily routine, therefore, although they might seem minor to us, are valued as highly as acts that involve the immediate performance of ritual or the upholding of the proper order of ranks.[18]

At the same time, actions that we would consider seriously disturbing to the order are valued rather less. For example,

> The residences and sleeping places of all Daoists, whether male or female, should be surrounded by four walls and built for single occupancy. There should not be several bunks [in the same room] either in front or behind each other. Whether sitting or sleeping, Daoists should always be alone and one per bed. Failure to comply carries a subtraction of 120 [days of life].

Punished only with 120 subtracted days, this ranks on the same level as not keeping the well or the privy clean or behaving arrogantly toward ordinary people. It is only slightly more serious than leaving one's water pitcher uncovered, a truly minor offense in our understanding that will not affect the entire community as much as a breach of celibacy might.

Any failure, moreover, can be made up by cultivating the proper positive attitudes, usually expressed in wishes or prayers the recluses are encouraged to have on behalf of the wider populace. Thus,

> All Daoists, whether male or female, whenever [encountering] fords and stream crossings, roads and ways that are blocked and impassable, or bridges and overpasses under construction or repair, should always be mindful and develop the good intention that all living beings, past and future, should be free from obstacles and obstructions. May they all attain good fortune without measure! This attitude carries an addition of 420 [days of life].[19]

Daoists can, therefore, not only estimate where they came from in terms of personal karma and where they are likely to be headed, but they can also figure out just how many deeds it will take to get there and how certain attitudes and behaviors will play out. They can both increase and diminish their life expectancy and good fortune in accordance with the rules and calculations. Placed in a precarious position within the larger cosmic framework, in strict accordance with the understanding of moral determinism, Daoists have the power to influence the quality and length of their lives, not to mention their status of rebirth and the good fortune of their families and states. More vulnerable than ordinary people, who too are subject to the same principles of supernatural rewards and punishments, they must watch not only over their ritual and religious acts but also be conscious of every physical detail of their day-to-day lives and try to maintain a positive and compassionate attitude to all around them. Daoists serving as models for the bulk of humanity, are idealized and thus more vulnerable figures under the sway of the celestial administration.

Notes

 1 Varma 1963, 26–7; 42–6.
 2 Holt 1981, 53–5; Sadhatissa 1970, 74; Gombrich 1971, 246.
 3 Holt 1981, 67.
 4 Kohn 1998a, 855.
 5 Kohn 1998a, 856.
 6 Kohn 1998a, 857.
 7 The passage is found in *Lunyu* 16.9. For a complete translation, see Lau 1979.
 8 Demiéville et al. 1978, 252.
 9 Kalupahana 1975, 129
10 Kohn 1998b, 22.
11 Kohn 1998b, 25.
12 Kohn 1998b, 16.
13 Kohn 1998b, 28–9.
14 Shahar and Weller 1996, 4; Eberhard 1971, 179.
15 Kohn 1998a, 846.
16 Translated Suzuki and Carus 1973.
17 See Brokaw 1991.
18 Kohn 1998a, 854.
19 Kohn 2004, 122, 179–80.

References

Brokaw, Cynthia. 1991. *The Ledgers of Merit and Demerit: Social Change and Moral Order in Late Imperial China*. Princeton, NJ: Princeton University Press.
Demiéville, Paul, Hubert Durt, and Anna Seidel. 1978. *Repertoire du canon bouddhique sino-japonais, edition de Taisho*. Tokyo: Maison Franco-Japonaise.
Eberhard, Wolfram. 1971. "Fatalism in the Life of the Common Man in Non-Communist China." In *Moral and Social Values of the Chinese*, edited by Wolfram Eberhard, 177–89. Taipei: Chengwen.
Gombrich, Richard F. 1971. *Precept and Practice: Traditional Buddhism in the Rural Highlands of Ceylon*. Oxford: Clarendon.
Holt, John C. 1981. *Discipline: The Canonical Buddhism of the Vinayapitaka*. New Delhi: Motilal Banarsidass.
Kalupahana, David J. 1975. *Causality: The Central Philosophy of Buddhism*. Honolulu: University of Hawaii Press.
Kohn, Livia. 1998a. "Counting Good Deeds and Days of Life: The Quantification of Fate in Medieval China." *Asiatische Studien/Etudes Asiatiques* 52:833–70.
Kohn, Livia. 1998b. "Steal Holy Food and Come Back as a Viper: Conceptions of Karma and Rebirth in Medieval Daoism." *Early Medieval China* 4:1–48.
Kohn, Livia. 2004. *The Daoist Monastic Manual: A Translation of the Fengdao kejie*. New York, NY: Oxford University Press.
Lau, D. C. 1979. *The Analects by Confucius*. London: Penguin.
Saddhatissa, H. 1970. *Buddhist Ethics*. London: Allen & Unwin.

Shahar, Meir, and Robert P. Weller, eds. 1996. *Unruly Gods: Divinity and Society in China*. Honolulu: University of Hawaii Press.

Suzuki, D. T., and Paul Carus. 1973 [1906]. *Treatise on Response and Retribution*. LaSalle, IL: Open Court Publishing.

Varma, Vishwanath P. 1963. "The Origin and Sociology of the Early Buddhist Philosophy of Moral Determinism." *Philosophy East and West* 13:25–48.

Part V
Perfection

14 Selfhood and spontaneity

All this leads to a unique understanding of the self in Daoism. The self is inherently a modern Western concept, something to be lost or found that requires the dichotomy of subject and object. It is a complex and intricate phenomenon, made up from personal identity, social relations, and specific ways of understanding the cosmos or larger universal connection. In Western thought, it goes back to René Descartes (1596–1650) with his emphasis on reason and the autonomy of the individual vis-à-vis God and nature. To him, self meant the inherent "thinking substance" of the person, the confirmation of existence due to thought (*cogito ergo sum*).[1]

In his wake, John Locke (1632–1704), a key thinker of the Enlightenment, created a new theory of mind that laid the foundation for modern concepts of the self. He calls it

> that conscious thinking thing (of whatever substance, made up of spiritual or material, simple or compounded, it matters not), which is sensible, or conscious of pleasure and pain, capable of happiness or misery, and so is concerned for itself, as far as that consciousness extends.

The self was thus seen mainly as a function of consciousness—which was not originally sinful but a blank sheet—a personal sense of reflection and awareness created actively by the thinking, rational ego. "Only that of which we were conscious belonged to our identical self."[2]

David Hume (1711–1776) was the first to deny the constant, substantial nature of the self, seeing it instead as a bundle or "collection of impressions and ideas, memories and personality patterns," comparing it to an ever-flowing river. This trend continued with Immanuel Kant (1724–1804), who found that an 'I' was necessary for empirical, coherent awareness, consisting of a certain level of consciousness determined by personal representation in relationships and integrated patterns.[3]

While modern philosophers such as Søren Kierkegaard (1813–1855), Gilbert Ryle (1900–1976), Jean-Paul Sartre (1905–1980), and Roderick Chisholm (1916–1999) have continued to speculate about the nature of the self in terms of substance and knowledge, psychologists have worked with it experimentally and divided it into various kinds. Thus, Sigmund Freud (1856–1939), the father of psychoanalysis whose vision has inspired generations of psychologists, both as followers and opponents, sees it as tripartite: id, ego, and superego. The id is our instinctual substructure, an unconscious and impulsive part, based on inherited, biological factors; it includes basic drives such as libido and aggression. The ego is the modification of the id under the impact of personal reality; it applies reason and has both conscious and subconscious parts, the latter including automated responses to outer and inner impulses. The superego is the higher self, characterized by internalized social values and ethics, the ideal vision of oneself that controls impulses.[4]

The American philosopher and psychologist William James (1842–1910), too, divides the self into three kinds: material, social, and spiritual. They include the way we define ourselves through body, clothes, and possessions; through family, friends, work, culture, and other relationships; as well as through God and the universe, a sense of inner wholeness and self-satisfaction. Each level involves multiple identities, defined as evolving and adaptable building blocks of the self. Together they create an "empirical self," the sum total of all that I can call mine. James also makes the important distinction of self as subject and as object: myself as thinking and doing certain things versus myself being evaluated and developed in specific ways.[5]

Selfhood

Both ancient and modern Chinese express the notion of "self" with *ziji*, a term that consists of two characters. These two characters, although frequently used interchangeably and both indicating "self," in their original definition and also when they are used separately in philosophical Daoist and Confucian documents, connote two different visions of the self: an organized and object-oriented selfhood (*ji*) versus one a contained and receptive spontaneity (*zi*).

Both words for "self" are radicals in the Chinese writing system, which means they are fundamentally meaningful parts of the Chinese language. The graph for *ji*, selfhood, originally represents "the warp and weft of a loom" and shows "two threads running transversely and another running lengthwise."[6] From its very beginning, *ji* therefore shows an organized structure, something one can see on the outside, something that can be made and controlled. Beyond its meaning of "selfhood," the character is used already in oracle bone inscriptions as the sixth of the ten earthly stems, a group of ten characters which were used to indicate the names of the ten-day week in the Shang dynasty. As sixth stem, *ji* is associated with the center of things and later with earth among the five phases. It is the organized, structured center of the world: what one thinks of as self.

Grammatically *ji* is used primarily in the object position. One can "right one's selfhood," as Mencius says (2A7); one can "conduct oneself," as Confucius has it in the *Lunyu* (5.15, 13.20). One can also compare others to one's self; and one can search for humanity or virtue within it. *Ji* as the self is therefore an object among other objects, it represents an organized person among other people. In this latter aspect, the word is often contrasted with *ren*, literally "people," but often just indicating others. "I shall not let the fact afflict me that others do not know my self," Confucius says repeatedly, also formulating the Golden Rule using the same contrast: "Do not do unto others what you would not wish done to your self."[7]

In the same vein, *ji* is often explained through, and used similarly as, the personal body (*shen*). This word, whose pictogram shows a human figure with a protruding belly, like *ji* occurs as a pronoun indicating oneself as opposed to others. Also like *ji*, the personal body is a constructed and organized object, something that develops and grows, not something one is equipped with spontaneously.[8] Daoists, as noted earlier (see ch. 4 above), contrast this socially defined notion of body as self with the naturally unfolding and much less consciously constructed physical body (*xing*), the basic shape or form one has in this world. Where the physical body is a basically cosmic entity, the personal body and thus the self is a human construction, formed through likes and dislikes, passions and desires, needs and emotions that the individual ego develops toward the objects of the world. In this sense, the personal body describes just as much an object-oriented, organized selfhood as that expressed with the word *ji*.

Both Daoist and Confucian thinkers assert that this psychologically developed self has to be adjusted, subdued, limited, cultivated, or even destroyed. "To subdue the self and recover full propriety constitutes benevolence," Confucius says, and continues, "If a person can, even for one day, subdue his self and recover full propriety, all under heaven will recover benevolence through him."[9] Similarly the *Daxue*, one of the famous "Four Books" of Neo-Confucianism, sees the key to human development in cultivating the personal body.

> In the old days those who wished to make bright virtue radiate throughout the world would begin by putting their states to good order. To put their states in good order they would first harmonize their families. To harmonize their families, they would first cultivate their personal bodies. To cultivate their personal bodies, they would first make their minds sincere.[10]

The *Daode jing* similarly advocates the control and reduction of the personal body, which it finds an outright affliction to life and major obstacle to one's attainment of the Dao.

> The reason why I have great afflictions is that I have a personal body.
> If I had no personal body, what afflictions would I have? (ch. 20)

That the personal body here indicates the object-oriented selfhood and not the physical body is made clear in a later interpretation, found in Sima Chengzhen's *Zuowang lun*. He says,

> "Not having a body" does not refer to not having this particular physical form. It rather means that the bodily structure is unified with the Great Dao, that one is never influenced by glorious positions and does not seek after speedy advancement. It is to be placid and without desires.[11]

In the same vein, the *Daode jing* insists that the sage should disregard his self and put himself in the background (ch. 7), that he should withdraw as soon as his work is done (ch. 9). More strongly than this, the *Zhuangzi* even pleads for the complete dissolution of all selfhood: "The perfect man has no self!" it states emphatically (ch. 1).

In other words, the self as an entity determined through the senses and defined in the relationship to outside objects, other people, and social demands should be cultivated, subdued, and eventually overcome. Doing so means becoming placid and without desires, a state free from strong emotional reactions and self-conscious evaluations, which opens the path toward a fluid way of being in the world, an inner sense of wholeness and ease.

Spontaneity

This, then, is expressed with the other word for "self," *zi*. The term indicates an individual's spontaneous inner being, the qualities one is endowed with by nature. Like the physical body as form, the spontaneous self is cosmic. It is the way one is spontaneously, the natural so-being of oneself, the way nature or heaven has made us before we develop ego-consciousness and desires for objects.

The graph for *zi* goes back to a pictogram that shows a human nose.[12] The nose is the most protruding part of the face and as such a person's central characteristic. Still today, people in East Asia point to their noses when they want to indicate themselves. And yet, the nose, however much it represents oneself, cannot be seen or known directly. One can only guess at the shape of one's own nose with the help of a mirror. It is something one is equipped with by nature, something one feels and uses, but cannot shape or control. The nose, as the center of oneself, is part of one's basic makeup; it points back at one's natural so-being, at the spontaneity of one's existence.

Grammatically *zi* is used exclusively in the reflexive position, i.e., before the verb; it never occurs as object.[13] Whatever one does, if done by the *zi*, is done of itself and by the self as a spontaneous, independent organism, not by an organized object-centered self. In this sense, the *zi* can give rise to an inner feeling of shame, as Confucius notes (12.23); it can have a spontaneous inclination toward good or back fortune, as Mencius indicates (2A4); and, as the *Zhuangzi* says, it can develop spontaneous knowledge or attain true spontaneity within (ch. 6).

The word *zi* in its reference to spontaneous so-being is most clearly present in the compound *ziran*, literally "self-so," but commonly translated as "naturalness" or "spontaneity." As such, it sometimes refers to the spontaneous part of the self. In Confucian texts the term denotes the given nature of the individual, that within a person not artificially constructed or controlled. In Daoist documents, it is immediately linked to Dao, indicating its ultimate independence and freedom from definition through relationships. Beyond that, the term refers to the spontaneous activity of all creatures, a way of being themselves that brings them most closely to Dao. The perfected in the *Zhuangzi*, free from evaluations and personal feelings, "just lets things be naturally the way they are and does not try to help life along" (ch. 5). By remaining in nonaction and free from thinking, feeling, and acting, everything will move along as naturally intended (ch. 21). There will be nothing that is not done, as the *Daode jing* repeatedly insists (chs. 37, 48).

The dichotomy between an organized, conscious, and object-oriented selfhood that has to be suppressed or cultivated and the true spontaneity of nature within pervades the understanding of the self in traditional and modern China. The spontaneous so-being of nature functions freely and constantly. Originally part of the depth of the human psyche, it cannot be known, felt, or manipulated. Overlaid increasingly by a mode of consciousness that centers on outer objects and expresses itself in egoistic desires, human beings tend to hide the spontaneity of their true nature under an organized selfhood, a socially defined entity that depends on outside stimulation and comparison for its very existence.

Only through prolonged efforts of cultivation and control of the formal selfhood can the spontaneity of nature be recovered. There is no way, really, to socialize people without giving them an organized selfhood or socially defined identity: it is a necessary stage of human development. In fact, were it not for the existence of the ego-centered self, neither Confucians nor Daoists would have anything to teach to the world. Both philosophies instruct their followers to find the True Way—true humaneness for Confucians, oneness with Dao for Daoists. Both emphasize the difficulty of the undertaking and the obstacles to be overcome. Spontaneity or naturalness, although an inherent human quality, is not easy to realize. While always and originally present, it is yet the endpoint of long and arduous training, the ultimate attainment of perfection within this world.

Social application

This mistrust of a strong, organized self in conjunction with the preference for naturalness in traditional China has led to a variety of social applications, a pervasive and continued effort to develop and perfect people's social awareness over their personal desires. In contrast to the West, there is really no true problematic of the individual self in ancient China. Questions like "Who am I?", "What am I?", or "Why am I?" are not asked. There is no sense of critical self-reflection nor is there the true tragic of an individual faced by an unresolvable dilemma. For some, there is no I at all as "self-identical substance," no self as a "fundamentally singular and independent entity."[14]

Chinese autobiography documents the point. Although an ancient and varied genre, it does not encourage critical self-questioning or self-analysis. The earliest autobiographies merely consisted of short summaries of a person's life. They were extremely schematic and made much use of comparison with traditional models. The individual emerges only as the conglomerate of different standardized patterns. Later, in the Song dynasty, a more complex and much longer kind of autobiography developed in the form of a chronological outline. Still, the predominant mode was a stereotypical description of the person and his actions, emphasizing the relation to classical models rather than individual idiosyncrasies. Critical evaluations and questioning searches of the self do not appear before the contact with Western culture.[15]

The same tendency toward stereotype and the predominance of established models appears in the literary self. Chinese literature does not dwell on quests for self-knowledge, extended self-pity, or self-mortification. Rather than facing severe moral choices, the protagonist of traditional Chinese fiction only follows the lessons of the ancients, his actions prescribed by his social situation. A hero, for example, who—in ignorance of the fact—was raised by the man who was responsible for exterminating his native family has no qualms whatsoever in killing his benefactor when he learns the truth. His social position as a member of his original family trumps his gratitude to his adoptive father. There is no self-questioning: the social role determines behavior and, one presumes and hopes, internal feelings. At the same time, characters that show some critical or assertive individuality tend to be villains and outsiders. They are shown to be self-obsessed, causing their own destruction by pursuing their egocentric desires. Positive heroes, on the other hand, practice self-denial for the sake of a larger good, be it Dao, world, society, or just the fulfillment of duty.[16]

The same rejection of independence and the individual in favor of community and social coherence is also found in traditional Chinese law, as it developed in the Confucian state. Entirely aimed at restoring social harmony after a breach, laws only served to determine punishment in regard to the severity of the disruption. In contrast to Buddhist karmic thinking, they disregarded whether the deed was done with or without harmful intent. In law, the individual did not count—only his or her impact on the whole of society. The same attitude is also evident in the high emphasis placed on confession in criminal proceedings. Wrung, if necessary, from the accused by torture, the confession was the essential testimony that a breach in social harmony had occurred and at the same time the first step to restitution. Its importance lay not in proving the guilt or innocence of anyone involved in a crime, but in the need to heal the network of social harmony.[17]

The high regard for social harmony is the concrete expression of the particular Confucian training and indoctrination that aimed primarily at the dissolution of the ego-centered self in favor of an understanding of oneself as a social figure, a servant to society and the world, a part of a larger whole. Confucius himself has described his efforts as a continuous process of life-long learning, and his followers have never tired of pursuing "a self-realization in which man fulfills all that is distinctly human while participating in the creative work of heaven and earth."[18]

Thus, adulthood in Confucianism means an unceasing progression toward "becoming human." In the end, after seventy years of effort, as Confucius says of himself, one can finally "follow one's hearts desire without transgressing the boundaries of right" (*Lunyu* 4.5). To be fully human in this context means to have internalized the rules of society to such a degree that one fulfills them spontaneously. The organized ego that had to learn, the self that related to society as an object among other objects, is dissolved. Society, the cosmic order, and the individual self are integrated into one great harmony. The "joy of a childlike heart," as Mencius describes it (4B12), the simplicity of naturalness, is found in the complete integration of self and society, in the harmonization of what one is and what one ought to be. The aim of Confucian cultivation is thus "to quiet down or curb selfish desires, while directing active emotions toward unselfish ends." Thus, social harmony and universal spontaneity are realized.[19]

This harmony ultimately means a loss of organized selfhood in favor of a larger unity: it means giving up personal thoughts, feelings, and actions. The individual is gradually freed from the object relationship to self and world, desires are dissolved, emotions lessened, the will of the ego is loosened. Where there was an ego-centered will before, now all willing is based on something higher and larger. As Herbert Fingarette notes,

> While the will that I direct toward the Way is personal regarding its initial locus of energy and control over its arousal, intensity, direction, and persistence, when it comes to the *ground* on which I choose and justify the direction for my will, and on which I elect to maintain that will vigorously and wholeheartedly, that ground is in no way one that has reference to me personally.[20]

The same concept, somewhat more cosmologically oriented, is also voiced in Guo Xiang's commentary to the *Zhuangzi*. He says,

> This life of mine, I did not bring it forth. Thus all that occurs throughout my life of perhaps a hundred years, all my sitting, getting up, walking, and staying, all my movements, all my quiet, all hurrying and resting of mine—even all the feelings, characteristics, knowledge, and abilities I have—all that I have and all that I don't have, all that I actively do and all that happens to me: it is never me, but principle only.
>
> (ch. 6)

The vocabulary varies, and where Confucians emphasize the importance of propriety and social harmony, Daoists stress principle and Dao. Still, the structure remains the same. Self-realization in ancient China meant the dissolution of the *ji* and the development of the *zi*, the giving up of selfhood in favor of naturalness or spontaneity, whether defined as overarching harmony and social integration or Dao and nonaction. Either way, the Chinese propose to reduce the limited ego of organized self and encourage a dissolution of personal identity in something wider and greater.

Object and observing self

A very similar distinction appears in contemporary psychological terms as the contrast between the "object self" and the "observing self." As described by Arthur Deikman, the object self is part of the natural evolution of human consciousness. At birth, the world is nothing but a blur of confusing sensory impressions of varying kind and intensity. In the first phases of life, human beings use their bodies as templates to understand the world. Their primary experience is based on the senses and expressed in physical needs or desires. The first rudiments of a self develop between these two. An object perceived with the help of the senses is understood entirely through the body. A first abstract, yet humanly fundamental concept emerges: object = body = self.[21] One's very own body, the agent that processes the sense data and translates them into needs and desires, is seen as an object in itself, as one more object to receive stimuli from and direct wishes toward.

Consciousness of the object self can be divided according to three distinct functions: thinking, feeling, and acting. The thinking self contains one's conception of who and what one is. It is a "me" defined by society and culture, it includes all the characteristics one attributes to oneself: tall, ugly, strong, shy, and so on. Thinking is bound by relativity and the dependence of opposites. It is based on measurements and comparisons, on the establishment of categories and classifications. The feeling self contains the emotions: anger, fear, worry, sadness, joy, and so on. All these are reactions of feeling toward a given object or objective. They are intimately linked with desire. I am joyful because something I have desired has actually happened; I am anxious lest something I desire now will not develop; and I am sad or angry because some object of my desire has passed away. The feeling self is the self of desire; it classifies the world according to whether it is desirable or undesirable at any given moment and reacts with feelings and emotions accordingly.

The acting or functional self contains all that we do. It is an awareness of oneself as an acting individual. I know that I do; I realize the capacity I have to act in the world. I feel my body as an instrument of outer activity; I direct my feet and hands, my facial muscles, as well as my vocal chords in a particular direction, producing a particular effect. The acting self manipulates the world around it. It pulls objects and objectives toward it or pushes them away. These three taken together constitute the object self. What thinking, feeling, and acting have in common is their conceptual basis of the world and the self as objects to be evaluated, classified, and manipulated in certain ways. They constitute the hard core of the ego in the center of the person, a core that is the measure of all things, yet always remains an object itself.[22]

Now, there is originally nothing wrong with developing a healthy sense of self-preservation and of conceiving of the world and oneself as objects. In fact, it is a necessary stage of human development, an evolutionary phase that is essential for survival of both individual and culture. On the other hand, as children develop, so evolution proceeds further. The vision of the world and oneself as objects eventually becomes only one of several possible modes of self-conception, from which the individual moves on to develop a greater acceptance of, and respect for, other human beings, attaining mutuality, harmony, and a fruitful inter-individual vision of life and the world.

This development eventually leads to another mode of self-awareness or personal consciousness, what Deikman calls the "receptive mode." A way of perception that diminishes the boundaries between self and world, it provides a sense of merging with the environment. An example would be the appreciation of a piece of music or a work of art. Looking upon anything artistic as a mere object one is bound to be bored by it, left cold and untouched. In order to really appreciate art, people must open themselves to it and merge with it to a certain degree. The same holds true for more intense relationships among people. No true understanding can take place if individuals keep themselves shut into a world of mere objects.[23]

The observing self, then, is the fulfillment of the receptive mode. Originally at the center of one's being, this self is the deep inner root of human existence, an ultimate and transcendent sense of being alive within. It is there, yet cannot be consciously known, felt, or manipulated: it cannot be objectified in any way. Rather than thinking, feeling, and doing things actively and with regard to an object, the observing self allows things to happen spontaneously. Instead of as objects, people then see themselves and the world as flowing streams of energy, intensely alive and perfectly individual, yet ultimately interconnected in a cosmic whole. The observing self has no limits; it is transcendent and yet most deeply immanent in all.

The observing self as Arthur Deikman describes it is in many ways similar to Abraham Maslow's concept of Being-cognition. Being-cognition is the opposite of Deficiency-cognition. Where the latter is constantly aware of something missing, something needed, the former is content and calm, receptive as it were, and merely observing. Being-cognition allows a wholeness of perception that is in itself enriching. Maslow claims that the more someone learns to perceive and act without Deficiency- determined purposes and remains free from value-judgments, the more beautiful, meaningful, and good the world becomes to this person.

Although perception in the receptive mode of consciousness is unifying and free from classification, thinking still takes place. Only, instead of clearcut value judgments and the evaluation of things as objects, there is now a sense of fluidity of values, openness to other points of views. Similarly, there is still feeling, but there are no emotions that are intrinsically related to the desires of the ego. In a state of Being-cognition, Maslow says, "the only possible emotions would be pity, charity, kindliness, and perhaps sadness or Being-amusement with the shortcomings of the world."[24]

Still, people in this state can and do act in the world. But their actions are not based on single-minded categorizations nor on ego-centered emotions. They act for the best of all, they do a job well for its own sake, and in general give others' needs precedence over their own. As Deikman says,

> There is no solution to the problem of meaning except to transcend the motivations of the object self. The path to that transcendence is service— real service, which means serving the task and, ultimately, serving what mystics call the truth.[25]

Notes

1 Taylor 1989, 147.
2 Locke quote in Locke 1997, 307; Taylor 1989, 162. Last statement from Mol 1976, 56.
3 Kupperman 1984, 37, 45.
4 See McLeod 2008.
5 Perinbanayagam 2012, 8–9.
6 Fazzioli 1986, 34; Kohn 1992, 129.
7 *Lunyu* 1.16, 4.14, 14.3, 15.18; 12.1; Fingarette 1979, 131.
8 Dobson 1974, 414–15, 599–600.
9 *Lunyu* 12.1.
10 Munro 1969, 91–6.
11 Kohn 2010, 95, 151.
12 Fazzioli 1986, 29; Kohn 1992, 131.
13 Dobson 1974, 751.
14 Kubin 1990; Trauzettel 1977.
15 Bauer 1964.
16 Lau 1985, 381.
17 Trauzettel 1977, 347–50.
18 DeBary 1985, 332.
19 Tu 1985, 115; DeBary 1985, 332.
20 Fingarette 1979, 135
21 Deikman 1982, 68.
22 Deikman 1982, 92–4.
23 Deikman 1982, 71.
24 Maslow 1964, 82–3.
25 Deikman 1982, 114–15.

References

Bauer, Wolfgang. 1964. "Icherleben und Autobiographie im älteren China." *Heidelberger Jahrbücher* 8:12–40.
DeBary, William Th. 1985. "Neo-Confucian Individualism and Holism." In *Individualism and Holism: Studies in Confucian and Taoist Values*, edited by Donald J. Munro, 331–58. Ann Arbor: University of Michigan, Center for Chinese Studies.

Deikman, Arthur J. 1982. *The Observing Self: Mysticism and Psychotherapy*. Boston, MA: Beacon Press.

Dobson, W. A. C. H. 1974. *A Dictionary of Chinese Particles*. Toronto, ON: University of Toronto Press.

Fazzioli, Edoardo. 1986. *Chinese Calligraphy: From Pictogram to Ideogram*. New York, NY: Abbeville Press.

Fingarette, Herbert. 1979. "The Problem of the Self in the *Analects*." *Philosophy East and West* 29.2:129–40.

Kohn, Livia. 1992. "Selfhood and Spontaneity in Ancient Chinese Thought." In *Selves, People, and Persons*, edited by Leroy Rouner, 123–38. South Bend, IN: University of Notre Dame Press.

Kohn, Livia. 2010. *Sitting in Oblivion: The Heart of Daoist Meditation*. Dunedin, FL: Three Pines Press.

Kubin, Wolfgang. 1990. "Der unstete Affe: Zum Problem des Selbst im Konfuzianismus." In *Konfuzianismus und die Modernisierung Chinas*, edited by Silke Krieger and Rolf Trauzettel, 80–113. Mainz: Hase und Köhler.

Kupperman, Joel. 1984. "Investigations of the Self." *Philosophy East & West* 34.1:37–51.

Lau, Joseph S. M. 1985. "Duty, Reputation, and Selfhood in Traditional Chinese Narratives." In *Expressions of Self in Chinese Literature*, Robert E. Hegel, 363–83. New York, NY: Columbia University Press.

Locke, John, 1997. *An Essay Concerning Human Understanding*, edited by Roger Woolhouse. New York, NY: Penguin Books.

Maslow, Abraham H. 1964. *Toward a Psychology of Being*. New York, NY: Van Nostrand Reinhold.

McLeod, S. A. 2008. "Id Ego Superego." www.simplypsychology.org/psyche.html.

Mol, Hans. 1976. *Identity and the Sacred*. New York, NY: Free Press.

Munro, Donald J. 1969. *The Concept of Man in Ancient China*. Stanford, CA: Stanford University Press.

Perinbanayagam, Robert. 2012. *Identity's Moments: The Self in Action and Interaction*. New York, NY: Lexington Books.

Taylor, Charles. 1989. *Sources of the Self: The Making of Modern Identity*. Cambridge, MA: Harvard University Press.

Trauzettel, Rolf. 1977. "Individuum und Heteronomie: Historische Aspekte des Verhältnisses von Individuum und Gesellschaft in China." *Saeculum* 28.3:340–64.

Tu, Wei-ming. 1985. "The Confucian Perception of Adulthood." In *Adulthood*, edited by Erik Erikson, 113–20. New York, NY: W. W. Norton.

15 The perfect human

The envisioned perfection of humanity in Daoism as realized through the self as spontaneity in many ways matches the understanding of the accomplished mystic in other traditions. Mysticism in general can be defined as the worldview that seeks the perfection of the individual through union with an agent or force conceived as absolute. It is usually the result of a quest that proceeds in several distinct stages, known in Christianity as the purgative, illuminative, and unitive forms of the mystical life. While the purgative phase is a period of purification, of emptying and cleaning out all the learned values of ordinary life, the illuminative stage fills the produced vacuum with the concepts and ideals of the mystical tradition, while the unitive stage sees the ultimate realization in complete oneness with the divine.[1]

The exact form this oneness and its underlying concepts take depends greatly on the agent of union. Western traditions tend to be theistic and transcendent while Eastern, especially Indian, forms are monistic and immanent, focusing respectively on ecstasy and embrace versus blur and spiritual dislocation.[2] Including the Chinese tradition, Lee Yearley has proposed three major forms of mysticism, matching the core of their worldview as focusing on change-only, monism, and real contingency.

That is to say, while Chinese thought acknowledges only creative change as real with no uncontingent reality behind it, Indian religions see the world as unreal and only one reality as existing, that of the unchanging. Western worldview, in contrast, acknowledges two realms—the real and unchanging plus the temporary and fleeting—which interpenetrate and depend on each other. The knowledge mystics work with differs accordingly. The Chinese see all knowledge as a learned system, a temporary crutch, and focus on unknowing: they acknowledge no fixed place to stand on, time to be in, or object to focus on. Indian thinkers center on the transcendent ideal: truth exists but it cannot be expressed in ordinary terms or with common senses, so that the only way to reach out toward is through negative theology and sensory withdrawal. In the West, finally, knowledge is analogous: it reflects something about what truly is, echoing and connecting but not entirely matching the realm of the ultimately real, so that mystical union is a combination of immanence and transcendence.[3]

Despite these conceptual differences, the ideal human in all mystical traditions is a superior person, closely connected to universal values and divine agencies, deeply integrated within and full of harmony without. A Rorschach study of spiritual practitioners bears this out. Asking for associations and patterns on the basis of inkblots, the test reveals a person's perception of reality and inner conflict structure. When examined in this manner, advanced practitioners of various spiritual traditions in a very similar manner tended to stress their belief in the oneness of all, the fundamental aliveness of the universe, and the importance of love and goodwill. Their "intrapsychic structure had undergone a radical enduring reorganization" that resulted in "a whole unified person whose internal psychic differentiation and organization would simply represent his diversified interests and abilities."

The most interesting results emerged from an enlightened Buddhist. First, he saw the inkblots themselves as a projection of the mind; second, he integrated all ten blots into a systematic description of his teaching, thus revealing a level of oneness with his beliefs that is extremely rare. A similar result was also found in the test results of an Apache shaman who similarly "used the ten cards as an occasion to teach the examiner about his lived worldview," revealing the degree to which the perfected human lives and thinks in unity.[4]

The great man

The Chinese tradition has various names for the perfected human. As described earlier (ch. 9), the sage of the *Daode jing* is a fully integrated being, at one with the universe, who also serves as a leader of society. The Confucian gentleman (*junzi*) plays a similar role. Both at times, moreover, are described with the epithet "great man" (*daren*), a term that occurs first in the *Yijing* under the first hexagram "Heaven," in the oracle of the fifth line: "The dragon soars into heaven. It is auspicious to see the great man."

Among the six lines of the hexagram, the fifth symbolizes the ruler. The great man therefore refers to the head of state, the king or emperor of China. This notion is consistent with the role of the ruler as the Son of Heaven, who stands at the pinnacle of human society and provides an immediate link with the ancestors and gods of the country. The great man of the *Yijing* thus takes up the Shang-dynasty role of the king as the head shaman. The later "Wenyan" (Words of the Text) commentary explains the expression:

> The great man is in harmony with heaven and earth in all his attributes. He is one with the sun and the moon in his brightness. He joins the four seasons in his orderly proceedings. He is in accordance with the spirit-like operations of providence with all that is fortunate and calamitous. He may precede heaven, and heaven will not act in opposition to him. He may follow heaven, but will act only as heaven itself would at the time. If heaven will not act in opposition to him, how much less will ordinary people?[5]

In this passage, the great man has realized complete personal freedom while at the same time working with heaven as does the sage of the *Daode jing.* Like the dragon, a symbol of the ruler, he can soar up into empty space at will and enter into heaven.

More specifically Confucian materials contrast the great man with the "small man," seeing a major divide between the gentleman or sage as a paragon of virtue and ordinary people. The texts do not commonly speak of the great man, and the term occurs only once in the *Lunyu,* denoting a person superior eve to the gentleman and on a par with the sages of old. The text has,

> Confucius said: There are three things of which the gentleman stands in awe. He stands in awe of the ordinances of heaven. He stands in awe of great men. He stands in awe of the words of sages. The mean man does not know the ordinances of heaven and consequently does not stand in awe of them. He is disrespectful to great men. He makes sport of the words of sages.
>
> (16.8)

Mencius characterized the great man more clearly as a sage. He appears as a paragon of virtue who has attained perfection in accordance with heaven, who is complete in the virtues of humanity. For example, he says that the great man will never perform "acts of propriety which are not really proper and acts of righteousness which are not really righteous" (4B.6). He is at one with nature and has "never lost the mind of a child" (4B.12), thus spontaneously doing and speaking what is right (4B.11). Beyond that, the great man, like the sage, has an immediate impact on his surroundings: as he rectifies himself, all beings are rectified through him (7A.19).[6]

The *Zhuangzi* characterizes the great man as the possessor of the state. As such, he cannot be a mere being, but must be greater and more powerful than all living things. Not content to live merely with others, the great man then soars above and beyond the known; all alone he reaches the peak of realization. Nevertheless, he is still there for the world. Even though a recluse in the wilderness, he will answer questions and help human seekers on their way. He may also hold an adept's hand and take him on an excursion into the nothingness of no-beginning. "He passes freely in and out of the boundless; he is as ageless as the sun and the moon. His face and body merge with the Great One; like the Great One, he is without self" (ch. 28). At one with the universe, he is free from all bondage, and yet sees all, knows all, and never dies. He embraces heaven and earth but is without definite social connections. He neither holds office nor becomes famous in the world; like the Dao he is beyond the definitions of language (ch. 24).[7]

The great man, therefore, represents the integration of ecstatic freedom and political order in the figure of the cosmic individual. He continues the sage of the *Daode jing,* described as being at the center of all life, the mediator among heaven, earth, and humanity, who also serves ideally as the ruler the world or at least his close adviser. The *Zhuangzi* connects this ideal with the freedom of the ecstatic journey and with the vision of an immortality "as ageless as the sun and the moon."

The perfected

While the great man like the sage has a social and political role, the purely perfect human, without any particular role, is the "perfect man" (*zhenren*), a figure central in *Zhuangzi* as much as later Daoism and Chan Buddhism. Rendered variously as "true man," "authentic person," "genuine human," or "real *mensch*," the term centers on the word "perfect," which indicates the true state of a thing as opposed to anything artificial, a way of being in utmost purity and sincerity. It reflects a state of being like a raw piece of jade as opposed to a finely designed ceremonial object, an uncarved block in contrast to an intricately executed masterpiece. Being perfect means to be whole and unaware as if completely drunk. As the *Zhuangzi* says,

> When drunks fall from a carriage, though it goes fast, they won't be killed. They have bones and joints like other people, but they are not hurt in the same way, because their spirit is whole. They had no idea they were riding, and they don't know they have fallen out. Life and death, alarm and terror do not enter their chest.
>
> (ch. 19)

The ideal state is thus one of complete unknowing, an utter lack of awareness of where one is or what one does, a way of being without a fixed identity. The text describes this in the case of Mengsun Cai and his attitude to change, evident when faced with the death of his mother. It says,

> He doesn't know why he lives and doesn't know why he dies. He doesn't know why he should go ahead; he doesn't know why he should fall behind. In the process of change, he has become a thing [among other things], and he is merely waiting for some other change that he doesn't yet know about. Moreover, when he is changing, how does he know that he is really changing? And when he is not changing, how does he know that he hasn't already changed?
>
> (ch. 6)[8]

Holding fast to the flow of energy through the cosmos, he is free from evaluations and emotions, has no consideration for disasters, events, or changes, life or death. This, in turn, provides an inner sense of integration, a naturalness of the self, which fashions a wholeness that extends to the physical, preventing any kind of upset or injury. The spirit is whole, and so is the person.

In this wholeness of spirit, at the pivot of Dao, virtue is the main force moving the individual. At one, natural, and spontaneous, perfect humans are carried by cosmic currents and flow along like water. Using their natural gifts properly, they act in full conformity with the heavenly patterns, naturally free, without control, special powers, or transcendence. Such people "take heaven as their ancestor and virtue as their roots;" free of emotions, they do "not use mind to oppose Dao, nor use human faculties to assist heaven;" in them, the human and the heavenly do not overcome one another but work in harmonious balance.[9] As the *Zhuangzi* says:

> When water flows downward, it doesn't *do* anything but just follows its inherent nature. Similarly, when the perfected fully realize inner power, they do not cultivate anything and yet there is absolutely nothing that could separate them from it. It is just like the sky is naturally high, earth is naturally solid, the sun and the moon are naturally bright—what is there to cultivate?
>
> (ch. 21)

Another way of describing this psychological state is in terms of being naturally at home in Dao as fish are in water (ch. 6), that is, completely aligned and comfortable to the point of being utterly oblivious of self, world, and others. "One is oblivious of the feet when the shoes are comfortable; one is oblivious of the waist when the belt fits just right. Knowledge obliterates all right and wrong when the mind is completely aligned with all" (ch. 19). This means, perfect humans are fully at home in the universe, as comfortable in their mind and spirit, inner nature and destiny, Dao and virtue as they are in clothes that fit well.

Since the match is perfect, there is no need to evaluate things or develop feelings about them. Being the only way they can be as determined by heaven and nature, perfected humans feel no urgency to change or develop regrets about not changing. Living without evaluation or judgment, they "enjoy everything as it is for what it is." Accepting everything that occurs as the way it should be, the "mind holds to and lets go of events as they arise" in each moment. They recognize life as "a series of new beginnings" and embrace each changing state when it comes, then let it go in complete presence.[10]

At rest in a place where "the relationship of consciousness to the sense organs is no longer one of destruction and overcoming, but one of permeation and transformation," where "the various drives and parts of person and world are integrated in an affirmative way," the perfected have a personality that is withdrawing and gentle. Thomas Merton calls this "cosmic humility"—based on the full "realization of one's own nothingness, this is full of life and awareness, responding with boundless vitality and joy to all living beings."[11] The *Zhuangzi* expresses this:

> The perfected of old did not resent being humble, did not take pride in success, and never plotted their affairs. From this basis, they could be without regret if things went wrong, remain free from self-congratulations

when they went right … They slept without dreaming and woke without concerns. Their food was plain and their breath deep.

(ch. 6)

Fully authentic people, such perfected humans are free from pride, bragging, and schemes; they hold neither fear nor regret. Without stress, they can breathe deeply; without anxiety, they have no nightmares; without ambitions; they live simple lives. Nor are they worried about life and death. "The perfected of old came to life without celebration, they left again without messiness. Calmly they came, calmly they went—and that is all. They never forgot where they came from; they never inquired about where they would end" (ch. 6). Death to the perfected is merely a "return to perfection," another transformation in the ongoing flow of existence.[12]

Withdrawn and unassuming, they furthermore manifest "blandness," a characteristic of Dao in the *Daode jing* (ch. 35), like being invisible, inaudible, and subtle (ch. 14). Blandness is an optimal and discreet equilibrium where all qualities coexist simultaneously, a state of neutrality where "one is not fixed within the confines of a particular definition." From here, the perfected renew themselves constantly, like heaven embracing the whole of reality while going along with its diverse patterns. Having access to the undifferentiated foundation of all existence, they live in original innocence, in true naivete, free from intention, able to "simultaneously encompass contradictory qualities," adapting to the changes and "realizing mastery of *all* their abilities."[13] Fully themselves yet also fully one with all beings, the nature of their existence is such that the joys and sufferings of others are their own, with no self-identity apart from the world. There is no limit to their ability to respond to diverse and changing circumstances.

This, however, is not an unconscious, reflexive, or instinctual pattern. "Able to watch the 'yes and no' pursue the alternating course [of things] around the circumference, the perfected retain perspective and clarity of judgment."[14] They are full of clarity, that is, understanding, illumination, lucidity, or enlightenment; their mind free from assumptions and preconceived notions, they possess an inner radiance of spirit that transcends all duality and works with "a correlative spiral rather than a hermeneutic circle." They are, again in the words of the *Zhuangzi*, people whose "inner being rests in the stability of cosmic peace and who thus spread a heavenly radiance" (ch. 23), always centered on their inner light, the pure radiance of spirit and virtue.[15]

Social interaction

Perfected humans have no individually determined, personally chosen life, but are heaven in action. That is to say, all their doings are not governed by personal preferences or egoistic desires, but by spirit and virtue working through the individual. By the same token, death is not the loss of a carefully crafted and ultimately artificial identity, but the mere change from one state of being to another, yet another transformation of many. As the *Zhuangzi* says,

> The life of the perfected is heaven in action; their death is a mere transformation. In stillness, their virtue matches yin; in motion, their flow matches yang. They do nothing to initiate good fortune; nothing to anticipate calamity. They receive an impulse, then respond; receive a push, then move. Only when there is no other way, do they stir themselves. Giving up all analysis and consideration of precedents, they intuitively follow the inherent order of the cosmos. For this reason, they are completely free from all natural disasters, attachments to things, opposition from others, and spiritual burdens.
>
> (ch. 15)

Freedom from natural disasters and calamities—immunity to the elements, invulnerability in the face of water and fire—is an important mark of the perfected. They "could climb high places without getting scared, dive into water without getting soaked, and pass through fire without getting hot" (ch. 6); they could "walk under water without choking, tread on fire without burning, and travel above the myriad things without fright" (ch. 19). More explicitly, they are people of pure spirit:

> The perfect are like spirit. Though the great swamps blaze, they cannot burn them; though the great rivers freeze, they cannot chill them; though swift lightning splits the hills and howling gales shake the sea, they cannot frighten them. People like this ride the clouds and mist, straddle the sun and the moon, and freely wander beyond the four seas. Life and death have no effect on them, how much less the rules of gain and loss?
>
> (ch. 2)

This feature of invulnerability, also known from other traditions—yogis, shamans, and medicine men whose minds are whole or in deep trance commonly survive being immersed in water and walking over hot coals—in Daoism is understood variously. Hagiographies of immortals and tales of the marvelous take it literally, linking it with the idea of ecstatic flight and the magical powers of shamans and mediums. Other sources read it more psychologically as demonstrating the power of mind over matter. Thus, the *Liezi* tells of a master who can perform amazing feats because he has strong belief and never lets fear enter his mind. "I forgot where my body was going; I forgot which things benefit and which harm me. I was single-minded" (ch. 2). It also describes a seeker's encounter with a stranger in the mountains who can pass through metal and stone and walk over fire without harm, again because he does not know.[16] Guo Xiang matches this understanding when he says that the perfected can perform such feats because "they mystically accept all they encounter and never rouse their mind; ... going along perfectly with the mildness and severity of heat and cold, they never let them impact on his mind."

Going beyond this, moreover, Guo Xiang also provides a yet subtler reading. First, he attributes the freedom from harm as the result of conscientiousness and simple prudence, noting that

> the perfected naturally walk on dry land without purposely avoiding water. They are naturally far away from fire, but do not intentionally run away from it. They might not feel heat as heat, yet they would never run toward a fire… or plunge into water, or in any way endanger their lives.
>
> (7.6ab)

In other words, perfected humans are smart enough to stay out of trouble.

Moving on, he also sees a more cosmic, destiny-oriented dimension to invulnerability. Once people are in a state of perfection, Guo Xiang says, in close and direct connection to Dao and virtue, in perfect synchronicity, they "always step into good fortune" and never encounter calamities. This is more than giving up psychological apprehensions, resting in oblivion, or being at peace with whatever happens; it is more than being prudent and avoiding potentially dangerous situations. It is being consistently fortunate and meeting only circumstances that are just right, because one is merged with universal principle, from which no wrong can ever come.[17]

Not in a position of leadership like the sage or the great man, perfected humans tend to stay out of worldly involvement.

> The spirit man hates to see the crowd arriving; if it does arrive, he does not try to be friendly with it. Not being friendly with it, he naturally does nothing to benefit it. The perfect man dwells corpse-like in his little four-walled room, leaving the hundred clans to their uncouth and uncaring ways, not knowing where they are going or where they are headed.
>
> (ch. 23)

Born in a body and living in society, they are "beings among beings," yet in their minds and spirit far beyond ordinary people. Inwardly free from the world, seeing fame and reputation as "so many handcuffs and fetters" (ch. 5), and steadfastly refusing to "become embroiled with it in questions of people and things, profit and loss" (ch. 26), they are yet also part of society and cannot not act. Being human means being socially responsible, and thus the perfected are active in the world, while "yet making sure that there is nothing they are very close or very distant to" (ch. 24).

All this means that the perfected also function in the world and have an inherent sense of morality,

> maintaining social responsibility without fail, accepting nothing even when in dire straits. Dedicated to observing the rules, they are not rigid

about them; extensive in their emptiness, they are not fanciful with it …
They consider punishments as the substance of government, propriety as
its supporting wings, wisdom as the key to good timing, and virtue as its
main guideline.

(ch. 6)

They live within society and observe its rules, at least as much as they jibe with
their overall sense of cosmic integration. Perfected humans are ethical yet not
slavishly so, having fine-tuned their sense of universal rightness and ultimately obeying Dao more than man. In other words, besides being fundamentally moral, they are transmoral or supramoral, going beyond the demands of
human society in a spontaneous sense of cosmic oneness.

   In addition, despite their reluctance to get involved and their vague
moral standing, their very existence makes the world a better place. Subtle
yet powerful, they model a way of living that is secure, joyful, fully present,
and supportive of everyone's growth. By just being who they are, they have
an impact not unlike the butterfly effect described in chaos theory, which
states that the flapping of a butterfly's wings in one place can, under the right
circumstances, lead to weather changes several oceans away. What happens
is that different actions and events in diverse settings become "fractally con-
gruent," i.e., match the subtle patterns that pervade all existence, thus allowing
a minute change in a complex system to have extensive amplification and vast
resonance.[18] The perfected with their self as spontaneity and their virtue in
wholeness thus closely reverberate with Dao and imperceptibly provide a
stimulus toward worldly harmony and universal goodness.

Notes

 1 Underhill 1911, 169–70.
 2 For early classifications, see Otto 1932; Zaehner 1961; Danto 1972.
 3 Yearley 1982, 440–3, 446–7.
 4 Brown and Engler 1984, 260.
 5 Wilhelm 1950, 382–3.
 6 Kohn 1992, 97.
 7 Graham 1989, 204.
 8 Coyle 1998, 202; Kohn 2014, 146–7.
 9 Graziani 2006, 273–7.
10 Yearley 2010, 126, 132–3.
11 Citations from Chong 2011, 337; Coyle 1998, 199; Merton 1969, 27, respectively.
12 Chong 2011, 327; Coyle 1998, 205.
13 Jullien 2004, 23 56, 60.
14 Merton 1969, 30.
15 Coyle 1998, 200; Kohn 2014, 149.
16 Graham 1960, 41, 46.
17 Kohn 2014, 195.
18 Jones and Culliney 1999, 648.

References

Brown, Daniel P., and Jack Engler. 1984. "A Rorschach Study of the Stages of Mindfulness Meditation." In *Meditation: Classic and Contemporary Perspectives*, edited by Deane N. Shapiro and Roger N. Walsh, 232–62. New York, NY: Aldine.

Chong, Kim-chong. 2011. "The Concept of *Zhen* in the *Zhuangzi*." *Philosophy East & West* 61.2:324–46.

Coyle, Daniel. 1998. "On the *Zhenren*." In *Wandering at Ease in the Zhuangzi*, edited by Roger Ames, 197–210. Albany: State University of New York Press.

Danto, Arthur. 1972. *Mysticism and Morality: Oriental Thought and Moral Philosophy*. New York, NY: Basic Books.

Graham, A. C. 1960. *The Book of Lieh-tzu*. London: A. Murray.

Graham, A. C. 1989. *Disputers of the Tao: Philosophical Argument in Ancient China*. La Salle, IL: Open Court Publishing.

Graziani, Romain. 2006. *Fictions philosophiques du Tchouang-tseu*. Paris: Gallimard.

Jones, David, and John Culliney. 1999. "The Fractal Self and the Organization of Nature: The Daoist Sage and Chaos Theory." *Zygon: Journal of Science and Religion* 4:643–54.

Jullien, François. 2004. *In Praise of Blandness: Proceeding from Chinese Thought and Aesthetics*. New York, NY: Zone Books.

Kohn, Livia. 1992. *Early Chinese Mysticism: Philosophy and Soteriology in the Taoist Tradition*. Princeton, NJ: Princeton University Press.

Kohn, Livia. 2014. *Zhuangzi: Text and Context*. St. Petersburg, FL: Three Pines Press.

Merton, Thomas. 1969. *The Way of Chuang Tzu*. New York, NY: New Directions.

Otto, Rudolf. 1932. *Mysticism East and West: A Comparative Analysis of the Nature of Mysticism*. New York, NY: Macmillan.

Underhill, Evelyn. 1911. *Mysticism*. London: Methuen.

Wilhelm, Richard. 1950. *The I Ching or Book of Changes*. Translated by Cary F. Baynes. Princeton, NJ: Princeton University Press.

Yearley, Lee. 1982. "Three Ways of Being Religious." *Philosophy East & West* 32.4:439–51.

Yearley, Lee. 2010. "The Perfected Person in the Radical *Zhuangzi*." In *Experimental Essays on Zhuangzi*, edited by Victor H. Mair, 122–36. Dunedin, FL: Three Pines Press.

Zaehner, Robert C. 1961. *Mysticism Sacred and Profane*. London: Oxford University Press.

16 Immortality

Immortality is the ultimate goal of Daoist cultivation, the final state of being. Building on the perfection of humanity and the development of sagehood, it is in addition a form of apotheosis, the assumption of the person into a higher realm and ascension into the heavens above. In this respect, it is similar to processes of deification and personal transformation in other cultures, including the godlike worship of Egyptian pharaohs, Greek hero cults, and the elevation of dead emperors in ancient Rome. Christians, too, believe that human beings are made in the image of God and, therefore, have the potential to become godlike. In Catholicism, this plays out in an after-death scenario, where people are reborn and resurrected to fully participate in the divine nature of God. In the Church of Jesus Christ of Latter-Day Saints, it appears in the belief in exaltation, the conviction that human beings are able to develop intrinsically divine qualities while still on this earth, to then be assumed into the Presence after death.[1]

Among indigenous cultures, the closest match to Daoist immortality is shamanism, a worldview based on the assumption that nature is a living force, where all entities are imbued with life energy and jointly participate in the greater cosmos. Dividing reality into the three levels of heaven, earth, and the underworld, such cultures rely on shamans as specialist mediators to go into trance in various ways and soul-travel to the upper or lower worlds to connect to spirit beings and collect information. This information not only describes the details of how the world is structured but also provides recipes for healing and advice for governance. Beyond this, shamans guide the dead to their proper level and ensure that all agents are in harmony and at peace. In some traditions, they also open themselves to the presence of divine entities, housing the spirits in states of possession. In addition, they typically gain assistance from natural forces, mountains, trees, and in particular from strong, powerful animals. Present among hunter-gatherer populations today and documented historically in cultures all over the world and going as far back as the Paleolithic, shamanism represents a fundamental level of human religiosity.[2]

Transformation

Integrating and developing this, Daoist immortals are recluses who engage in ecstatic excursions and attain divine status upon ascension. This is borne out by the very word for "immortal," which shows a man next to a mountain or, in an older version, a figure dancing with flying sleeves. Immortals appear on the scene in the late Zhou and early Han dynasties, when concepts of an ancestral afterlife were expanded to include more physical forms of longevity, various indigenous tribes were found to possess arts of making the body stronger and lighter, and contacts with other cultures enhanced the belief in a magical paradise of pure power where wondrous figures live that nourish on energy and can appear and disappear at will.[3]

Unlike shamans who tend to resist the calling to divine service and divinized humans who depend on their descendants or divine grace to secure them a place in the pantheon, Daoists intentionally undergo a process of transformation that ensures the attainment of superhuman powers and active ascension into heaven. This process begins with fundamental ethics, expressed in various sets of codes as well as in hagiographic tales of tests adepts have to undergo. Although eventually transcending all morality, they have to develop basic ethical qualities before being accepted as worthy disciples and allowed to undergo training. A popular story that tells of a series of tests is the hagiography of Lü Dongbin, leader of the Eight Immortals and inspiring patriarch of Complete Perfection.

> Once at the time of the New Year, Lü was leaving his house to be accosted by a beggar demanding alms. He handed over all [the presents for his family] he carried, cash and gifts. But the beggar remained dissatisfied and threateningly demanded more, using the most abusive terms. Yet Lü kept a smiling face and again and again apologized to him politely.
>
> Then again, he was looking after some sheep in the mountains. A hungry tiger came upon them, with the result that the flock scattered in all directions. Lü interposed his own person between the tiger and the terrified sheep. The tiger gave up the chase and crept away.[4]

Like other in the series, these texts focus on Lü's degree of attachment to material things and social customs as well as on his fear of death and his compassion for helpless creatures. The aspiring immortal must be generous with his possessions and independent of social approval, has to have courage in the face of death and other threats or beguilements (one test also has Lü encounter a sensuous beauty), and be willing to sacrifice himself on behalf of weaker beings. These moral virtues, however, are not required for their own sake or to develop a particularly moral type of person but serve to indicate the stamina and determination necessary for the utter overcoming of body and self on the path to otherworldly immortality. They serve the same function as the abuse heaped on aspiring Zen practitioners when they first enter the training monastery: standing here, freezing, hungry, and miserable—how much do I *really* want to do this? If the answer is, "more than anything," the candidate is ready.[5]

The path itself, then, proceeds with the transformation of energy levels in body and mind, basically reverting the individualized self and personal identity to more cosmic levels while recovering the original organism of physical interconnectedness and the vast abyss of the pure spirit. Present in Daoist environments from an early age, it was standardized in the Song dynasty into a system known as internal alchemy and as such still forms the dominant form of specialist Daoist cultivation today.

Adepts, who ideally live in monastic communities but may also work as hermits or in small practice groups, typically begin with longevity techniques to make their body strong and supple as well as concentrative meditation to make their mind tranquil and stable. Then they start the transformation process by focusing on essence, the materially tangible form of *qi* that develops in the human body as it interacts with the world and appears most obviously as sexual energy—semen in men and menstrual blood in women. To revert this to pure *qi*, they train themselves to become aware of its movements, then reverse its natural downward flow and move it up along the spine, across the head, and along the front of the torso in a cycle known as the small heavenly circuit or microcosmic orbit. After prolonged practice, the *qi* is stabilized and manifests in the first seed of immortality, called the Pearl of Dew.

In a second stage, adepts transform this pure *qi* into spirit by evolving the Pearl of Dew into the Golden Flower. To do this, they identify yin and yang as specific forms of energy in the body, circulating them around each other and merging them in different ways, continuously refining them to subtler levels. These increasingly purer dimensions are described with different metaphors, including heart, fire, dragon, lead, and the trigram Li for yang, as well as kidneys, water, tiger, mercury, and the trigram Kan for yin.

Texts that outline such practices tend to be rather obscure and highly metaphoric. For example, the *Huandan ge zhu* (Annotated Songs on Reverting Cinnabar) says:

> The Bird is harmonized and nurtured; it brings forth the Golden Flower.
>
> The Red Bird is the phase fire. Among directions it corresponds to the south and to the position *bingding*. In the sky it is the planet Mars; on earth it is fire; in human beings it is the heart…. It greatly encompasses heaven and earth, minutely reaches into the smallest nook and cranny. Control it and it will obey, let it go free and it will run wild. In the scriptures it is called the bright fire….
>
> To harmonize it, isolate pure water from the Jade Spring Palace in the upper elixir field. Join this with the fire of the heart and refine it until it enters the lower elixir field. Secure it behind the Jade Lock Pass. Once locked in, refine it further with yin. Naturally a new spirit soul and a separate sun and moon emerge. After nourishing them for a long

time, their color will turn brilliant. They combine to form the Golden Flower.[6]

The Golden Flower is the root core of the immortal embryo or holy fetus in the lower elixir field. Once present, adepts switch their practice to employ a method called embryo respiration to nourish it for ten months. This is an internal form of breathing, combined with the meditative circulation of *qi*, which allows the embryo to grow and makes the adept increasingly independent of outer nourishment and air. Unlike the first phase, which was easier for men, the process at this stage is easier for women because they are naturally endowed with the faculty of gestation. After ten months, the embryo is complete.

Adepts then proceed to the third stage. The as yet semi-material body of the embryo is now transformed into the pure spirit body of the immortals, an entity of pure, divine yang with no yin counterpart, that is, of cosmic life different from life as opposed to death. To attain its full realization, the embryo is carefully nurtured for three years so it can grow into its own and learn to move about independently. Gradually and in close cooperation with the adept's spirit soul, it starts to exit the body, moving first along the spine, then leaving through the top of head, a point known as the Heavenly Gate. From here, the adept through the immortal child engages in vivid journeys through the otherworld and the heavenly spheres, gradually learning to blend his existence with that of the gods and flow along with cosmic emptiness. This part typically takes nine years of deep meditation. Finally, the adept becomes an immortal spirit of pure yang and merges completely with Dao, taking up permanent residence in the heavens above.[7]

The process shifts significantly from an overarching alignment with nature to its transcendence. Thus, in the preparatory stages, adepts strive to establish harmony with the natural cycles and activate seasonal renewal through alignment in diet, exercise, meditation, and ritual celebration. The foods they eat, the clothes they wear, the colors they choose, and their daily activities all differ depending on the month and the season. In addition, Daoists have great awareness of the circadian rhythm of the day, matching their meditations to the energetic dominance of yin and yang and the functioning cycle of the internal organs and their meridians—often practicing the early hours around midnight when yang is on the rise. Applying various medical and longevity techniques, they recover and enhance their inborn life expectancy and health levels. Still moving along the trajectory of natural entropy, they yet increase the quality of their physical, mental, and spiritual well-being.

Once the transformation from essence into *qi* and spirit is underway, Daoists work on increasingly subtler levels and begin to overcome and even reverse the natural patterns. Rather than letting energy sink down and transform into essence, they move it upward and revert it to a more primordial state. Doing so, they activate cosmic purity on increasingly higher planes, intentionally going against the natural flow, actively reverting entropy and sexual maturity in a return to a stem-cell level of being, a recovery of the original source of all.

Supernatural powers

Once they have attained the level of pure spirit, they reach a level called spirit pervasion, which comes with several abilities that go beyond ordinary senses and abilities. That is, immortals are able to make themselves light or heavy, minute or vast, taking on any energetic form or shape while knowing of and controlling various objects and creatures around them. For example,

> Master Yellow Hut was good at curing and healing. Even at a distance of one thousand miles, if he only knew the name of the sick person, he could cure him. All would get well, even if he never saw the patient's body.
>
> He also excelled at exorcising with the help of *qi*. He would get rid of tigers, wolves, and all kinds of nasty insects. None of them would dare to move when he was around. And he could make rivers flow backwards as far as a mile.
>
> Easily reaching the age of 280, he was able to lift a ton without any trouble and walked as fast as other people rode on horseback. Around his head there always was a five-colored halo, which made him look about ten feet tall.
>
> At times of drought, he could enter deep into the springs and summon forth dragons. Controlling them, he ordered them to ascend to the sky and produce rain. Numerous times, he worked miracles like that. One day he said farewell to his family and friends, mounted a dragon and ascended, never to return.[8]

Another immortal of multiple powers is the Lady of Great Mystery. She possessed complete immunity to the elements, could enter water and not get wet, sit in a blazing fire and not burn. Able to travel far distances in an instant and adept at bilocation, "she could change her appearance at will: one moment she was an old man, then again a small child." She also transformed material objects.

> Whatever she pointed at would vanish into thin air: doors, windows, boxes, or caskets that were securely locked needed only a short flexing of her finger to break wide open. Mountains would tumble and trees would fall at the pointing of her hand. Another gesture would resurrect them to their former state."[9]

The powers of immortals divide into two different dimensions: those applying to themselves and those working transformations in the outside world. Having full control over their own *qi*, they are shape-changers who can appear in any form they please. They can multiply themselves into many different people, bilocate to be present in more than one place at once, become visible and invisible at will, travel thousands of miles in an instant, see through walls and into distant locations, read the minds of others, and predict the future. They have complete mastery over their appearance, health, and vitality, and are able to live for as long as they like, eventually ascending smoothly to the subtler realms of the heavenly spheres.

Controlling not only themselves, immortals also have power over nature and the outside world—an integral part of the unified world of *qi*. Like wizards, they can make rivers flow backward and mountains tumble; plants, animals, and people die at their command and come back to life if they tell them to do so. They transport buildings to far-off places, open up mountains to reveal grottoes. Like shamans, they can heal the sick, exorcise demons or beasts, make rain or stop it, foretell or prevent disasters, and call upon wild animals as helpers. They have full integration of *qi*, manifest in control over the body, a subtle harmony with the forces of nature, as well as an easy relationship with gods and spirits, ghosts and demons.[10]

Today known as extrasenory perception (ESP), these abilities include first an enhanced level of sensory awareness, the ability to connect to the world in more subtle ways or through multiple venues such as in forms of synesthesia. Next, they involve an increase in attention, a powerful focus on, and heightened awareness of, the "nonlocal hyper-dimensional space-time in which we live." This leads to states of nonsensory knowing and the reception of information as manifest in the classic psychic or "psi" phenomena of telepathy, clairvoyance, and precognition. Moving beyond perception, there is also the powerful direction of intention into the holographic, interconnected universe, leading to a direct impact, an active modification of the world in the major psi manifestation known as psychokinesis.[11]

Within this framework, telepathy is direct mind-to-mind communication, also known as the perception of the entire field of mental and physical reality. Clairvoyance is the unmediated knowledge of distant events, today most strongly activated in remote viewing, while precognition is the awareness of future events, also called feeling the future. Psychokinesis, moreover, is the power of mind over matter, the ability to influence physical reality by sending focused intention, activated in qigong demonstrations, spoon bending, and— most powerfully—in spiritual healing.[12] These phenomena all work due to the nonlocal, holographic nature of the universe, its fundamental characteristic of quantum entanglement, which Daoists describe in terms of *qi*, where all is interconnected and separation is an illusion. Psychically connected to all existence on a subliminal level, all people "are constantly submerged in a sea of telepathic suggestions," leading to sympathy pains, mass hysteria, and other linked events. The gross world of matter and the subtle world of cosmic consciousness closely intersect, each flowing and working together in intrinsic harmony, beyond the ken of ordinary people but under the full control of the immortals.[13]

Ascension

Once immortals have reached their goal, they divide into several types. Celestial immortals ascend directly to the heavens to serve in the celestial administration; earth immortals, though ready for ascension, still remain on earth to enjoy life to the fullest; those liberated by simulated corpse (*shijie*) leave a substitute such as a sword or staff behind. In all cases, they eventually undergo ascension, a feat that most strongly expresses the transcendence of individual personality and social relations. Whether a given immortal observes his own funeral, a high Daoist master exhibits his ultimate transformation to his disciples, or the person just vanishes—in all cases the break with normalcy, the overcoming of personalized individuality and social integration is complete. Ascension is thus a key phase that separates Daoist mystics as perfect humans from immortals as members of the administration of heaven and attendants on the higher deities of Dao.

Ascension comes in different forms. The highest is by celestial chariot. Receiving a summons to office among the heavenly bureaucrats, the immortal readies himself and on the appointed day is formally met by a dragon-drawn cloudy chariot and escorted up to heaven by a large entourage of celestial guards, supernatural horsemen, and divine lads. The second-best way is by vanishing completely. Again, a divine invitation is received, but rather than in a formal reception, the immortal ascends upward on his own, using clouds and streams of air for support. Here, too, the celestial-to-be announces his supernatural state and gets ready for departure, but the entire setting is decidedly less formal. This form of ascension, not as celebrated and rather less well prepared, often leaves friends and family in a state of confusion.

Third is ascension through liberation by simulated corpse, a rather crude way, since it requires that the immortal leave some physical token of his worldly presence behind. It shows that he has ascended but not fully dissolved into the heavenly spheres. A yet different way is used by Daoist masters who sit in meditation and exit in their spirit, leaving their body behind. A sign that ascension has occurred is that the corpse does not decay but remains fragrant, pink clouds come to hover over it, and strands of celestial music sound.[14]

The most famous chariot ascension is that of the Yellow Emperor. According to the *Shiji* (Historical Records) of the first century BCE, he was received into the heavenly host by a divine dragon. He mounted it with seventy of his followers, and with people still trying to cling to the dragon's beard and claws, was taken off into the empyrean. Another famous case is Liu An of the Han, who took an alchemical elixir and ascended into heaven on a cloudy chariot, followed by the dogs and chickens of his court that lapped up the dregs of the drug.

A well-known case of vanishing is Qu Baiting who ascended to heaven in broad daylight in the 5th month of 773. He was eighteen at that time and apprenticed to the 15th patriarch of Highest Clarity. The event took place in the courtyard of the Peach Blossom Monastery in full view of monastic and lay onlookers: while holding on to a chestnut tree, Qu's physical form dissolved completely, and he vanished into thin air.[15]

Deliverance through the corpse is a handy way to leave family and friends while going off on a further quest for eternal life. As the *Shenxian zhuan* recounts, for example, Fei Changfang, an apprentice of the Gourd Master, after learning the basics, expresses his desire to follow the master:

> "I have the strong wish to join you, but I would prefer my relatives not to know that I have gone off. Is there anything we can do about this?"
>
> "But that's easy," the Master said and handed him a fresh stick of bamboo. "Take this stick," he instructed, "and go back home. Then complain of some sickness and place it in your bed. Come away in secret and watch what happens."
>
> Fei did as he was told. After he had left, his relatives believed that he had died, seeing as they did his corpse in the bed. They wailed and sobbed, and duly buried the body.[16]

In the aftermath, Fei continues his training but does not pass one of the severe tests. With regret, the Gourd Master informs him, "You will not attain immortality, but you can wield the powers of a demon master on earth and will get to live for several hundred years." Fei duly returns home, riding on another stick of bamboo. His relatives are shocked by his reappearance but reassured when the exhume his corpse and find the original bamboo.

An example of the transfiguration of Daoist masters is the case of Sima Chengzhen, who reportedly announced that he would shortly take up a position in the heavenly administration. On the date specified a pink cloud surrounded him and he rose up as a full immortal to the sound of heavenly music. His disciples duly proceeded to bury his robe and cap. Another is the Flower Maiden who similarly foresaw her ascension and instructed her disciples to leave the coffin open and only cover it with a thin piece of gauze. Then, a few days after her death,

> Suddenly the disciples heard a massive stoke of thunder. When they looked at the coffin, there was a hole about as big as a hen's egg in the gauze, and in the coffin itself only the Maiden's shroud and some wooden tablets were left. In the ceiling of the room, there was a hole big enough for a person to pass through.[17]

Ascension, however desirable, thus always means passing through a death-like experience; the successful transition to celestial status needs ample preparation and hard practice. Adepts not only work diligently on energetic transformation and steep themselves in visualization, but also undertake numerous ecstatic excursions through the immoral child to gain easy access to and direct communication with the otherworld. Whichever form it takes, then, ascension signals the final dissolution of mundane ties and forms of identity, the adoption into the greatness of the divine realm. It does not happen according to the individual's wishes, either, but occurs only after the person's life expectancy has been fulfilled or when a summons to celestial office arrives, thus allowing him receive a rank in the hierarchy above and serve in the celestial administration of this and the other world.

Deification

All this means that Daoist immortals essentially take on the role of deities and become gods. However, they are fundamentally different from other divine beings. They are not nature gods such as stars and planets, rivers and lakes, mountains and fields, rain and wind, who form part of the universe from creation or pure forces of Dao, such as yin and yang, personified in the Queen Mother of the West and the King Father of the East.

Nor are they transformed ancestors, humans deified on the basis of merit, elevated by popular consent and ratified through a lengthy process of official recognition.[18] A well-known example here is the city god of Shanghai, a meritorious local official of the fourteenth century who was promoted to his supernatural position upon popular petition and increased his stature under colonial rule to the point where he now presides over a vast shopping mall in the city center. Another important case is that of Mazu, the vastly popular protector of fishermen, merchants, and travelers. The Song-dynasty daughter of a fisherman, she was able to enter into a deep trance and travel spiritually to where her father and brothers were in peril, dispelling the winds and bringing them to safety. After an early death, she was venerated locally, then increasingly more widely, to eventually rise into the Daoist pantheon. Honoring her with a Daoist title and official mission, Lord Lao empowered her to slay demons, dispel disasters, and rescue humans from all kinds of difficulty.[19]

All these various deities stand in a close relationship with humanity. They receive regular nourishment through food, wine, incense, and incantations, and in return send good fortune and provide protection. The relationship is strictly reciprocal, and disasters and illnesses in life are often attributed to neglect of one's devotional duties. These gods tend also to be ranked in an organized hierarchy and serve in various departments under the Jade Emperor. Thus, for example, the Department of Destiny supervises human affairs, its officials—divided according to the twelve signs of the zodiac—keeping track of people's good and bad deeds and making suitable additions to and subtractions from the life expectancy. Another section is the Celestial Treasury, where divine administrators issue a certain amount of credit to everyone at birth, that is, bestow primordial *qi* in the form of currency, which then has to be repaid over one's lifetime in good deeds and through the burning of spirit money.[20]

Immortals may be deputized to one or the other of these departments, but they are not part of the reciprocity system since they have gone far beyond the yin-yang patterns of life. More commonly, they reside in heavens of their own, enjoying banquets, chanting poetry, and engaging in graceful dance. They can, if they wish, appear on earth and engage with people, but that happens entirely on their own terms. Thus, for example, as recorded in the Han-dynasty *Liexian zhuan* (Immortals' Biographies), Lord Horsemaster cured animals far and wide and once even relieved a celestial dragon of an atrocious tooth-ache, while the wonderworker Zuo Ci, enjoying a banquet with a local ruler, procures the most wonderful foodstuffs from far-off places within an instant.[21]

Often immortals are described as eccentrics, using their powers to make fun of people or to extricate themselves from difficult situations—coming close to the trickster figure known from other cultures. They show how not to take life and death quite so seriously, maintaining childlike innocence, and living playfully in the world. Thus, the highly popular Eight Immortals tend to be happy-go-lucky fellows who hang out drinking and playing board games, write silly verses on the walls of taverns and shock contemporary citizens with their unconventional behavior.

Highly popular among them is Zhang Guolao, an old man with a long white beard, who smiles a great deal and travels around riding backwards on a white donkey. He has powers over life and death. When he arrives in a town and does not need his donkey for a while, he blows his *qi* on the animal and shrinks it to pocket-size; when he wishes to travel onward, he blows it up again to regular dimensions. Another favorite is Ironcrutch Li. He started out as an expert in ecstatic excursions and once decided to go up into the heavens, leaving his corpse-like body behind for an entire week. To make sure nothing happened to it, he ordered a disciple to keep watch, but the boy got called away. Assuming that his master would not return anyway, he cremated the body. When Li returned, he found his own body gone and entered that of a recently dead man who happened to be an old, crippled beggar. To help himself get around, he then used an iron crutch, thus his name. Despite this change, he lost none of his vigor or magical powers, fighting rogues and bandits with high martial skill. Others are more artistic types, performing magic, playing music, and arranging flowers.[22]

Immortals, therefore, whether in heaven or on earth, enjoy life to the fullest in their own eccentric way, relieving human suffering and making the world a more enjoyable place. Quite independent of what others may think, they often exhibit strange behaviors. They sing at funerals, pinch wine and meat from the gods at sacrifices, drink and make merry whenever they get a chance, and laugh at anything and everything. Accepting life and death as a single flow, they take neither seriously and make the best of all they meet. Their happy attitude, their playful way of being is what makes them so popular, still depicted widely on good-luck cards, in paintings on the walls of restaurants, as well as in movies and comic books. They are, more than anything, the popular face of Daoism in the world today.

Notes

1 See Kharlamov 2012.

2 Eliade 1964; Winkelman 2002, 72–5.
3 Yü 1964, 87.
4 Yetts 1916, 794.
5 Wetering 1974.
6 Kohn 2001, 146–7.
7 For more details, see Ho 2018.
8 Kohn 1993, 290; Johnson 2014, 259.
9 Kohn 1993, 291.
10 Kohn 2016, 181.
11 See Targ 2012.
12 For definitions, see McTaggart 2007, xxviii; Targ 2012, 7–9.
13 Panati 1974, 105–6, 137; Targ 2012, 203, 212
14 Kohn 1990, 18–20, 2016, 176–7.
15 On the Yellow Emperor, see Campany 2002, 238. For Qu, see Kohn 1993, 328–32.
16 Kohn 1993, 124; Campany 2002, 161.
17 On Sima, see Engelhardt 1987, 52. For the Flower Maiden, see Kirkland, 1991; Kohn 1993, 332.
18 On deification and immortality beliefs, see Puett 2002.
19 Boltz 1986, 224.
20 See Hou 1975.
21 Kaltenmark 1953, 47; Campany 2002, 280.
22 See Yetts 1916.

References

Boltz, Judith M. 1986. "In Homage to T'ien-fei." *Journal of the American Oriental Society* 106:211–52.

Campany, Robert F. 2002. *To Live as long as Heaven and Earth: A Translation and Study of Ge Hong's Traditions of Divine Transcendents*. Berkeley: University of California Press.

Eliade, Mircea. 1964. *Shamanism: Archaic Techniques of Ecstasy*. Princeton, NJ: Princeton University Press.

Engelhardt, Ute. 1987. *Die klassische Tradition der Qi-Übungen. Eine Darstellung anhand des Tang-zeitlichen Textes Fuqi jingyi lun von Sima Chengzhen*. Wiesbaden: Franz Steiner.

Ho, Chung-tao. 2018. *Internal Alchemy for Everyone*. St. Petersburg, FL: Three Pines Press.

Hou, Ching-lang. 1975. *Monnaies d'offrande et la notion de tresorerie dans la religion chinoise*. Paris: Memoires de l'Institut des Hautes Etudes Chinoises.

Johnson, Jerry Alan. 2014. *The Secret Teachings of Chinese Energetic Medicine: Volume 2: Energetic Alchemy, Dao Yin Therapy, Healing Qi Deviations, Spirit Pathology*. Pacific Grove: International Institute of Medical Qigong.

Kaltenmark, Max. 1953. *Le Lie-sien tchouan*. Peking: Université de Paris Publications.

Kharlamov, Vladimir. 2012. *Deification in Christian Theology*. Cambridge: Cambridge University Press.

Kirkland, J. Russell. 1991. "Huang Ling-Wei: A Taoist Priestess in T'ang China." *Journal of Chinese Religions* 19:47–73.

Kohn, Livia. 1990. "Transcending Personality: From Ordinary to Immortal Life." *Taoist Resources* 2.2:1–22.

Kohn, Livia. 1993. *The Taoist Experience: An Anthology*. Albany: State University of New York Press.

Kohn, Livia. 2001. *Daoism and Chinese Culture*. Cambridge, MA: Three Pines Press.

Kohn, Livia. 2016. *Science and the Dao: From the Big Bang to Lived Perfection*. St. Petersburg, FL: Three Pines Press.

McTaggart, Lynne. 2007. *The Intention Experiment: Using Your Thoughts to Change Your Life and the World*. New York, NY: Free Press.

Panati, Charles. 1974. *Supersenses: Our Potential for Parasensory Experience*. New York, NY: Quadrangle.

Puett, Michael J. 2002. *To Become a God: Cosmology, Sacrifice, and Self-Divinization in Early China*. Cambridge, MA: Harvard University Press.

Targ, Russell. 2012. *The Reality of ESP: A Physicist's Proof of Psychic Abilities*. Wheaton, IL: Theosophical Publishing.

Wetering, Janwillem van de. 1974. *The Empty Mirror: Experiences in a Japanese Zen Monastery*. Boston, MA: Houghton Mifflin.

Winkelman, Michael. 2002. "Shamanism and Cognitive Evolution." *Cambridge Archaeological Journal* 12.1:71–101.

Yetts, Percifal. 1916. "The Eight Immortals." *Journal of the Royal Asiatic Society* 1916:773–807.

Yü, Ying-shih. 1964. "Life and Immortality in the Mind of Han-China." *Harvard Journal of Asiatic Studies* 25:80–122.

Conclusion
Contemporary connections

Daoism, the indigenous higher religion of China, has a set of unique perspectives on key questions asked in philosophy and religion, concerning the nature of reality, the position and role of humanity, ideal forms of community, moral and ethical requirements, as well as specific visions of perfection, the best and most harmonious way to be as within one's person, in the world, and in an ultimate state. The core notion that lies at the root of all its concepts and pervades all its visions is the understanding of the universe, the world, and everything as being essentially one, consisting equally of a cosmic, vital energy described as *qi*. *Qi* is everything; it can flow faster and slower, be denser or subtler, and manifest in a variety of ways, some more tangible than others, yet there is always only one *qi*, and all that exists, has ever existed, and will ever be is nothing but energy.

The Daoist take, in addition, formulates this vision not only in terms of energetics, matching Chinese cosmology and medicine, but also in social and ethical terms, closely relating to Confucianism and Buddhism. Beyond that, it gives it a particular slant by expressing the energy-nature of the universe in more mythological terms, ranging from pure deities of Dao through celestial bureaucrats and body gods to demons and specters. It is important to understand that, however colorful and fantastic the Daoist pantheon may be, its denizens essentially represent different forms of more or less subtle energy and can be dealt with accordingly.

Living in an interconnected, holographic universe, Daoists find themselves responsible for their own well-being as well as that of the world. Their ethics reflect this, combining virtue ethics with social responsibility and a sophisticated system of rewards and punishments that extend from the individual throughout the entire network of time and space. In all this, moreover, the human body is central, a denser form of *qi* than the mind yet fundamentally one with it, modified through various forms of cultivation into subtler and more cosmic levels. The ultimate, then, is immortality, a state that involves the internal transformation toward a more natural, spontaneous self, the realization of this self in a mystical state of unified awareness, a vastly expanded life expectancy, and the transcendence of all through ascension into the higher spheres.

With these core characteristics, the Daoist take on life and world has much to offer modern philosophy: in fact, some of its key features are already central issues in twenty-first-century thinking. Thus, the universe as energy matches the vision of quantum physics, the importance and cultivation of the body is central to the new fields of energy medicine, and the idea of extended longevity and even immortality is at the forefront in the battle against disease and old age.

The quantum world

The quantum world, discovered in a series of experimental and conceptual breakthroughs in the early twentieth century—from Albert Einstein through Niels Bohr, Werner Heisenberg, Erwin Schrödinger, David Bohm, John Bell, and others—is in no way like the world we know in ordinary life. Neither solid, stable, nor continuous, it comes as what David Bohm called plasma, a fourth state of matter akin to ether that is rather similar to *qi*. Neither solid nor liquid or gaseous, it is composed of infinitely small particles in constant agitation. The tiny particles consist of quanta, the energy that electrons absorb or emit when changing energy levels, as well as gluons, the forces that hold atoms together. The most basic subatomic particles behave like both particles and waves, and many of these particles take part in universal supersymmetry—a law that demands all elements of nature must come in pairs—and form sets like yin and yang, where one cannot exist without the other.[1]

These particles, moreover, are not entities but process, continuous motion of inward collapse and outward expansion.

> An electron is not one thing but a totality or ensemble enfolded throughout the whole of space. Sustained by constant influx from the implicate order, a particle may appear to be destroyed but is not lost. It has merely enfolded back into the deeper order from which it sprang.[2]

In itself a manifestation of the whole universe, the particle/wave seems inherently random. It is impossible to know both its exact momentum and location at the same time—in fact, there is an inverse relationship in that the more information one has about the former, the less is known about the latter, and vice versa. The whole of the universe being present in each of its parts at all times, quanta like *qi* can be at more than one place at a time. Not manifest until observed as particles, they cease to exist in one place and appear in another without any obvious way of getting from here to there, and any observation affecting one also affects its twin, no matter how far apart they are.[3]

In other words, the subtlest units of reality are in one state of being at a time but can exist on multiple levels and in multiple states, like Schrödinger's cat—latent or manifest, dead or alive, or anything in between—representing a plethora of possibilities. This means that everything in the universe is in a state of constant flux and ongoing change and transformation. The cosmos consists of unlimited possibilities in a vast quantum field that consists of vibrating energies, waves and particles, which change their state trillions of times in one second. Still, they tend to cluster and pattern in certain ways, centering at magnetic field lines and creating harmoniously oscillating structures.

David Bohm describes these structures terms of two levels of order—quite akin to the two aspects of Dao in ancient Daoist thought. One is the external, visible order of things in this world; the other is the underlying structure, orderly in its own way but much more subtle: explicate and implicate or unfolded and enfolded.

> In the [*implicate* or] *enfolded* order, space and time are no longer the dominant factors determining the relationships of dependence or independence of different elements. Rather, an entirely different sort of basic connection of elements is possible, from which our ordinary notions of space and time, along with those of separately existent material particles, are abstracted as forms derived from the deeper order. These ordinary notions in fact appear in what is called the *explicate* or *unfolded* order, which is a special and distinguished form contained within the general totality of all the implicate orders.[4]

This essentially means that not only is there an underlying order in the greater universe and all its parts, but also that "each event and each appearance in the world is a manifestation of a much larger process." The larger process is ubiquitous and pervasive, linking everything together in closely integrated wholeness, i.e., ultimate oneness.

> The quantum world is fundamentally holistic … and indivisible. In every observation, the observer and the observed are linked by a quantum. Since the quantum cannot be broken apart in any way, during an observation, the observer and the observed must be considered an indivisible whole.[5]

Quantum concepts imply that the world acts more like a single individual unit, in which even the "intrinsic" nature of each part (wave or particle) depends to some degree on its relationship to its surroundings. This also means that our traditional boundaries of local and nonlocal, mind and matter, body and consciousness are overcome, giving instead rise to the notion of an overarching subtle energy field whose strings vibrate in different frequencies yet are always one. Daoist descriptions and practices of *qi* thus closely match to quantum and offer ways to integrate it into our lives, both in theory and practice.

Energy medicine

The practical dimension comes to the forefront in energy medicine, a cluster of research in biology, physiology, and physics that has opened up new ways of looking at the body. Rather than seeing it in terms of solid structures and mechanical components, its representatives focus on biomagnetic fields and bioelectricity. Biomagnetic fields are human energy centers that vibrate at different frequencies, storing and giving off energies not unlike the inner organs and elixir fields in the Daoist system. Their energetic output or vibrations can be measured, and it has been shown that the heart and the brain continuously pulse at extremely low frequencies. It has also become clear through controlled measurements that biomagnetic fields are unbounded so that, for example, the field of the heart vibrates beyond the body and extends infinitely into space, verifying the Daoist conviction that people and the universe interact continuously on an energetic level.

Similarly, bioelectricity manifests in energy currents that crisscross the human body and are similar to the meridians of acupuncture. Separate from and, in evolutionary terms, more ancient than the nervous system, these currents work through the so-called cytoskeleton, a complex net of connective tissue that is a continuous and dynamic molecular webwork. Also known as the "living matrix," this webwork contains so-called integrins or transmembrane linking molecules which have no boundaries but are intricately interconnected. When touching the skin or inserting an acupuncture needle, the integrins make contact with all parts of the body through the matrix webwork. Based on this evidence, wholeness is becoming an accepted concept, which sees "the body as an integrated, coordinated, successful system" and accepts that "no parts or properties are uncorrelated but all are demonstrably linked."[6]

The living matrix is simultaneously a mechanical, vibrational, energetic, electronic, photonic, and informational network. It consists of a complex, linked pattern of pathways and molecules that forms a tensegrity system. A term taken originally from architecture where it is used in the structural description of domes, tents, sailing vessels, and cranes, tensegrity indicates a continuous tensional network (tendons) connected by a set of discontinuous elements (struts), which can also be fruitfully applied to the description of the wholeness of the body.

> The body as a whole, and the spine in particular, can usefully be described as tensegrity systems. In the body, bones act as discontinuous compression elements and the muscles, tendons and ligaments act as a continuous tensional system. Together the bones and tensional elements permit the body to change shape, move about, and lift objects.[7]

This understanding of the body as a tensegrity system allows for the analysis of physical and movement therapies, such as qigong and taiqi quan. Bodily posture and modes of movement are essential to the way people feel and act. Straighter posture and better balance allow bioelectric energies to flow more freely, improve the ability of the body to adapt to changing situations (plasticity), and enhance the efficiency of the body's use. Also, correct movements may contribute to the release of traumas and tensions stored in the joints and muscles of the body, providing access to greater health and well-being.

Not only exerting an impact on the environment, human beings are also subject to its vibrational tendencies. Thus, and again matching Daoist notions of alchemy and herbal remedies, health is enhanced with the use of plants, metals, and minerals, most notably crystals since they correspond to the inherently crystalline nature of living tissues. "Living crystals, composed of long, thin, pliable molecules," are found in the body

> "in arrays of phospholipid molecules forming cell membranes and myelin sheaths of nerves, collagen arrays forming connective tissue and fascia, contractile arrays in muscle, arrays of sensory elements in the eye, nose, and ear, arrays of microtubules, microfilaments, and other fibrous components of the cytoskeleton.[8]

Mental attitudes and emotional states, too, play an important role, much as in Daoism seen as directed vibrations that can have a disturbing or enhancing effect on health. Mental attitudes give rise to specific patterns of energy so that magnetic activity in the nervous system of the individual can spread through his or her body into the energy fields and bodies of others. This understanding, closely linked to the emerging science of epigenetics, accounts for the presence of different diseases in identical twins as well as the survival of certain people under extreme circumstances. It also explains the efficacy of therapeutic touch and distant energy healing, during which the practitioner goes into a meditative state of mind and directs healing thoughts toward the patient. Measuring experiments have shown that the field emanating from the hands of a skilled practitioner can reach a million times the strength of the normal brain field; it can also contain infrared radiation, creating heat and spreading light as part of the healing effort.[9]

Energy medicine thus brings Daoist-style understanding of body and mind as energy into the modern world, explaining the powers of qigong masters as much as of ancient immortals and opening the path to a new and higher level of health and wholeness.

Immortalism

Health and wholeness, then, lead to an expanded life expectancy and ultimately open the path to immortality. As a concept today, this is at the center of thought among the so-called immortalists, a group of twentieth-century scientists who—very much like Daoists—believe that old age is a disease to be cured and that human beings with the help of genetic engineering and medical techniques can live for several hundred years and even forever. The immortalist movement began in the 1960s with Wilson Ettinger, a professor of physics at the University of Michigan who was injured in World War II.

Hospitalized for three years, he had ample opportunity to confront his death and decided that he wanted to live forever, then set out to find the means to do so. He wrote *The Prospect of Immortality* (1969) to outline his vision, thereby beginning a cultural trend that is still flourishing. Today, after Ettinger's passing, this trend is most prominently represented by Alan Harrington, author of *The Immortalist* (1979).

Their argument against the naturalness of old age and death grows from the continuous increase in life expectancy over the past millennia. After all, in ancient Greece people on average only lived for twenty-two years, and even a hundred years ago the median life expectancy was forty-six, as opposed to the eighties in industrialized countries today. Of course, these numbers reflect a high infant mortality rate in earlier centuries, and even in traditional cultures, some individuals made it to sixty, seventy, or eighty. But this does not deny the fact that today people live longer, stay young into older years, and that the fastest growing segment of the population in the industrialized world are the centenarians—Queen Elisabeth II, who writes a personal note to every one of her subjects who celebrates his or her hundredth birthday, only wrote about 300 cards a year just a few decades years ago. Now she, or rather her staff, have to send out several thousand annually, and the numbers are rising—leading, potentially, to the demise of the practice.

Immortalists, bolstered by these statistics, embrace the idea is that there is an inbuilt clock of aging in every person. They strive to discover its location and mechanism, then work to slow it down or stop it altogether. The recent mapping of the human genome has given them much support, as have studies on human growth hormones, the effect of very low-calorie diets on mice and men, and the increasing health benefits of work-outs in western society. Immortalists hope to see everyone attain a very long life and eventually grow into immortality. They argue that survival is a key feature of nature, that the death of cells is very slow and can and should be slowed down even more.

They take the scare out of immortality by making it a universal and general feature. No longer are immortals freaks who are different and alien and threatening, but our entire society grows into advanced old age, centenarian living, and eventually the state of no-death. Immortalists see this as a very positive development. They argue that, with people living longer and remaining youthful and active, the problems of the planet and society would stand a much better chance of solution, since that people would be around long enough to see the disastrous impact of present-day decisions. There would also be more balanced moral values, since people living for long periods would have to realize that doing things that are good for themselves had better also benefit others. In addition, people would take fewer risks and move with more caution, since they would have so much more life to lose. And, most importantly, everyone would have so much more fun, so much more freedom, and a great deal less urgency to get things done.

However, this sunny vision is met by staunch opposition. Opponents of the immortality program warn that extending human life into unknown dimensions is tampering with nature and can have many unexpected side-effects; that long life and immortality are good only as long as one has youth and vigor. After all, didn't Tithonus, a prince of Troy in Greek myth, have his wish for immortality granted by the goddess Aurora but forgot to ask for youth and vigor? And see what happened to him! He vegetated forever as an old man until he was eventually rescued by being transformed into a grasshopper and allowed to die. Then, again, what would people do with all the time they have on their hands. Even today people get bored by age forty and barely make it to seventy, let alone 170. More of the same, every year, the next year, and on for many more years—why bother?

They also do not see the reduction of urgency as a boon. To them it is bad enough today if you want to get some work done tomorrow. What if your plumber or computer man lived to 200 and had absolutely no reason to work today—*mañana* forever? No more repairs? No more progress? And the idea of more caution: aren't we strangulated by safety regulations already? Living even longer would make people overprotective to the point where they would only venture out wearing padded clothes and face masks!

These attitude changes aside, as the world is already beginning to experience, longer lives mean a drastic increase in population, which translates into more pollution, diminishing resources, less social security money, retirement benefits stretched to the limit. Except, of course, that retirement would no longer happen at sixty-five or seventy any more. Instead, people would work far into their eighties and nineties—taking jobs away from younger folks who, too, expect to have very long and fruitful careers. The latter, come to think of it, could be eased by creating a whole new life cycle: be young and in education for the first sixty years (attend college for ten or twenty years instead of four), go to work for the next sixty, and spend another sixty in retirement—or any number of years: eighty, a hundred, two hundred.

Society would change. With so much time to live, people would not have one or two families, but—given the divorce rate—three or four, adding enormous complexity to relationships and family structures. In the longer run, birth control would become essential, and new arrivals on the planet would have to be strictly limited, bringing society into a state of managed care, as described in Aldous Huxley's *Brave New World* (1998) with its official predestinators and already practiced in Communist China where couples have to have a permit to get pregnant. At the other end of life, with people not dying naturally anymore, exit strategies would need to be developed and suicide education provided. After all, it is always possible that someone, even presented with the opportunity to go on forever, might not want to continue and need a way out—an issue potentially resolved by energy transformation and ascension into the higher spheres. Alternatively, society, following the model of some prehistoric groups described in myths and tales, might make the decision: you've been around long enough, time to make room. Whether it's an automatic death sentence at a certain age or a form of euthanasia by sifting out weaker and less productive specimens, death would have to be controlled—or, in the case of true immortality, birth would have to be prohibited.

Modern Immortalists, again closely echoing traditional Daoists, are not scared by these scenarios. They claim that consciousness will adjust to the new realities and develop new standards. People will grow older while remaining healthier, they will work longer years and be more productive, and methods of replacing body parts, cloning oneself, and deep-freezing the body until science is ready will happen anyway as research goes on. Humanity is on the fast track to immortality, and nothing will stop it, but hopefully it will gain some measure of perfection in the process.

Notes

1 Peat 1997, 25, 48, 65.
2 Talbot 1991, 47.
3 Nadeau and Kafatos 1999, 197.
4 Bohm 1980, xv.
5 Peat 1997, 106.
6 Oschman 2000, 49.
7 Oschman 2000, 153.
8 Oschman 2000, 129. On mind in health, see Lipton 2008.
9 See Gerber 1988.

References

Bohm, David. 1980. *Wholeness and the Implicate Order*. London: Routledge & Kegan Paul.

Ettinger, Wilson. 1969. *The Prospect of Immortality*. New York, NY: Macfadden-Bartell.

Gerber, Richard. 1988. *Vibrational Medicine: New Choices for Healing Ourselves*. Santa Fe, NM: Bear and Company.

Harrington, Alan. 1979. *The Immortalist*. London: Abacus.

Huxley, Aldous. 1998 [1932]. *Brave New World*. New York, NY: Perennial.

Lipton, Bruce H. 2008. *The Biology of Belief: Unleashing the Power of Consciousness, Matter, and Miracles*. Carlsbad, CA: Hay House.

Nadeau, Robert, and Menas Kafatos. 1999. *The Non-Local Universe: New Physics and Matters of the Mind*. New York, NY: Oxford University Press.

Oschman, James. 2000. *Energy Medicine: The Scientific Basis*. New York, NY: Churchill Livingstone.

Peat, F. David. 1997. *Infinite Potential: The Life and Times of David Bohm*. New York, NY: Helix Books.

Talbot, Michael. 1991. *The Holographic Universe*. New York, NY: HarperCollins.

Index